IMPERFECT EQUILIBRIUM

NEW PERSPECTIVES ON EASTERN EUROPE AND EURASIA

The states of Eastern Europe and Eurasia are once again at the centre of global attention, particularly following Russia's 2022 full-scale invasion of Ukraine. But media coverage can only do so much in providing the necessary context to make sense of fast-moving developments. The books in this series provide original, engaging and timely perspectives on Eastern Europe and Eurasia for a general readership. Written by experts on—and from—these states, the books in the series cover an eclectic range of cutting-edge topics relating to politics, history, culture, economics and society. The series is originated by Hurst, with titles co-published or distributed in North America by Oxford University Press, New York.

Series editor: Dr Ben Noble—Associate Professor of Russian Politics at University College London and Associate Fellow at Chatham House

KIRILL SHAMIEV

Imperfect Equilibrium

Civil–Military Relations in Russian Defense Policymaking

HURST & COMPANY, LONDON

First published in the United Kingdom in 2026 by
C. Hurst & Co. (Publishers) Ltd.,
New Wing, Somerset House, Strand, London, WC2R 1LA
© Kirill Shamiev, 2026
All rights reserved.

The right of Kirill Shamiev to be identified
as the author of this publication is asserted by him in accordance
with the Copyright, Designs and Patents Act, 1988.

A Cataloguing-in-Publication data record for this book
is available from the British Library.

ISBN: 9781805264279

EU GPSR Authorised Representative
Easy Access System Europe Oü, 16879218
Address: Mustamäe tee 50, 10621, Tallinn, Estonia
Contact Details: gpsr.requests@easproject.com, +358 40 500 3575

www.hurstpublishers.com

CONTENTS

List of Figures and Tables	vii
Maps	ix
Acknowledgments	xv
Introduction	1
1. Russian Civil–Military Relations after the USSR	17
2. Civil–Military Relations and Russian Military Culture	33
3. Winds of Change? Russian Military Development in 2000–7	61
4. From Combat Effectiveness to Oversight Overload: Russia's Military Development in 2007–21	115
5. Russian Civil–Military Relations and the Full-Scale Invasion of Ukraine	165
Conclusion: The Tug-of-War in Russia's Civil–Military Relations	185
Appendix 1: List of Interviews	193
Appendix 2: Adapted Advocacy Coalition Framework	197
Appendix 2.1: Operationalization of Factors Used in Analysis	198
Appendix 3: Defense Policy Agenda	200
Notes	207
Selected Bibliography	257
Index	259

LIST OF FIGURES AND TABLES

Figures

1.	Model of civil–military relations in defense reform (simplified)	8
2.	Survey of Russian elites, support for order at any price	44
3.	Perception of combat readiness among the Russian public	67
4.	Coalitions in 2000–3	78
5.	Coalitions in 2004–7	98
6.	Coalitions in 2007–12	129
7.	Coalitions in 2012–21	150

Tables

1.	Relatively stable parameters	198
2.	Coalition opportunity structures	199
3.	External contextual factors	199
4.	Agenda for the 2001–3 reform: Priorities in military development according to the 2000 Military Doctrine	200
5.	Agenda for the 2004–7 period	201

LIST OF FIGURES AND TABLES

6.	Objectives for military development from 2010	203
7.	Defense policy priorities in the 2013–20 period	204

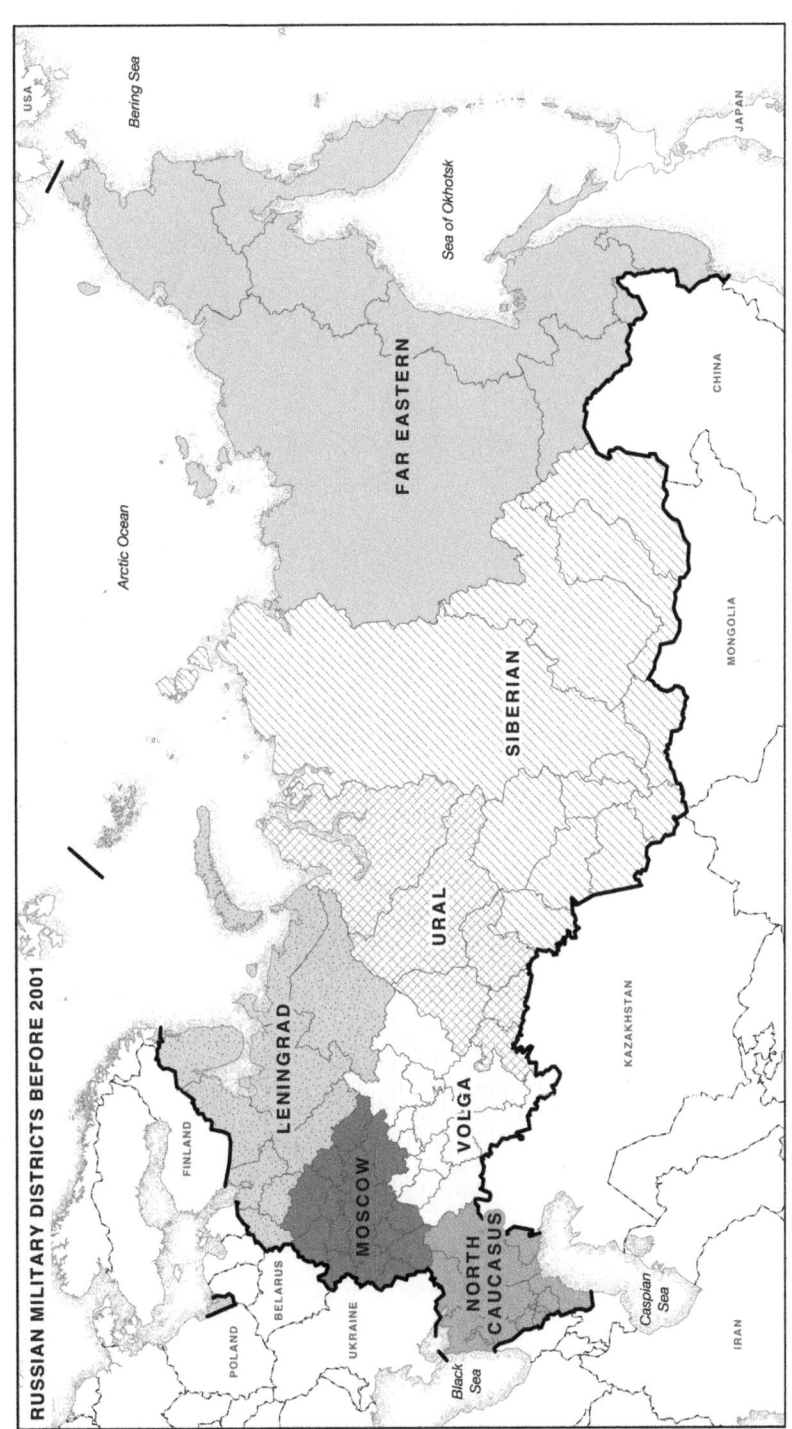

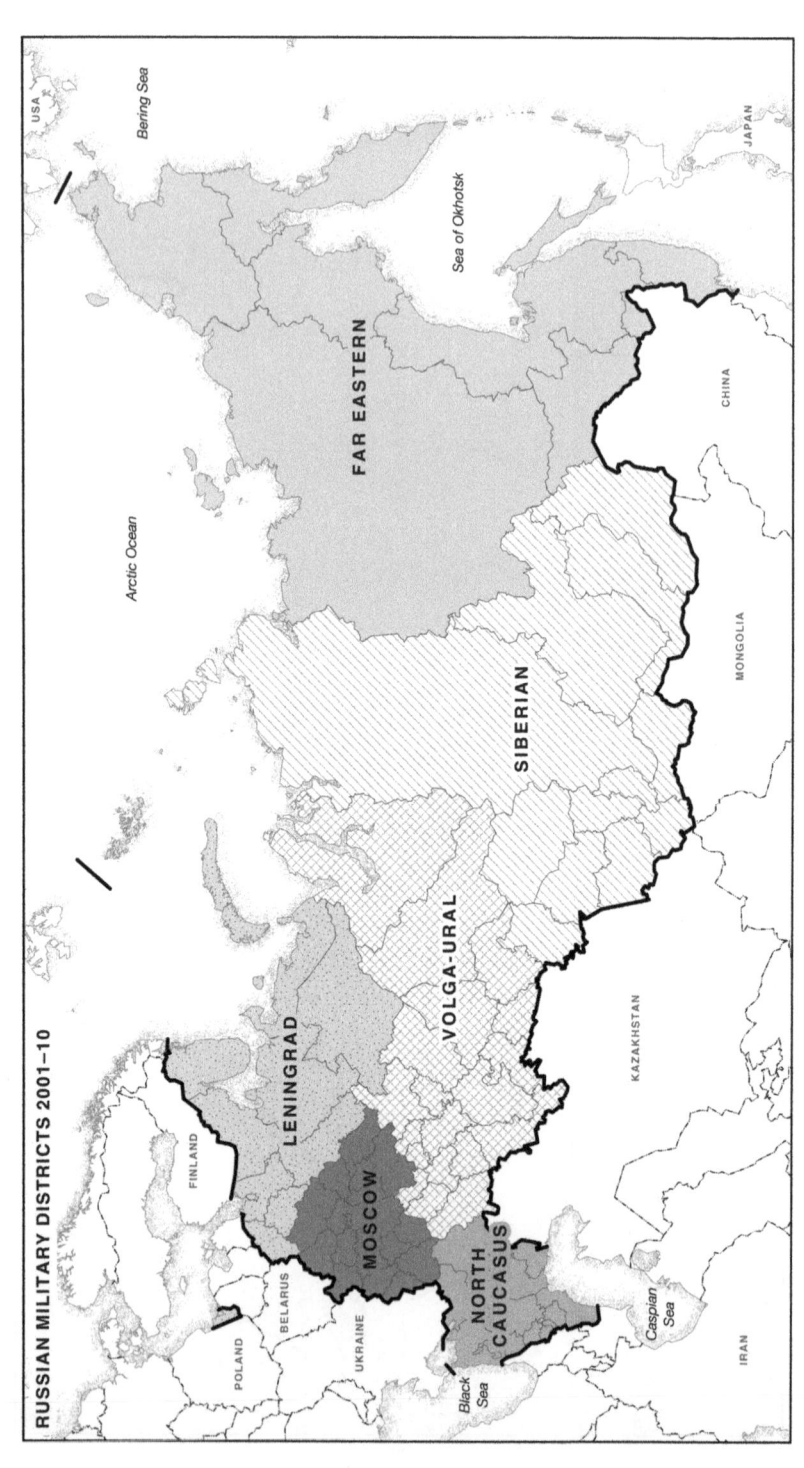

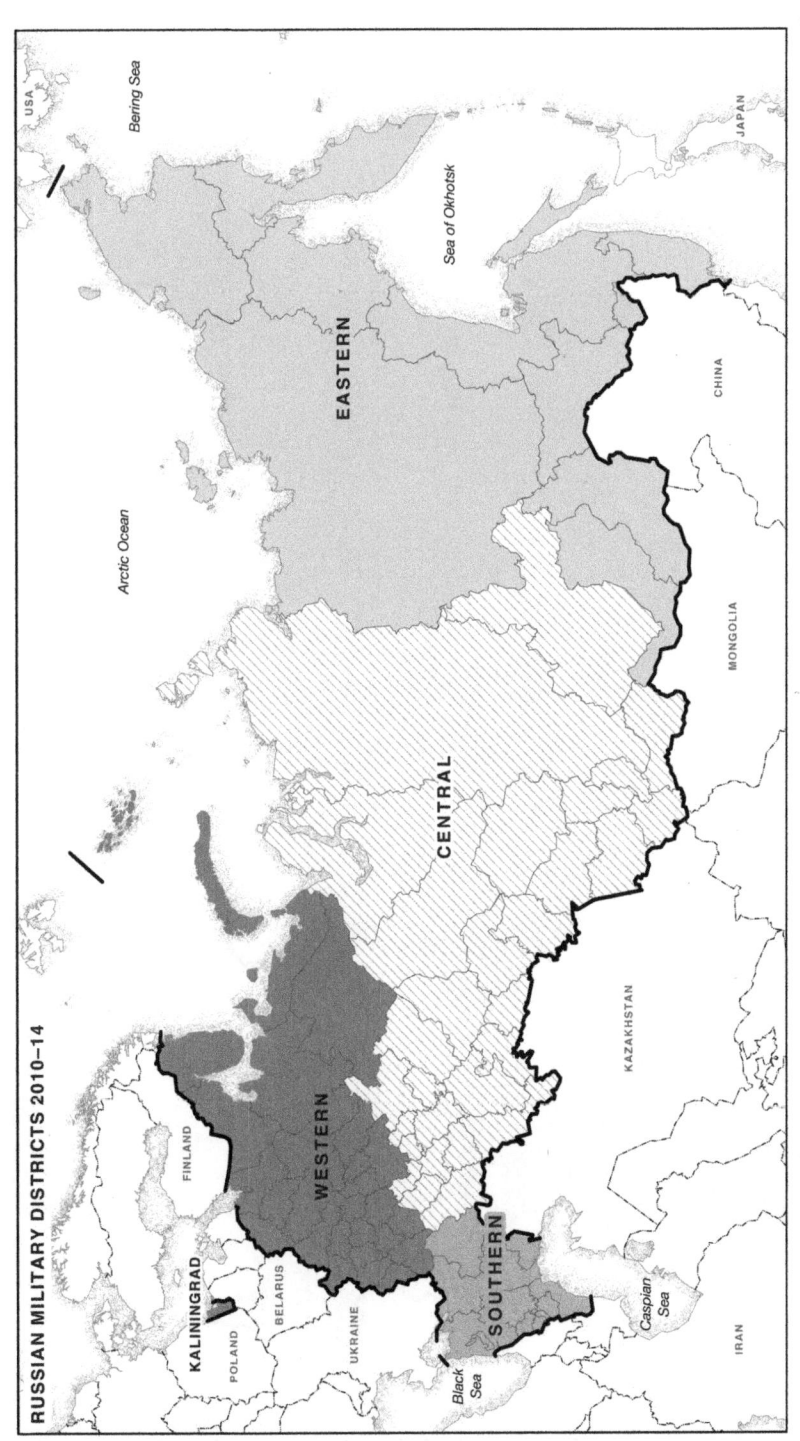

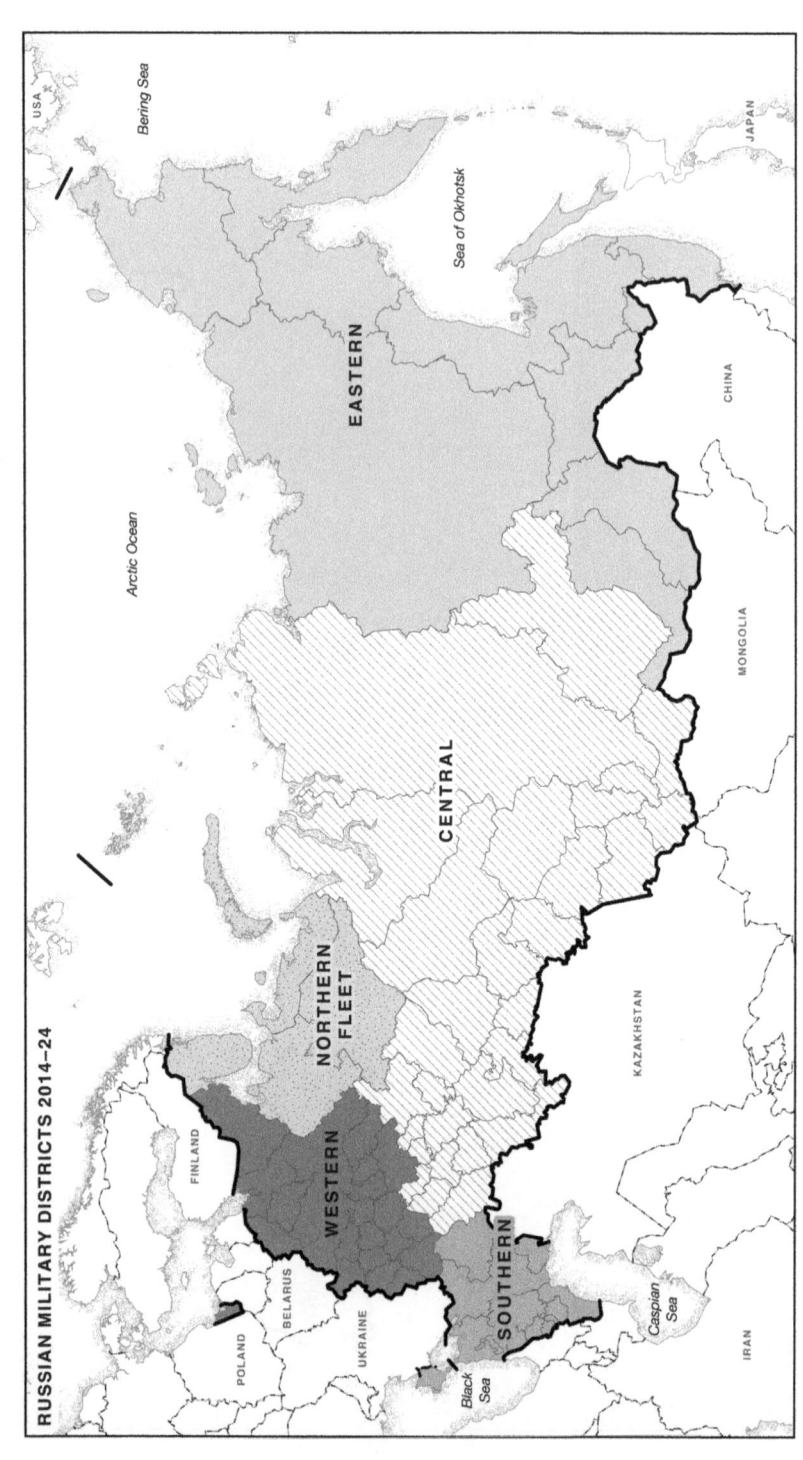

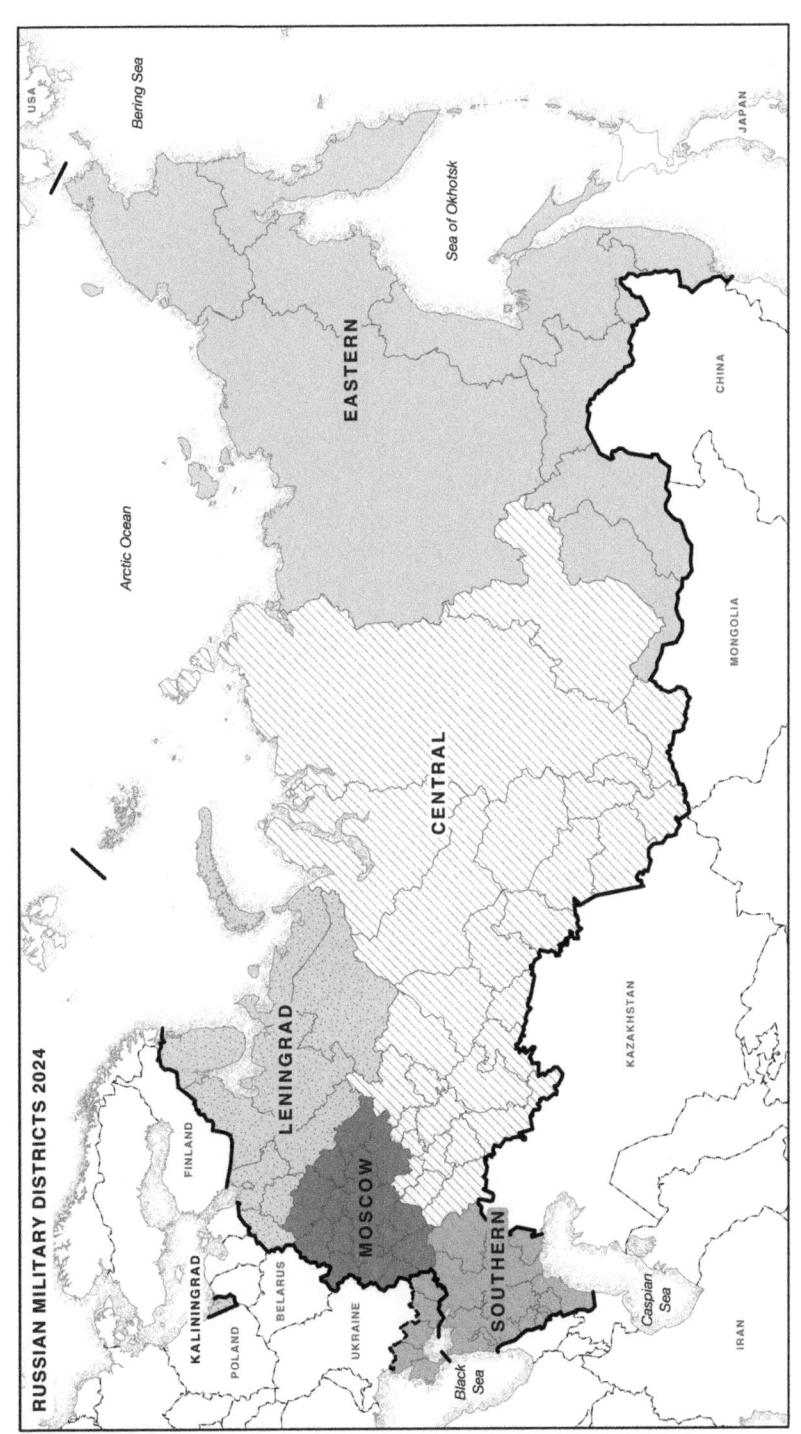

ACKNOWLEDGMENTS

My interest in civil–military relations began more than a decade before I wrote this book, though I did not know the term then. One of my earliest childhood memories is of a BTR-80—a 14-ton armored personnel carrier—passing by on a cold morning in the 1990s in Russia's Far East. Its 2.9-meter hull seemed monstrous and absolutely intimidating to my two- or three-year-old self. As a high school student, I watched thousands of officers resign and openly criticize the military leadership during the 2008–12 reforms. I still remember the angry faces of veterans of the Soviet–Afghan and Chechen Wars and their disgust at the defense minister and reforms they could not accept.

While they spoke, I kept thinking how every young Russian male in my community feared military service. Few aspired to be officers, and almost none wanted to serve as conscripts. The military seemed not just "uncool" but also dangerous, plagued by violence, poor supplies and mismanagement. Officers disagreed with and resisted the reforms, while civilians stayed away from the armed forces entirely. Explanations of the causes of this gap were unconvincing. Officers accused the minister of treason or corruption; civilians saw disgruntled service members as corrupt and unfit for job.

I could not understand why no one had sought to reconcile these perspectives. Even the anti-Kremlin protesters of the Snow Revolution of 2011–12 ignored the military's criticism of the minister. This pushed me to study political science and ultimately

ACKNOWLEDGMENTS

write this book as an attempt to answer the question I first asked more than a decade ago.

Most of this work was done during my PhD at Central European University (CEU), which gave me the resources and space to pursue it. I thank my supervisors Christopher David LaRoche and Julia Buxton for their guidance. Christopher helped me build the data-driven core and sharpen my argument. Julia shaped my analytical thinking, advising me to write for the public good and to question mainstream assumptions in academia and politics. My committee members Cristina Corduneanu-Huci and Carsten Q. Schneider provided rigorous feedback that anchored the research in political science. I am grateful to Bettina Renz for sharing her expertise with me during my fellowship at the University of Nottingham; Bettina's articles first introduced me to Russian civil–military relations and led me to discover the classical works of Samuel Huntington and Morris Janowitz on civil–military relations. The feedback of Risa Brooks from Marquette University was crucial in linking my argument to the wider civil–military literature and preparing it for publication. Meeting all these wonderful people and doing my fieldwork would not have been possible without CEU's generous commitment to supporting open academic discovery.

Collecting data connected me to dozens of experts, veterans, journalists and civic activists in Russia. One interviewee was sanctioned by Western governments in 2022 for pro-Kremlin war reporting. Others fled to avoid prosecution; one received a long prison sentence; another died of COVID-19 soon after our interview. I am grateful for their time and openness.

I thank Ben Noble at University College London, editor of the New Perspectives on Eastern Europe and Eurasia series at Hurst Publishers, for his extensive help in editing the book. Without him, it would have taken a very different shape. I also thank the two anonymous reviewers for their incisive feedback and the Hurst team for their support throughout the publication process.

My dear Rasa saw me in the most hopeless writing moments and miraculously managed to transform them into periods of encouragement and support. Our flat-coated retriever, Džiaugsmas (Joy), taught me that a moment without joy is a moment wasted—

ACKNOWLEDGMENTS

and pushed me to walk even when I needed to write, which supported my physical and mental health and made my Garmin shine. Thank you, Joy, for not eating my laptop and holding yourself back from licking my face during TV appearances.

I am deeply grateful to my parents, Veronika and Vyacheslav (Slava), whose support made it possible for me to learn English, study at a top Russian university and then earn a degree abroad. Without their confidence in my abilities, I might never have left my remote hometown in Russia's Far East. I also thank my friends Andrey, Anna, Freya, George (Yegor), James, Konstantin, Liza, Mack, Ruslan and Tetiana, who read parts of the book or discussed it with me at various stages.

I am grateful to the many organizations that gave me opportunities to present my work and publish my analysis. Special thanks go to the Inter-University Seminar on Armed Forces and Society (including its *Armed Forces & Society* journal and biannual conference), the European Council on Foreign Relations, the Center for Strategic and International Studies, the Center for Naval Analyses, George Washington University, PONARS Eurasia, the Royal United Services Institute, the Higher School of Economics in Saint Petersburg, the Austrian National Defense Academy, the Finnish National Defence University and Scuola Normale Superiore in Florence, Italy.

I hope this book will serve as a useful resource for anyone interested in Russia's politics and history. It may also serve as a reference for studying civil–military relations in other contexts. In an era of rapid defense innovation and growing integration of civilian and military technologies, critically assessing civil–military relations is essential for building more effective, accountable and efficient armed forces.

INTRODUCTION

At dawn on 24 February 2022, thousands of Russian soldiers, together with tanks, artillery systems, aircraft and battleships, began a striking campaign and land incursion into Ukraine. By the end of the day, their commanders had begun receiving reports that local civilians and the enemy's armed forces had stopped some of the advancing columns. The first casualties appeared hours after the start of an operation that would ultimately prove a catastrophe for the Russian military.

Yet something similar had happened before:

> At dawn on [REDACTED], the combined detachment began to move, but by noon alarming reports were received: at the bridge at the entrance to [REDACTED], the column was stopped by local residents, led by armed men [REDACTED] who burned ten of our vehicles and overturned six. At 17:15 the chief of staff reported that in the area of [REDACTED] from the side of the forest the column of vehicles was fired at from automatic weapons. The first casualties appeared.[1]

This is how the Russian general Gennady Troshev described the beginning of the First Chechen War in December 1994. The war was a conflict between the Russian central government and the Republic of Chechnya, which declared independence in 1991 following the Soviet collapse. Moscow sought to regain control over the region via a swift military operation, which resulted in a brutal urban and guerrilla war. Troshev became the commander of the Joint Group of Forces in Chechnya after several generals before him had refused to lead military forces against their own compatriots.

Troshev grew up in Chechnya and knew its capital Grozny well. But his skills and knowledge of the terrain were of little help. Bogged down in cold and squalid mud, the Russian troops suffered casualties, and the operation turned into a decade-long conflict. Moscow signed a temporary ceasefire agreement with the rebels in 1996 before unleashing even more firepower three years later in what became known as the Second Chechen War.

Almost thirty years passed between the beginning of the First Chechen War and Russia's full-scale invasion of Ukraine, a period in which the Russian defense budget almost tripled, from $23.79 billion to $68.65 billion (in 2023 US dollars).[2] Yet despite spending over $1.1 trillion on its military and making numerous attempts at defense reform, Russia's armed forces have been hampered by similar limitations: inadequate strategic assessment of the adversary, poor command-and-control skills, insufficient intelligence, weak force integration, limited precision-strike capabilities and poor equipment maintenance. At the time of writing, hundreds of thousands of Russian soldiers have been killed or wounded in a war against Ukraine that was supposed to last just three days.

Why has Moscow been unable to make its armed forces more effective? An effective military is one that is successful in fulfilling its purpose: defeating the enemy in given economic, technological and sociopolitical circumstances. This goal requires keeping the military at a sufficient size, constantly improving its cohesion, being responsive to domestic and external environments and maintaining the motivation and competencies of its personnel as well as the quality of its weapons and equipment.[3] This seems not to have happened in Russia despite Vladimir Putin's and Dmitry Medvedev's efforts to strengthen the military and the billions of dollars spent on more than twenty years of reform.

Before Russia's 2022 invasion of Ukraine, the perception of Russian military capabilities bore little resemblance to the reality. Many observers thought the Russian military was very powerful, which in part reflected its recent performance and operational experiences. In 2014, Russia deployed thousands of military personnel to Crimea, quickly annexing the peninsula and occupying Ukrainian government buildings and key military bases. In the same year, Russian forces supported pro-Russian rebels in Eastern Ukraine, effectively occupying parts of Ukraine's Donetsk and Luhansk regions and forcing Ukraine to accept a ceasefire agreement on Moscow's terms. In 2015, Russian troops were deployed to Syria, saving the autocratic regime of Bashar al-Assad from losing the civil war and weakening the Syrian rebels and Islamist terrorist groups. In 2020, Moscow deployed a peacekeeping force in Nagorno-Karabakh to support a ceasefire agreement between Azerbaijan and Armenia. And just a few months before going into Ukraine, Russian forces appeared in Kazakhstan, helping Kassym-Jomart Tokayev's nascent regime suppress a major anti-regime uprising. All this happened against a backdrop of Russian military intelligence interference in democratic elections, hacking of Western digital infrastructure, disinformation campaigns and assassinations of political opponents, defectors and former rebel commanders in Russia and abroad. The Russian military seemed to have become a serious and powerful opponent. The war in Ukraine has thus shown that it is difficult for bystanders as well as Western intelligence agencies, presidents and even the Ukrainian government to make a clear assessment of the development of Russian military power.

However, although the Russian military's strength was clearly overestimated before the 2022 invasion, it is important to avoid swinging to the opposite extreme and underestimating Russia's military capabilities. While there are clear deficiencies in Russia's defense sector, overemphasizing these deficiencies risks overlooking areas where the military has adapted and improved. A balanced analysis is one that recognizes Russia's weaknesses and its capacity for institutional learning and change.

Imperfect Equilibrium examines Russia's civil–military relations to explain why Russia's efforts to reform its armed forces have often led to imperfect and incomplete policy outcomes, notwithstanding certain improvements in its defense sector. These relations are shaped by three key coalitions—presidential, military and civilian—with differing levels of stability and coordination, each advancing its own group interests. Russian defense policy is the result of the balance of power between these coalitions, influenced by their internal composition, institutional mandates, cultural norms and shifting political opportunities. Each policy change ultimately creates a new equilibrium, a condition when civil–military coalitions achieve a level of power they are unable to alter without a major policy change. In the end, neither the civilian nor the military leadership has been satisfied with the condition of the Russian military, but they have not been able to improve it either. This is what I call the imperfect equilibrium of Russian civil–military relations.

Imperfect equilibrium

One of the state's main roles is to defend its citizens.[4] The police are used to protect the public at home, and the armed forces are used to defend the state from threats beyond its borders. But who keeps the military from going rogue and taking control of the state it is supposed to protect? In non-democratic countries, the armed forces are sometimes used to suppress civil society and help the sitting regime stay in power. In Argentina, for example, President Juan Perón (1946–55, 1973–4) used the military to suppress the opposition, particularly left-wing groups; in Chile, President Salvador Allende (1970–3) used the military to maintain internal security and suppress the opposition.[5] However, the same forces can act against the ruling leader. President Perón was ousted by a group of generals who sided with multiple anti-regime opposition groups and established military rule. In Chile, General Augusto Pinochet organized a successful coup and established a military dictatorship that lasted until 1990.

But military coups alone do not explain the distribution of power between civilian and military actors in the policymaking process. Russia has not had any successful military coups since 1801. Previous work has claimed that Russia has enjoyed non-interference from the military due to the country's organizational culture and institutional counterbalancing or factionalism,[6] which weakens the incentives for a coup.[7] However, historically, the military has had a strong presence in the Russian policymaking process, being present in discussions on issues ranging from defense reforms and industry to veteran affairs and education.[8] Indeed, Putin has appointed officials with a military and security background to multiple positions in the federal government.[9] Yet despite this military involvement, the Kremlin has struggled to reform the Russian military.

Unlike much contemporary thinking on militaries in authoritarian regimes, I argue that the Russian military's role extends beyond repression and the prevention of coups. A seemingly politically obedient Russian military has acted as a veto-player in the policy process, thwarting attempted reforms by the civilian leadership, even in Putin's highly centralized authoritarian regime. The expectations of the Russian military and its civilian leadership frequently diverge when it comes to the role of the military and future conflict; they also follow different management and relationship patterns and focus on separate strategic priorities, leading to conflicting visions of national security, defense policy and the desired composition of the armed forces.

The Russian government has had to take account of the military's position because no military reform can be developed and implemented without military expertise, including from the General Staff, and access to defense sector data. Russian military advice has affected what and how many resources the government has designated for reform, the policy programs it has implemented and how it has evaluated the results of its reforms. Without strong oversight, the Russian military has been able to dilute, amend or simply ignore government orders. The paradox of Russian civil–military relations is that Russia's hierarchical and highly centralized armed forces fit poorly into the hierarchical and highly centralized Russian political system.

The development of the Russian military between 2000 and 2022 can be divided into three distinct periods. The first, from 2000 to 2007, took place during Putin's first two presidential terms and was a period of stability for the armed forces following years of post-Soviet decline. The Russian government was unable to implement reforms in the face of military objections, and neither Putin nor Minister of Defense Sergei Ivanov was interested in pushing for substantial change.

The second, from 2007 to 2012, coincided with Medvedev's presidency. This period was defined by ambitious defense reforms aimed at modernizing the Russian military's structure and capabilities. The war with Georgia in 2008 exposed severe deficiencies, including logistical failures, outdated equipment and poor coordination, with the Russian military suffering significant losses, many due to friendly fire and road accidents. In response, Minister of Defense Anatoly Serdyukov, backed by key civilian experts, launched sweeping structural reforms that aimed to enhance the armed forces' combat readiness. The Kremlin shifted the equilibrium and restructured civil–military relations by tightening civilian control during the reform. However, the reforms provoked strong resistance from the military bureaucracy, non-military security agencies and retired officers, ultimately leading to Serdyukov's dismissal in 2012 and the restoration of the imperfect equilibrium in the Russian defense sector.

The third period, between 2012 and 2022, marked a shift toward the assertive use of military power as a key instrument of Russian foreign policy in which the armed forces played an increasing role in conflicts abroad. During this period, the Defense Ministry benefited from substantial federal funding, which facilitated the rearmament of the military, the introduction of new command-and-control systems and large-scale infrastructural investments. However, the government proved unable to change the imperfect equilibrium. By relying on the military bureaucracy to oversee the reform process, Defense Minister Sergei Shoigu diluted many of the changes from the previous period, and the Kremlin failed to establish a functional system for monitoring and evaluating military-led development. The pace of military modernization stagnated accordingly, leaving the Russian armed forces in a state of strategic inertia before the full-scale invasion of Ukraine.

The imperfect equilibrium in Russian civil–military relations stems from the Kremlin's inability to establish a functional framework in which presidential, military and civilian coalitions have been able to cooperate effectively and address their disagreements through pragmatic compromise to pursue shared policy goals. Instead, both the president and the military have been reluctant to disclose critical information about the true state of the armed forces. The military retains strong institutional control over information flows within the government, preventing independent oversight. It has inflated the perceived significance of published policy programs, theoretical studies in military journals and scripted exercises, creating a distorted picture of Russian military capabilities and contributing to overestimations of its strength.

Three factors had to coincide to make military reform successful. First, the Russian president needed a strong political will.[10] Despite Putin's public appearance as a strong, militaristic man, he has, in fact, rarely been ready to exercise his political will in the defense reform process. Second, the president needed an assertive and militaristic geopolitical orientation that would elevate the importance of the armed forces as a foreign policy tool. The Kremlin has not really been interested in preventing and solving numerous serious and violent crimes in the Russian military so long as they have not directly affected Putin's foreign policy. Finally, reformers needed administrative access to the president. Without these three factors, any military reform was always doomed.

Analytical approach

The imperfect equilibrium describes the quality of relationships between the presidential, military and civilian coalitions that affect defense policymaking in Russia. The norms, values, institutional rules and resources available to each coalition determine the balance of power within the coalition. This power balance usually rests in equilibrium because no side can change it without a major political process, such as reform, a federal government reshuffle or major federal elections. The balance of power also influences which ideas are available to decision-makers, who participates in the policymaking process and whether reform goals will be accepted by the military. In essence, civil–military relations serve as both the foundation and the filter through which defense policy is formulated and executed. This means that the relationship between civil–military relations and defense reforms in Russia is cyclical: civil–military dynamics shape reform outcomes, which in turn reshape those very dynamics

(Figure 1). Once a reform is initiated, its implementation inevitably alters the institutions and culture—norms and values—governing civil–military relations. However, these transformations are not always intentional: deviations from the initial reform program, bureaucratic resistance and external factors, such as economic or natural disasters, protests and revolutions, international affairs and the death of political leaders, can shift the policy's trajectory and unintentionally reshape the defense sector. Thus, every defense reform in Russia is both a product of existing civil–military dynamics and a catalyst for their evolution. This interaction ensures that Russian civil–military relations remain fluid, adapting to the political and strategic environment in which they operate.

This framework of civil–military relations can be applied to other countries, where such relations may, in some cases, function effectively rather than being dysfunctional or unbalanced. However, in Russia, the Kremlin has rarely achieved the reform outcomes it has sought, underscoring the imperfect status of the equilibrium in Russian civil–military relations. Figure 1 outlines how I analyzed the development of civil–military relations.

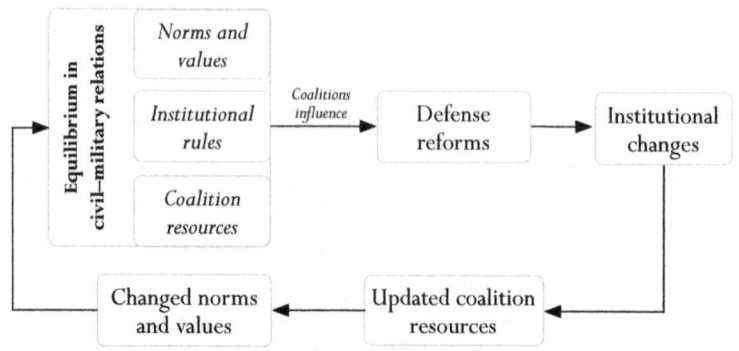

Figure 1: Model of civil–military relations in defense reform (simplified)

To analyze how coalitions function in this civil–military cycle, I adapted the classical advocacy coalition framework (ACF) used to study policy change (see Appendix 2).[11] The ACF's central premise is that defense policy results from the jostling of competing interests, shaped by structural factors and private agendas. To achieve their objectives, Russian political, military, administrative and civil society actors formed coalitions with varying degrees of stability and coordination, and the coalitions faced constraints and employed strategies to achieve their policy goals. Below, I discuss the framework's key assumptions: the balance between structural influence and actors' rational agency, and how Russian civilian and military actors operated in separate coalitions. Chapter 1 describes the framework in more detail and applies it to the process of Russian defense reform.

Actors and coalitions

The key element of the ACF is the way actors unite and cooperate within coalitions. Actors—political leaders, military officers, bureaucrats and members of civil society—form coalitions based on their organizational affiliations and shared policy beliefs. These coalitions consist of a case-specific number of actors with varying degrees of unity and coordination.[12] The types and numbers of actors involved often determine the success of a given reform, as different actors have different levels of access to key decision-makers, such as the minister of defense, the chief of the General Staff and, ultimately, the president.

Russian civil–military relations revolve around three primary coalitions. The presidential coalition includes the president, the Ministry of Defense (MoD), other executive agencies and judicial and oversight bodies that are directly accountable to Putin and, for a short period between 2008 and 2012, Medvedev. The civilian coalition consists of actors outside the presidential group, such as members of the State Duma (Russia's lower house of parliament), civil society activists and other civilians who are not directly subordinate to the president. The military coalition, led by the chief of the General Staff, includes uniformed military personnel and, in some cases, representatives of the military-industrial complex. In the civil–military domain, members of the military coalition have distinct policy beliefs that have developed over years of education and service; they also serve in a strongly regulated, disciplined and exclusive community with hierarchical coordination rules, strict procedures and pre-defined practices. The military coalition is therefore unique and can be relatively easily separated from other societal groups.

President Putin was never part of the military coalition. At the beginning of his presidency, he relied on his former KGB colleagues, which was a logical choice for an ex-KGB officer with limited experience of federal politics. Over time, he has increasingly used repressive measures of varying intensity against his opponents, requiring the creation of compliant and powerful domestic security agencies. However, to consolidate power, Putin has always needed to maintain a balance among the Russian security services.

All coalitions have their own set resources for the intercoalition interactions that lead to policy decisions. These resources include favorable public opinion about the supported policy, access to administrative and insider information, supportive allies, financial resources and political expertise. However, a formal decision on paper may not always become a functional institutional rule that will regulate actors' behavior. Few changes in the defense sector can be implemented without military specialists and expertise. Russian defense policies have sometimes been thwarted when the presidential coalition has lacked sufficient resources and capacities to create practical policies able to overcome the military's objections, despite its nominal support for civilian supremacy in defense affairs.

Structures and agency

Military officers and civilian specialists shape policy, but structural constraints and external events inevitably influence their actions.[13] These constraints—socioeconomic, legal, political and international—define power relationships, set expectations for behavior in various roles (e.g., military officer and politician) and influence decision-making at all levels. Studying these structures helps us see beyond individual personalities or actions, revealing the deeper forces shaping institutional functions and behavioral patterns. For example, after the Cold War, civil–military relations in Russia became more dynamic and interactive, requiring a constant reassessment of security threats such as domestic terrorism and separatism, response mechanisms, strategic objectives and coordination with civilian authorities.

But structures alone do not fully determine behavior. Political leaders, military commanders and soldiers retain agency, continuously adapting and learning from past policy decisions. While they acknowledge external constraints, they also make strategic adjustments based on available information. That is why the military's control over information about the armed forces is so important. By manipulating this information and restricting access to internal assessments, the military can influence the adjustments to the defense sector the president and civilians are able to make. At the same time, individuals operate under cognitive limitations, relying on mental shortcuts shaped by pre-formed beliefs and values.[14]

These mental shortcuts are embedded in cultural norms, that is, shared beliefs about what is right or normal. Military culture, for instance, valorizes courage, discipline and loyalty, reinforcing patterns of individual behavior and group cohesion. Together, structures and culture create the context in which institutional decisions are made. Effective leaders recognize that policy or strategic changes must account for these broader frameworks. Implementing a new command structure, for example, requires an understanding of how it aligns with existing norms and organizational structures. Chapter 2 explores the critical role of education and socialization in shaping beliefs and values, ultimately influencing military culture and institutional behavior.

How the research was conducted

My focus on the Putin era is intentional: the institutional instability of the 1990s would require examining informal practices and micro-level relations in the weakness of formal civil–military rules—a formidable task that would be of limited validity given the profound structural changes in Russia after the turn of the century (see more in Chapters 1 and 2). The formal nature of defense policies in Russia allows me to identify both expected policy directions and deviations from those expectations, such as changes, delays or outright stops in implementation. For example, even when a presidential decree mandated a change, analysis of its implementation sometimes revealed delays and deviations from the original plan. The military was often able to resist the political leadership by changing timelines, leaking sensitive information, documenting irregularities or discouraging active participation in reforms.[15]

The information for this analysis was collected through a multi-stage approach that combined interviews (see Appendix 1) and surveys with analysis of memoirs, amendments to federal laws and reputable Russian military blogs. I initially analyzed media publications, Russian-language research and public statements from the 2000–2 period. I focused on understandings of the formal elements of the Russian military, constitutional structures and official national security goals. This initial sweep of material also helped me to compile a list of key actors involved in defense sector development.

To examine military culture in Russian civil–military relations, Chapter 2 draws on semi-structured interviews conducted in 2020 with retired and active-duty Russian military officers, members of soldiers' rights advocacy groups and former members of oversight bodies, including the Presidential Council for Civil Society and Human Rights. These interviews provided valuable insights into the experiences and perspectives of military and civilian experts involved in defense policymaking and officer education. Given the challenges of accessing this group, snowball sampling techniques—asking respondents to introduce me to other interviewees—were used to build trust and gain insider perspectives. To check the truthfulness of these accounts, the analysis includes elite opinion polls,[16] memoirs, public speeches, policy documents and legislative changes.

To analyze defense reforms and the policymaking processes for Chapters 3–4, I conducted expert interviews between 2018 and 2021 with scholars, insider journalists and former policymakers who directly participated in or closely observed these reforms. I also scraped around 16,000 parliamentary speeches from the Russian State Duma's website and identified around 1,000 references to military-related terms. This analysis tracked the evolution of parliamentary discussions on defense, reflecting shifts in the balance of power in Russian civil–military relations. Although the Russian parliament is not a democratic institution, it still functions as a platform for policymaking and for certain groups to voice opposition to government policy. Parliamentary actors seek to advance their interests within a regulated yet often informal authoritarian political system. Their speeches therefore reflect what they are trying to accomplish.

Legislative changes and reputable military blogs serve as the last two sources of data. Legislative amendments to federal laws provide insights into the institutional distribution of power within the government. For example, the federal law "On Defense" regulates the powers of the president, minister of defense, the federal government and regional and local governments in the defense sector.[17] Amendments to the articles of this law can redistribute the responsibilities in the defense sector, formally empowering or weakening different government bodies and positions.

Blogs offer unfiltered insights into underreported trends and the experiences of service members. They are usually run by retired service members or military enthusiasts with inputs from retired and active-duty service members. Unfortunately, by 2021 these blogs had become less relevant as the Russian government prohibited the publication of independent information about the military. Information from these blogs was cross-checked with similar evidence from media sources and interviews.

Analytical challenges

Russia's armed forces and civil–military relations are inherently sensitive topics, which partly explains the limited scholarly attention paid to the subject prior to the 2022 invasion of Ukraine. The most significant body of research was produced between the 1990s and 2010–12. Accessing defense-related empirical data has always been difficult, requiring considerable investment in reputation-building and networking, such as publishing defense-related articles in Russian media, attending conferences and exploiting networks with former and active government officials. This has become even more difficult since 2014, when the Russian government began restricting access to information about its security services and the military in response to investigative pieces on Russian losses in Ukraine, and even more so since the invasion of Ukraine in February 2022. At the time of writing, the dissemination of defense-related information from independent, unauthorized sources is legally prohibited in Russia. This ban affected my research: several military-related blogs no longer exist, and response rates during my final round of fieldwork in 2021 dropped significantly. However, I was able to collect most of the necessary data before these restrictions were enforced.

Prior to the full-scale invasion, the academic community largely ignored the Russian security sector, which was another major challenge in this study. For example, Russian civilian scholars often viewed the military purely as a rent-seeking institution focused on accumulating wealth. Others framed the armed forces as little more than Putin's loyal soldiers, unquestioningly executing his directives. As the war has vividly demonstrated, both perspectives fail to capture the complexity of the Russian military.

Since 1991, the Russian armed forces have actively engaged in war, with service members dying in combat or fulfilling their duties in peacetime even when funding was scarce, such as during the Chechen Wars. The full-scale invasion of Ukraine further illustrated their loyalty, with Russian soldiers frequently undertaking suicidal missions that had little chance of success, and even high-ranking generals risking and losing their lives in combat. This persistent readiness to absorb losses and take extreme risks, despite inadequate support and equipment, suggests that the Russian military's motivations go beyond financial incentives alone. By July 2025, at least 160,000 Russian service members, most of whom had not been forcefully mobilized, had died fighting in Ukraine and will never be able to make use of the financial benefits the state had prepared for them.[18]

At the same time, as I aim to show, the military was never a passive recipient of defense policy; Putin has never been able to unilaterally impose decisions without negotiation and agreement from the military elite, despite his enormous powers to steer the country's development. As I aim to demonstrate, senior military commanders not only slowed or undermined elements of various reform programs but at times even voiced open disagreement with

INTRODUCTION

the president (see Chapters 2, 3 and 4). Putin was unable to punish these commanders directly, in part due to their high status and the challenges of assigning clear blame to individual actors.

Road map for the book

Chapter 1 introduces the state of civil–military relations before and after the fall of the USSR, highlighting how the Soviet institutional legacy and strategic thinking continue to shape its military affairs. The chapter introduces the analytical framework in detail and applies it to the description of defense reform in Russia.

Historically, the Russian armed forces have been subordinated to the political will of civilian rulers, whether under the imperial government, the Soviet Politburo or the president. Chapter 2 examines how the military has cultivated an organizational culture that views any active involvement in domestic politics as illegitimate, even during periods of political or economic crisis. At a cultural level, military officers recognize the information asymmetries involved and assume that political leaders are better equipped to govern.

It should not be assumed that politicians will always maintain full control over a politically obedient military. Russia's large military, extensive military-industrial complex, classified regulations and exclusive education and welfare systems for defense professionals create layers of autonomy that complicate civilian oversight.

Under Putin, the Russian approach to military development has involved two steps. In the first, the president formulates policy ideas in line with his broader foreign and security agenda. At this stage, both military and civilian influences shape the president's geopolitical orientation, while the Kremlin must anticipate potential resistance from the military leadership, which retains significant institutional autonomy. Chapter 3 examines this dynamic in the 2000–7 period, when President Putin sought to avoid a militarization of foreign policy but faced a military establishment that retained considerable influence over defense policy development.

In the second step, the military is tasked with implementing reform programs. As shown in Chapter 4, the minister of defense and the chief of the General Staff played a central role as gatekeepers in the 2012–21 period. The minister translated presidential directives into defense policy, while the chief of the General Staff oversaw policy implementation and consolidated military needs for the minister. However, disparities in the information available to the president, military leadership and civilian actors, combined with different capacities to assess this information, complicated decision-making. Moreover, the legal system in Putin's Russia subordinates accountability mechanisms to political priorities, limiting the effectiveness of defense reforms and undermining overall military capabilities.

Chapter 5 compares the previously assessed reforms with each other and explains the reasons for their successes or failures. It argues that the balance of power between civilian and military actors in Russia's civil–military relations was shaped by their administrative capacities. It analyzes the institutional and cultural factors affecting Russia's military performance in Ukraine and explains how the military's exclusive expertise allowed it to resist unwanted reforms. The conclusion suggests that there is potential for Putin's authoritarian regime to learn from its mistakes, rebuild its military and re-emerge as a more intimidating regional military power.

1

RUSSIAN CIVIL–MILITARY RELATIONS AFTER THE USSR

In 1992, Francis Fukuyama proclaimed "the end of history"— the universality of liberal democratic values after the fall of Communism. But the concept of the end of history did not apply to Russian civil–military relations.[1] For Russia, the collapse of the Soviet Union marked the beginning of a new period in its struggle over civil–military relations. This chapter provides an overview of Russian civil–military relations and defense reforms as a basis for the detailed analysis in the remaining chapters.

Russian civil–military instability

In 1985, perestroika, a package of reforms aimed at making the Soviet economy more efficient and the political system more accountable, led to a profound shift in the Communist system that ended with the Soviet disintegration of 1991. This political process included an attempt to reduce the prerogatives of Soviet security agencies and replace Communist Party rule with a new form of civilian control.

Perestroika destabilized the "relatively stable parameters" that regulated Soviet civil–military relations.[2] These parameters included the values and norms relating to civilian (party) control, strategic military and security objectives and ultimately the Soviet Constitution. The changes were monumental because these parameters were usually stable and had remained largely unchanged for dozens of years.[3]

The core norm of civil–military relations is the degree of civilian supremacy over the armed forces. This norm determines the extent to which civilians can implement policies independently, without seeking approval from security agencies. During perestroika, senior military officers became more active in Soviet politics, as they were now allowed to run for political office. This shift politicized the officer corps, leading some to participate in elections while still on active duty. For example, in March 1989 Colonel General Boris Gromov, who was awarded the title of "Hero of the Soviet Union" and commanded the withdrawal of the 40th Army from Afghanistan, was elected to the Congress of People's Deputies (CPD)—the highest state body in the Soviet Union between 1990 and 1991—while serving as the commander of the Kiev Military District of the Soviet Armed Forces. In addition, between 1990 and 1991, he was a member of the Central Committee of the Communist Party of Ukraine.[4] Such a degree of military politicization is highly unusual, whether in democratic systems or in contemporary Russia, as it assigns popular political legitimacy to military officers while they are still commanding troops. Naturally, this contributed to the weakening of civilian control in early post-Soviet Russia, with some senior military officers assuming overtly political roles.

The deterioration of civilian control culminated in the attempted coup of August 1991, when tanks started to roll into Moscow. A coalition of Soviet hardliners, including five civilian officials, the KGB chief, the defense minister and the interior minister, declared a state of emergency and placed Mikhail Gorbachev, the last Soviet leader, under house arrest. Their plan collapsed within three days. Notably, then-captain Sergei Surovikin was reportedly in an infantry fighting vehicle (IFV) that was fleeing the city and fatally ran over three civilian protesters.[5] Thirty-one years later, Surovikin, now known as "General Armageddon," gained notoriety for his brutal but effective leadership during the full-scale invasion of Ukraine.

Once both feared and revered, Soviet generals refused to use troops against civilians during the 1991 coup. In Leningrad (now Saint Petersburg), Russia's second largest city, Mayor Anatoly Sobchak, backed by his then unknown aide Vladimir Putin, publicly condemned the plotters and negotiated with the commander of the Leningrad Military District, General Viktor Samsonov, to prevent military deployment in support of the coup. The mass protest on 20 August, which attracted hundreds of thousands of demonstrators, made clear that the coup was not supported by the city's residents.[6]

The failed coup ultimately triggered the dissolution of the Soviet Union and exposed Gorbachev's and the Communist Party's loss of authority. Known for its formidable military and intelligence apparatus, the state disintegrated as army IFVs fled the capital and elite airborne troops were stopped by unarmed civilians.

The Russian Federation inherited all of the Soviet Union's international powers and obligations, including nuclear weapons, a substantial proportion of the Soviet armed forces, the central and former offices of the Soviet security services and the former Soviet elite.[7] However, the collapse of the USSR was an ideological, organizational and structural disaster for the Russian armed forces and security services. The military lost its huge defense budget and social prestige, was forced to reorganize from the remnants of the Soviet armed forces and had to adapt to a new strategic environment during a tumultuous transition to a market economy.

Russia's Constitution of 1993, which established the new institutional framework for civil–military relations, granted the Russian president extensive authority over the security agencies and armed forces. In practice, they became "the presidential ministries," directly controlled and managed by the president. As a result, defense policymaking in Russia became highly personalized, shaped by the president's priorities and level of political commitment rather than institutional oversight or broader civilian input.

Russia's strong presidential powers stem from the 1993 constitutional crisis—a confrontation between the executive and legislative branches over the distribution of authority and the direction of economic reforms. In September of that year, Russia's first president Boris Yeltsin issued a legally disputed decree to dissolve the parliament. In response, the parliament declared Yeltsin impeached and appointed Vice-President Alexander Rutskoy—a retired major general of the Soviet air force, Hero of the Soviet Union and veteran of the Afghan War—as acting president.[8] Yeltsin then ordered tank formations to fire on the Russian parliament, which was based in the White House—a tall white building on the banks of the Moskva River—crushing the opposition to presidential rule; Rutskoy was subsequently arrested. Ironically, the same building had symbolized resistance to the Soviet coup plotters just two years earlier. After the crisis, Yeltsin formalized "super-presidential" powers by enacting the new Constitution.[9]

Despite the military's critical support for Yeltsin during the constitutional crisis, it received no special privileges and continued to suffer from inadequate funding and subsidies. Just one year later, in 1994, underprepared and underfunded troops were deployed to Chechnya, sparking a decade-long insurgency with thousands of casualties. The leader of the Chechen nationalist movement was Dzhokhar Dudayev, a Soviet air force general and a veteran of the war in Afghanistan. Between 1991 and 1994, Dudayev's Chechnya suffered from high levels of crime, ethnic-based violence and economic degradation. Moscow used this as an opportunity to support the anti-Dudayev opposition with military force.[10]

Service members, unaccustomed to domestic roles, reportedly despised the mission, compounding the military's existing challenges. The Chechen War was a pivotal moment for Russia's strategic military and security objectives, exposing the disconnect between its traditional focus on large-scale warfare against NATO and the actual threats it faced: domestic terrorism, armed secessionism and regional conflicts in the former Soviet republics. A military trained to execute a rapid combined-arms advance to the English Channel after nuclear-first strikes instead found itself mired in protracted guerrilla warfare against its own citizens in the Chechen countryside.

The military struggled to define its role in a new Russia. It instead sought to reshape the country to resemble the Soviet system to which it was accustomed. Salaries were meagre, equipment was outdated and frequently inoperable, morale was low and desertions common. Officers faced deep uncertainty: some moonlighted as taxi drivers to survive, while others, in despair, took their own lives. Military service, a prestigious career in the Soviet Union, became an unappealing and unstable profession. This institutional crisis profoundly shaped Russian civil–military relations and defense policy.

Unlike other Soviet republics, Russia, as the successor of the USSR, inherited most of the central political and law enforcement structures that provided continuity in the development of the defense sector. Yeltsin successfully consolidated civilian control, but this proved ineffective in driving meaningful defense reforms. For nearly two decades after the Soviet collapse, the military remained underfunded, ineffective and plagued by corruption, while the problem of the balance of civilian leadership and military autonomy in the new political system remained unresolved.

Fake democrat, absent commander

When the Soviet Union collapsed, the Russian government faced serious civil–military challenges: appointing civilian defense ministers and staff to the military-dominated ministry; separating and subordinating the General Staff from the MoD; establishing institutions to manage defense policy, budgets and procurement; and establishing parliamentary committees and procedures for defense policy oversight.[11]

Yeltsin decided to partition the former KGB and the Ministry of Internal Affairs into various security agencies and to create the Security Council to regulate the dysfunctional security agencies.[12] Replacing Communist Party control with unilateral presidential control over the security sector complicated Russian civil–military relations. Without a strong political leader, the mechanisms for civilian control over the security agencies' activities were unclear, shattering their compliance with formal laws and regulations. The General Staff operated with limited oversight from the MoD and enjoyed direct access to the president. Senior active-duty and retired generals frequently voiced their disagreement with civilian policy decisions in the media and, at times, openly defied President Yeltsin's orders.

Between 1992 and 2001, Russia had three ministers of defense, all of whom were career military officers. The defense minister is the key actor responsible for overseeing the military in the presidential coalition. Yeltsin's decision not to appoint a civilian to head the MoD—contrary to Organization for Security and Co-operation in Europe (OSCE) standards for democratic civilian control—prevented meaningful reform of civil–military relations.[13] Yeltsin instead used the military to achieve short-term political goals, a decision that had lasting consequences for Russia's political development. I describe the role of the minister in detail in Chapters 4 and 5; I briefly introduce the pre-Putin ministers below.

Defense Minister Pavel Grachev (1992–6) played a key role in important military actions during President Yeltsin's tenure. He supported Yeltsin during the 1993 constitutional crisis by ordering the 13th Guards Tank Regiment to fire on the Russian parliament. Grachev also implemented Presidential Decree no. 2137 of 30 November 1994, which authorized the deployment of federal troops to Chechnya and marked the beginning of the First Chechen War, a decision that was opposed by several high-ranking officers and led to the resignation of many service members who were unwilling to fight their own compatriots, let alone without adequate preparation and support.

Operational planning was carried out by the United Group of Forces, based in the headquarters of the North Caucasus Military District (now part of the Southern Military District). However, the General Staff failed to provide accurate information about the readiness of the Chechen rebels led by Dudayev. Overconfident assessments portrayed the Dudayev regime as vulnerable, weakened by corruption, clan-based violence and crime.[14] Weeks before the invasion, Russia's Federal Counterintelligence Service (the predecessor to the Federal Security Service or FSB) conducted an unsuccessful covert operation to provide tank support to anti-Dudayev forces. President Yeltsin, who reportedly detested Dudayev, finally gave the historic order to launch the operation.

During a difficult re-election campaign in 1996, President Yeltsin dismissed Grachev and appointed General Igor Rodionov (1996–7) as minister of defense. Rodionov, backed by the influential secretary of the Russian Security Council, General Alexander Lebed, launched a public campaign criticizing the government's chronic underfunding and neglect of military issues. He openly quarreled with Yurii Baturin, the civilian secretary of the Defense Council, an extra-constitutional advisory body established by Yeltsin to oversee defense reform. Rodionov argued for comprehensive reforms requiring substantial financial investment to modernize the armed forces, warning that continued underfunding could lead to the military's decline or collapse as an organized force. Baturin advocated for reforms within existing budgetary constraints and the importance of strengthening civilian oversight. Ultimately, the reform effort stalled, and Yeltsin dismissed Rodionov for slowing the defense reform in May 1997.

The last military general to serve as defense minister was Igor Sergeyev (1997–2001), a general from the Strategic Missile Forces. Sergeyev's tenure was marked by structural reforms that ignited intra-military disputes, particularly with Chief of the General Staff Anatoly Kvashnin (1997–2004), over the delegation of severely limited financial resources to nuclear forces instead of conventional forces, especially ground troops, the traditional spearhead of the Soviet and then Russian army. Sergeyev introduced "permanent readiness" units to improve rapid deployment capabilities, merged the Siberian and Trans-Baikal Military Districts and controversially disbanded the Ground Forces General Command to centralize military command to the ministerial level, a decision that was reversed in 2001.[15] Sergeyev did not oppose the launch of the Second Chechen War in August 1999—a better-prepared operation that culminated in the defeat of the insurgency under President Putin.

The instability of Russian civil–military relations in the 1990s stands in stark contrast to the apparent stability observed between the invasion of Ukraine in 2014 and the full-scale war in 2022. In 2014, Russian troops occupied Crimea in a matter of hours. Later that year, unmarked servicemen equipped with artillery, heavy vehicles and weapons supported separatists in Eastern Ukraine, decisively defeating Ukrainian forces. In September 2015, Russia's deployment of troops to Syria marked a turning point in the Syrian civil war in favor of the Assad regime. Meanwhile, Western governments attributed assassinations, cyberattacks and malicious information campaigns in Europe to Russian military intelligence. What explains this change in Russian civil–military relations?

A strongman with weak hands

Putin inherited an unstable system of relations with the security community from Yeltsin, and this predetermined his search for a new institutional balance. From the beginning of his presidency, Putin prioritized the centralization and personalization of political control, especially in the defense sector. His administration gradually sidelined the already weakened parliament and consolidated the president's position as the main decision-maker in military and security matters. By doing so, Putin changed the key component in Russian civil–military relations: the degree of civil–military consensus required for policy change.

This consensus is largely defined by the prerogatives available to the military, including any formal veto power it may have in the policymaking process. In an ideal world, military personnel are expected to resign if they disagree with civilian decisions. But this is not always the case, as security coalitions may engage in bargaining, sabotage or even the vetoing of civilian policies, thereby influencing the degree of consensus required for effective policy reform.

The Russian president holds extensive legal authority over the military and security services, unilaterally appointing and dismissing senior officers, approving military doctrine and chairing the Security Council. He directly oversees conscription, mobilization and the restructuring of military units while also defining the priorities and structure of security agencies, such as the National Guard, the FSB, the Foreign Intelligence Service (SVR) and the Federal Guards Service (FSO). He also issues decrees on military training and determines which organizations operate in the interest of national defense.[16]

Putin's role in the military is consistent with the Stalinist belief that loyal, reliable individuals matter more than institutions or procedures, the so-called "cadres decide everything" principle.[17] He wields direct control over the leadership of the armed forces, security agencies and military policy without needing to consult other political bodies. Putin has appointed officials with a background in the security services to roles in government and state-owned enterprises.[18]

Putin's control extends to all security services, which serve as a counterbalance to potential political challenges from within the military.[19] The president leads the FSB, Russia's primary counterintelligence agency, appointing its director and coordinating its activities. He defines the goals of the foreign intelligence services, including the SVR, and oversees the FSO, which ensures his personal security. As commander-in-chief of the National Guard, he defines its mission, structure and personnel size.[20]

Yet while Putin has near-total legal control over Russia's military and security apparatus, the reality of centralized command is more complex, as various institutional dynamics shape decision-making and implementation.[21] For example, coordinating the work of the Russian security agencies can be a challenge, as these bodies have different mandates, institutional cultures and conflicting interests, and their staff often come from different educational backgrounds.[22] The military itself has different branches and regional districts, as well as complex relationships with the military-industrial complex. As a result, civilian authorities can never be completely sure whether the military will faithfully execute orders ("work") or deviate from expectations ("shirk").[23]

To make the military work, civilian leaders establish specialized mechanisms to monitor and evaluate military performance. These mechanisms are critical in shaping civilian leaders' understanding of military capabilities and challenges. The optimal configuration of these mechanisms is one that "minimizes the incentives and opportunity for the agent to flout the principal's wishes, at the least cost to the principal and while preserving the efficiencies of specialization that come with delegation."[24] Ineffective or poorly designed mechanisms disrupt the balance of civil–military relations, creating conditions for unrealistic civilian demands and inadequate military performance.

Despite the armed forces' apparent subordination to Putin's orders and the militarization of the country through culture, propaganda and high-level defense spending, the Russian military has remained one of the few sectors Putin has been unable to fully control. The military has defended its institutional autonomy and has often blocked civilian appointees from implementing meaningful reforms. The MoD and military generals have fiercely guarded classified military information, resisted the involvement of civilian outsiders in defense management and have often shifted the blame for failures and disasters onto civilian leaders. Overall, Russian defense reforms during this period fell short of achieving the Kremlin's aim of gaining military superiority against potential adversaries.

The imperfect equilibrium of Russian civil–military relations

As in democracies, armed forces in authoritarian states can play a strong role in shaping public policy, as many defense policies require military expertise for effective development and enforcement. In 1957, Samuel Huntington, one of the "founding fathers" of civil–military relations studies, suggested that the military must develop a certain degree of professionalism that requires institutional autonomy from civilians in military buildup and command and control over the forces to be able to use complex military tactics and weaponry. Civilian authorities are indeed interested in the successful development of the military, but, at the same time, they are also concerned by the possibility of military involvement in civilian affairs. Thus, there is a natural incentive to find a status quo that will maximize military effectiveness and minimize the chance of military interference in civilian politics.[25] In Russia, non-interference by the military has been achieved, but maximization of military effectiveness has failed. The Russian military has exerted legitimate, though worrying, pressure to get what it wants in military policy, sometimes disregarding the government's official position.

The Russian military's involvement in Russian defense policy takes place over two distinct stages. The first involves the selection of policy options in line with the president's foreign policy agenda. Military and civilian actors' access to the presidential decision-making process has largely determined the effectiveness and direction of subsequent reforms. However, the military has had a stronger position as a defense actor due to its institutional autonomy in organizational development. Therefore, the minister of defense and the chief of the General Staff serve as critical gatekeepers, mediating the president's influence over the armed forces.

All Russian officers were trained within the traditional military education system, which fostered skepticism of innovative proposals. This resistance highlights a common challenge in military reform, where proponents of progressive change have to contend with traditionalist military leaders.[26] A key normative concern among these leaders was the fear that reforms would undermine the military's structure and combat effectiveness, even when critical problems within the force were evident. Moreover, traditions are highly valued in the Russian military, and any perceived violation of established symbols or operational practices has often provoked irritation and criticism, even from active-duty officers.

In the second stage, the military is tasked with implementing the reform programs. However, Russian oversight and accountability mechanisms have hindered effective monitoring of reform implementation. Similar to other functions, the Russian president is again the key player in selecting the leadership of important accountability bodies. He proposes candidates for the positions of prosecutor general and deputy prosecutors to the Federation Council—the upper chamber of the Federal Assembly (Russia's bicameral legislature)—which is controlled by the president and has the power to appoint and dismiss regional prosecutors. In addition, the president appoints judges to the Constitutional Court, the Supreme Court and other federal courts. This centralization places the entire system of military oversight and accountability firmly under presidential control. Given the complexity and size of the Russian military, such a narrowly focused approach to oversight has repeatedly proven insufficient to ensure effective reform and accountability. The president, military leadership and civilian actors have essentially received different information on the state of the armed forces and have had unequal processing capacities for assessing it.

The president, as the key leader and overseer of all security services in Russia, can decide whether to go after high-ranking officials for alleged mistakes or even crimes or let them go. For example, a year and a half after the *Kursk* nuclear submarine disaster in August 2000, with the death of all 118 crew members (just a few months after Putin was sworn into office following the 2000 presidential election), several senior officers of the Russian navy's Northern Fleet faced only disciplinary action. Admiral Vyacheslav Popov, commander of the Northern Fleet, who was criticized for delays in launching rescue operations and for his reluctance to accept international assistance, was simply relieved of his command. Vice-Admiral Mikhail Motsak, chief of staff of the Northern Fleet, who was involved in planning naval exercises and coordinating the response to the disaster, was demoted and forced to resign. Both led active public lives after the disaster: Popov served as a senator for the Murmansk region as well as being deputy head of the Defense and Security Committee (responsible for the preliminary legal review and consultation on national security matters) of the Federation Council from 2002 to 2011; and until 2012, Motsak worked as deputy head and advisor to the Presidential Plenipotentiary Representative Office in the Northwest Region. Putin created the presidential plenipotentiary representatives in May 2000 to enhance presidential oversight over the enforcement of federal decisions, national security and sociopolitical conditions in the districts and to manage presidential personnel policy at a regional level.

The quest to achieve an equilibrium in Russian civil–military relations materialized in various shapes over the 2000–22 period. First, in the 2000–7 period, the Kremlin was reluctant to invest in military effectiveness despite numerous civilian attempts to lobby for changes. The reform agenda was rather conservative, and President Putin appointed a minister of defense, Sergei Ivanov, who abstained from policy conflicts (more on him in Chapter 3). Russia's most notable success came during the 2007–12 reforms, which introduced crucial structural changes. Subsequent efforts, which focused on technological modernization, were less successful. However, the 2007–12 reforms caused a crisis in civil–military relations. The MoD implemented policies bluntly and chaotically, while the military tried to slow the process. Since 2012, civil–military relations have seemingly improved, but the adoption of intrusive monitoring mechanisms, such as snap exercises, photo/

video reports and video surveillance, was expensive and overlooked the roots of the military's problems. Over time, the military learned how to overcome the centralized monitoring system, and the pace of change in the Russian military stagnated as a result. In short, Russian civil–military relations shifted from one imperfect equilibrium to another, resembling qualitatively different episodes instead of a continuous development of the same defense system.

Policymaking context

Is Russian defense policymaking unique in the broader context of reforms in Russia? Unlike the Soviet Union, where the military had significant resources by default, the pre-2022 Russian armed forces were relatively economical, and their needs have not been automatically prioritized. Military development has been influenced by the priorities and needs of other ministries, agencies and broader socioeconomic conditions. I therefore take into account the impact of other policies and socioeconomic factors, including budgetary constraints, production capacities and public opinion. Changes in socioeconomic conditions shape the incentives and resources available to coalitions in policymaking. Typically, deteriorating socioeconomic conditions increase competition for limited resources. Public opinion is another critical factor, as the popularity of civilian or military leaders, such as the minister of defense or chief of the General Staff, can influence the likelihood of accountability for military actors. The popularity of politico-military leaders shields them from criticism from the executive.[27]

In the late 1990s, Russian society was financially poor and deeply critical of the government. The state struggled to provide basic public goods, and many citizens viewed the political situation as "critical or explosive."[28] As political scientist Vladimir Gel'man has noted, Putin faced three key challenges in consolidating power: restoring Russia's coercive and redistributive state capacity, subordinating fragmented federal and regional elites and maintaining high levels of public support.[29] Achieving the first two goals was impossible without an effective security apparatus. Russia needed a functioning military and law enforcement system to end the war in Chechnya, combat organized crime and restore its foreign policy standing.

Public opinion had little impact on military policy in Putin's Russia before 2007. The first reform of the armed forces from 2001 to 2007 was largely unsuccessful, while civilian-led initiatives to modernize Russia's public administration were relatively successful. The public administration reform centralized the federal executive by eliminating or reforming thousands of government services and creating a three-tier system of federal bodies. The ministries became responsible for strategic policymaking, services were focused on oversight and federal agencies were dedicated to implementing state policies.[30]

The economic environment during this period was favorable, supported by rising oil prices, which allowed Russia to offset interest payments and establish the Russian Stabilization Fund in 2004. The fund acted as a rainy-day sovereign wealth fund, accumulating tax income from excess oil revenue to be spent during periods of low oil prices.[31] Russia's federal state budget was also strengthened by measures against tax evasion, as well as through reforms to the tax code and the Federal Tax Service.

While civilian experts advocated changes in the defense sector, military reform fell short of its stated goals, despite this supportive economic and political context.[32] The core issue stemmed from the composition of the presidential and military coalitions. Ivanov, the defense minister, was surrounded by traditionalist military generals, while Chiefs of the General Staff Kvashnin and Baluyevsky openly disagreed with the proposed reforms. When a significant number of individuals with a military background have been present in Russia's governing coalition, the military has had a greater capacity to shape defense policy, often resisting changes that challenged established structures and traditions.

Russia's most successful defense reform happened during Medvedev's presidential term from 2008 to 2012. This is somewhat paradoxical because Medvedev's presidency has often been characterized disparagingly as "a mixture of fake reforms and half-measures."[33] Politicians and analysts have described Medvedev's broader reform agenda as symbolic or ineffective, with efforts such as the 2010 civil service reform stalled due to a lack of dedicated funding,[34] and police reform—conducted within a small circle of Internal Affairs Ministry officials—largely failing.[35] Medvedev's leadership style and public image also contrasted sharply with Putin's bold, militaristic persona: as president, Medvedev often emphasized "humanistic" values as essential to Russia's development—principles not typically aligned with the military's ethos.[36]

Under Medvedev, the presidential coalition purged the sitting military leadership and made the new appointments implement the changes proposed by the MoD. The reform represented a challenging large-scale effort to modernize Russia's armed forces by trying to create a new force structure, procuring new equipment and improving military morale and education. The reform brought tangible results by 2014 and beyond (more on this in Chapter 4).

However, the reform remained incomplete when Putin returned to power and appointed a new defense minister, who halted and even reversed some of the most radical changes. Between 2012 and 2022, the Russian military received significant quantities of new equipment, but deliveries lagged projections due to economic shocks and sanctions imposed after the annexation of Crimea and the war in Eastern Ukraine, and the effectiveness of this equipment was undermined by persistent issues in military education, training and morale. As with the broader Russian economy, the armed forces once again fell into stagnation, consistently failing to meet development targets and, ultimately, suffering serious defeats in the first year of the full-scale invasion of Ukraine in 2022.

Conclusion

Russian civil–military relations exhibit a Janus-faced nature, balancing between formal civilian control and significant military influence over defense policy. While the military remains officially subordinate to civilian leadership, it actively shapes strategic decisions, resists reforms and safeguards its institutional interests.

This is typical of both authoritarian and democratic countries with a long tradition of civilian control. The United States exemplifies the pronounced dual role of the military: on one hand, it adheres to civilian authority, while, on the other, it has a strong influence on strategic decision-making.[37] The US military exercises this influence through senior commanders' rhetoric on the use of force, targeted lobbying for preferred strategies, such as presenting a limited menu of military options, and the accumulation of operational objectives that gradually displace broader strategic priorities (such as in Afghanistan, when the desire to defeat the Taliban militarily overshadowed the United States' inability to stabilize the country politically).[38]

In Russia, this duality generates ongoing tensions between military autonomy and civilian oversight and complicates the government's internal assessments of military development, as civilian institutions often lack both full access and the necessary expertise to conduct robust evaluations. Nevertheless, both the president and the military leadership have tolerated this imperfect civil–military balance, viewing it as a means of preserving political stability and a functional military. Actors who have sought to challenge this arrangement have been systematically excluded from the policymaking process and denied access to the armed forces. The next chapter examines the cultural underpinnings of these relations, focusing on the beliefs and strategic interactions between Russian civilian and military actors.

2

CIVIL–MILITARY RELATIONS AND RUSSIAN MILITARY CULTURE

Introduction

On 31 January 2022, retired three-star general Leonid Ivashov published an appeal to President Putin. Ivashov warned of the inevitable human casualties, widespread destruction and long-term suffering for Ukraine and Russia if the president launched a full-scale invasion of Ukraine. Ivashov argued that the ensuing war would isolate Russia on the world stage, attract severe economic sanctions and potentially provoke a wider conflict involving NATO countries.[1]

Ivashov's appeal was unusual. Russian generals, including retired ones, rarely criticize Putin in the media. Yet Ivashov argued against the mainstream government position in the media, was skeptical of Russian military superiority and criticized Putin's likely course of action. As we now know, the appeal was unsuccessful: Putin launched the invasion anyway, and Ivashov's prediction of casualties, sanctions and international security dynamics was fully realized.

The general's appeal highlights a common misconception: that the Russian military fully supports the president and his strategy. A deeper analysis of Russian civil–military relations reveals that civilian and military cultural values have always diverged in Russia, and this has jeopardized Russia's efforts to build a powerful military.[2]

This chapter examines the values and norms of Russia's civilian and military leadership as they relate to the defense sector. It explores how differing views on statehood, the military's role in national development and the place of the civilian leadership in setting military policy have influenced the trajectory of Russian defense reforms under Putin.

Why does military culture matter? The military fights wars, and its members are expected to kill the enemy or be prepared to die in combat. Given limited time, resources and information, soldiers cannot always rely on manuals and regulations to make decisions. In combat, cultural norms help service members make quick decisions, save their lives and complete the mission. For this reason, military academies and general training rely heavily on instilling the appropriate norms and values that will guide service members' behavior, even when no one is watching, whether in a foxhole or at an office desk. Military culture is "the software" of the armed forces: it provides the "values, norms, virtues, habits and beliefs, meanings and styles, the informal restrictions and permissions—including punishments and rewards—that make the machinery work."[3] In peacetime, the alignment of values between the military and civilian sectors influences their communication and cooperation.[4]

In Russia, civilian and military values and norms have not been compatible for most of the post-Soviet period. In the 1990s, a deep cultural divide with the civilian government prevented effective military reform. As my interviewees recalled, they were duty-bound to serve in the military but felt they no longer had a country to serve. Their national identity and expectations about the future disappeared together with the military's prestige, high wages and generous welfare. Instead, the Russian military became a decaying Soviet relic, adrift in the turbulent waters of Russia's post-Soviet transition. Military command publicly acknowledged hundreds of non-combat casualties from suicides, hazing and violation of safety protocols and struggled with severe recruitment and retention problems.

Hazing is defined as physical or psychological conduct perpetrated by one or more experienced service members without proper formal authority against less experienced service members, causing them to suffer or be exposed to cruel, abusive, humiliating, oppressive or harmful treatment. The Russian military has had a serious problem with hazing, with officers often seeing it as a necessary mechanism to build unit cohesion (to break recruits' individualism). However, hazing has sometimes resulted in serious psychological and physical trauma, death, absence without leave, desertion or even mass shootings.

Putin's rise to power narrowed the divide between the military elites and the civilian government. His rule brought with it values and norms that seemed closer to traditional military values: patriotism, unity, camaraderie and a focus on national interests. Yet the military leadership believe that the Russian armed forces play a historically "exclusive role" that ensures the survival of the Russian state. Therefore, in their view, the military has a legitimate right to make Russian citizens more militaristic and demand changes in the civilian part of the government before reforming the armed forces.

The 2008 war in Georgia shattered that perception and triggered abrupt, civilian-driven changes in the military. The war was a brief conflict between Russia and Georgia in August 2008 over the breakaway regions of South Ossetia and Abkhazia, which escalated after Georgian forces launched an assault on Tskhinvali, the capital of South Ossetia. Russia intervened militarily, repelled Georgian forces, invaded the Georgian-controlled territory and later recognized South Ossetia and Abkhazia as independent states.[5] Although Russia officially won the war, its military demonstrated a poor state of readiness, with low-quality equipment, a lack of intelligence and serious equipment and human losses.

However, the military bureaucracy counterattacked in ministerial offices, and most of the reforms implemented following the war have since been reversed, such as the consolidation of military academies, cancellation of the warrant officer rank (and removal of thousands of officers) and the fragmentation of divisions into brigades, thus restoring the imperfect equilibrium of civil–military relations in Russia.

Under an imperfect equilibrium, Russian military autonomy from the civilian leadership invigorated its sense of cultural exclusiveness. Some senior military leaders—for example, chiefs of the General

Staff—were aware of the problems in military readiness, morale, infrastructure and equipment and even discussed various policy proposals in the media.[6] Yet, innovative reform proposals in the 1990s and 2000s from civilian and retired military experts show that potentially positive policy ideas were culturally alien to the Russian military leadership, as they threatened military traditions and norms.[7] This exclusive military culture became detrimental to Russian military effectiveness as military elites blamed civilians for the failures of the military-driven reform. At the same time, Russian civilian experts blamed the generals for fighting over financial resources, and in making clear their unwillingness to waste efforts and sacrifice their careers to reform the military, entrenching an imperfect but mutually accepted equilibrium in the outcomes of reform.[8]

Making sense of Russian military culture

Culture is often misused as an all-purpose explanation of anything that defies mainstream expectations. To avoid this, and before going into the details of the Russian case, I define military culture and divide the concept into "deep core beliefs"[9] and "policy core beliefs,"[10] which directly regulate military relations with civilian leaders and other sectors of society.[11] As mentioned in the Introduction, military culture is a set of interdependent values, norms, beliefs, meanings and traditions, along with the informal constraints and permissions that regulate human behavior in the military.

Russian military culture is shaped by a legacy of over seventy years of Soviet development, during which the armed forces served as both the principal guardian and a central actor in advancing the socialist project. Today, North Korea represents an extreme case of such totalitarian militarization, where its "military-first" doctrine positions the armed forces as integral to every aspect of national life. Soldiers are systematically indoctrinated to view themselves as key pillars of the regime, with responsibilities extending across the state, society, economy and even popular culture.[12] In Türkiye, the military has traditionally assumed a strong ideological role, viewing itself as the guardian of secularism, national unity and sovereignty. This self-perception led to multiple successful coups, justified as responses to perceived threats against the secular republican order. The failed coup attempt in 2016, however, marked a turning point, prompting a sweeping overhaul of civil–military relations and a significant curtailment of the military's guardian role in domestic politics.[13]

Russia's military culture is neither totalitarian, like in North Korea, nor activist, as was previously the case in Türkiye, but is built upon the idea that national security is a basis of national sovereignty and the wellbeing of the people. This idea is so foundational that there is a strong belief that, without strong national security and the military to provide it, there would be no Russia. Due to Russia's location, history and territorial extent, Russian sovereignty is perceived to be constantly contested by foreign actors. However, this view coexists with the notion that the military has no legitimate role in active politics and should instead act within the governance framework defined by the Kremlin's political leadership.

Russian deep core beliefs

Deep core beliefs are fundamental, shaping the self-understanding of the state that the military serves.[14] These beliefs represent deeply ingrained values that are highly resistant to change,[15] guiding expectations of human behavior, the rules of social interaction, justice and the balance between security and development.[16] They remain stable over time, influencing military and political decision-making.

Russian service members swear to "defend the freedom, independence and constitutional order of Russia, the people and the Homeland."[17] As in other nations with professional militaries, these deep-seated values are reinforced through commemorative holidays, official historical narratives, mass culture, statements by opinion leaders—veterans, public figures and political leaders— and educational curricula in schools and military academies. When civilian and military deep core beliefs diverge, a fundamental civil–military divide emerges, making effective policy cooperation nearly impossible. Bridging such gaps has not only required policy adjustments but often a reshuffling of key personnel within the presidential coalition, the Security Council, the MoD and the General Staff.

The military and its militarism

To better understand how the Russian military leadership views the normative ideal of military service, I asked all my respondents to name the best representation of service in mass culture. They unanimously pointed to the Soviet film *Officers*. This was surprising because unanimous agreement among respondents is rare in research, especially when it comes to vague questions about cultural references. The *Officers* movie romanticizes military service as a higher calling—one dedicated to unconditional national security—and is famous for its iconic line: "There is such a profession—to defend the homeland."

The film follows a lineage of military officers, beginning with those who served in tsarist Russia, continuing through the Russian Civil War and extending to their children and grandchildren, who also chose a military path. Regardless of Russia's hardships, these officers prioritized service above all else, including their families, and faithfully executed civilian decisions on the use of force. The narrative highlights the devastating losses of the Great Patriotic War (the June 1941–May 1945 part of the Second World War),[18] where officers' children died in battle, leaving them to raise grandchildren who would also go on to serve. The film elevates the military to a core component of Russian national identity.

Some of the military respondents I interviewed came from longstanding military dynasties, while others described being immersed in a militarized social environment from an early age. They recalled frequently seeing fit and disciplined service members in public spaces, participating in basic military training programs at school and encountering local recruitment officers who actively engaged with students and their parents to promote military service. A survey of Russian elites, a repeated cross-sectional study initiated in 1993 and conducted across eight waves up to 2020 by researchers from the University of Michigan, Hamilton College and Stanford University, indicates that Russia's military leadership largely adheres to a statist vision of governance, prioritizing a strong and stable state, even at the expense of civil liberties. While many respondents expressed nominal support for political competition, they were willing to sacrifice it in favor of stability, particularly during times of political and economic uncertainty.[19]

By putting a strong emphasis on the Great Patriotic War, Soviet socialization pre-formed positive ideas about military service: "My mother told me I had to serve. My grandfather died in Stalingrad. Moreover, I served there [in the Stalingrad battle region] later, and she wrote to me in every letter that we should be proud."[20] Even though the interviewed officers often recalled some negative experiences, such as hazing, violence, commanders' mistakes, financial hardships in the 1990s and challenges with resocialization after retirement, they still described their military life as positive and praiseworthy:

> I still believe that service, especially as an officer, means a serious platform in life, serious material security, on the one hand. On the other hand, a man is engaged in a serious job, this is some kind of organization of life, and in general the groundwork for the future.[21]

This belief exists among Western military veterans too.[22] However, while their Western counterparts experienced free media, independent mass culture and the appeal of civilian success in business, government or culture, Soviet citizens were surrounded by a much more insulated, militarized and government-regulated culture from kindergartens to high-level political events. This isolated, homogeneous and heavily ideologized experience made the values and beliefs of military members particularly salient in post-Soviet Russia.

Politicization of the military

The fall of the Soviet Union created a deep cultural divide between civilian and military elites. As Soviet political structures disintegrated, the late Soviet government politicized the military by allowing service members to run for election and even voice their opinion on state policies in the liberalizing media. In the difficult aftermath of the Soviet collapse, the military found itself in an unusual position, assuming a greater role in civilian politics as the last "guardian" of the state.[23] This experience had a lasting impact on post-Soviet Russia, shaping the military's role in governance and its relationship with the civilian leadership.

In December 1988, Gorbachev introduced two legislative reforms, the law "On the Election of People's Deputies" and amendments to the Constitution, formally permitting military officers to run for the Soviet CPD.[24] The CPD was the highest organ of state power in the Soviet Union from 1989 to 1991, established during the perestroika period. The Russian republic followed suit and set up its own CPD in 1990 as its supreme legislative body within the USSR. One retired service member recalled being delegated by the aviation regiment to participate in the commission that nominated Galina Starovoitova to the Russian CPD,[25] noting that "the country was falling apart, there was no medicine" and hoping for positive changes with her election to the CPD.[26]

Similar instances occurred throughout the Soviet Union, with active-duty officers running for various political positions at local, national and union levels. A notable example is Ruslan Aushev, a decorated Soviet hero and Afghan War veteran who was elected to the Soviet CPD while still serving as a motor rifle regiment commander in Russia's Far East.[27] He became the head of Ingushetia in 1993, earning widespread recognition for maintaining political stability and military security in the republic during the wars in neighboring Chechnya. This experience reshaped the military's self-perception of its role in national development. Suddenly, the Soviet army, which had been a subordinate tool of the Communist Party since the October 1917 Revolution, got powers to compete in elections and take part in policy debates.

One of the first major political shocks for the military occurred in 1991 when the Soviet leadership tried to use military force to prevent the collapse of the USSR. Throughout the late 1980s and early 1990s, the territorial disintegration of the Soviet Union was accompanied by episodes of military intervention to suppress nationalist protests in the union republics, such as in Tbilisi (April

1989) and Baku (January 1990). This period also saw regime change within the Russian republic itself, placing the Soviet leadership in a dilemma: the state they had sworn to defend was unraveling. As one interviewed officer noted, "before, there was a union state and a Soviet army with representatives from all fifteen republics. But once the national divisions emerged, conscription ended, and only Russian representatives remained."[28]

The crisis culminated in a coup attempt in August 1991. When the coup plotters were confronted with the reality of turning their guns on unarmed civilians defending barricades, no one in the military was willing to take responsibility for firing the first shot. Few mobilized to preserve the Soviet Union, and far more rallied in defense of democratic change. The conspirators' attempt to save the USSR lacked support not only among the broader civilian population but also among lower-ranking military personnel. This disconnect ultimately doomed their efforts and underscored the weakening of the Soviet-era alignment between the military and the political leadership.

Instead of preventing the Soviet collapse, the coup hastened it. It left the military without a national identity, guided by a weak government and surrounded by a liberalizing society. The transition to a market economy and weak democratic state unleashed social forces and patterns of behavior that had previously been marginalized. The transition opened new opportunities for civilian elites, but, for the military, it was a completely unknown environment. One officer described the 1990s as a period that "destroyed the former state ... [They] tried to level out patriotism, to reduce it to zero, to dissolve the country and its identity."[29]

Another shock followed in the 1993 constitutional crisis, mentioned earlier. Although the military formally carried out the order to attack the White House, it displayed neither enthusiasm nor a clear commitment to the mission. My interviewees described an atmosphere of confusion and anxiety within the military, exacerbated by an informational blockade that left troops disoriented. Military respondents later expressed regret that civilian leaders had used them for domestic political purposes while shifting all the blame onto the armed forces. In his memoirs, for example, General Troshev described the initial post-Soviet years as being characterized by:

> brainless and ruthless economic reforms, the officers' indiscriminately running away from the army and then the bloody, soul-breaking autumn of 1993 [shelling of the parliament by Yeltsin], to top it off—the demand to urgently send troops to Chechnya. In general, Russia found itself in a deep coma without "waking up from a dream" [by "the dream," he likely meant the Soviet Union—ironically—whose propaganda frequently depicted its development as a path toward a socialist dream].[30]

These events deepened the divide between the military and civilian leadership, reinforcing a perception within the officer corps that politicians were exploiting the military for their own ends. As one respondent put it: "[The military oath] says we serve not Stalin, not Peter the Great, but the state handed to us. Politicians come and go, but the state remains."[31] This growing distrust of the civilian leadership laid the foundation for Russia's contemporary civil–military relations.

Military marginalization

The economic and political freedoms made possible by the Soviet collapse created plentiful political and business opportunities for civilians. Some of them, however, blamed senior military officers for perpetuating brutality, corruption and disregard for human rights in Russia.[32] As one civil society leader put it: "And for them, the Afghans who came to power, Grachev and the whole team, Chechnya was a piece of territory where people were outlawed. Do whatever you want, test your weapons, people there were prey. Like Anna Politkovskaya wrote, the prey. I saw it myself."[33] The interviewee referenced General Pavel Grachev and journalist Anna Politkovskaya—two individuals whose personalities and public roles could not have been more different.

Grachev was an army general who served as defense minister from May 1992 to July 1996. A decorated airborne officer, he rose to prominence during the Afghan War and later became first deputy minister of defense during the USSR's dissolution. Grachev supported Yeltsin during the August 1991 coup and later commanded troops to shell the Russian White House during the constitutional crisis. From 1994 to 1996, he commanded Russian forces in the First Chechen War, infamously promising to quell the conflict in "a couple of hours" using a single airborne regiment. His tenure was also marred by corruption allegations—famously involving the misappropriation of foreign cars during the withdrawal of Soviet troops from Germany, earning him the nickname "Pasha Mercedes." Following the disastrous outcome in Chechnya, Grachev was dismissed and later served as a defense advisor until his death in 2012.[34]

Politkovskaya was a famous Russian journalist who covered the Second Chechen War (from 1999) and took a highly critical stance toward Putin's government and the FSB. In 2001, she visited the 45th Special Purpose Airborne Regiment in Chechnya, where she observed pits allegedly dug for detaining Chechens suspected of collaborating with rebel forces. According to her account, just two minutes after speaking with the regiment's commander, she was detained and interrogated—presumably by FSB officers—who accused her of aiding the rebels. Later that night, she was subjected to a mock execution, during which a multiple launch rocket system was suddenly fired near her.[35] Later subject to death threats, she was ultimately murdered in her Moscow apartment building in 2006. It is still not known who organized the assassination.[36] The stories of Grachev and Politkovskaya exemplify the diverging paths of civil society and military leaders in the first years of post-Soviet Russia.

The survey of Russian elites (Figure 2) also revealed a divergence between military and civilian perspectives, with military respondents consistently downplaying the role of human rights in political stability compared to their civilian counterparts. Figure 2 illustrates that, across all periods, the military consistently placed a higher priority on maintaining domestic order than on protecting human rights. However, these findings should not be overgeneralized, as the survey is not representative of the entire spectrum of Russian elites. The results are best used for the discussion about the differences (trends) between time periods and between the military and civilian elite groups.

IMPERFECT EQUILIBRIUM

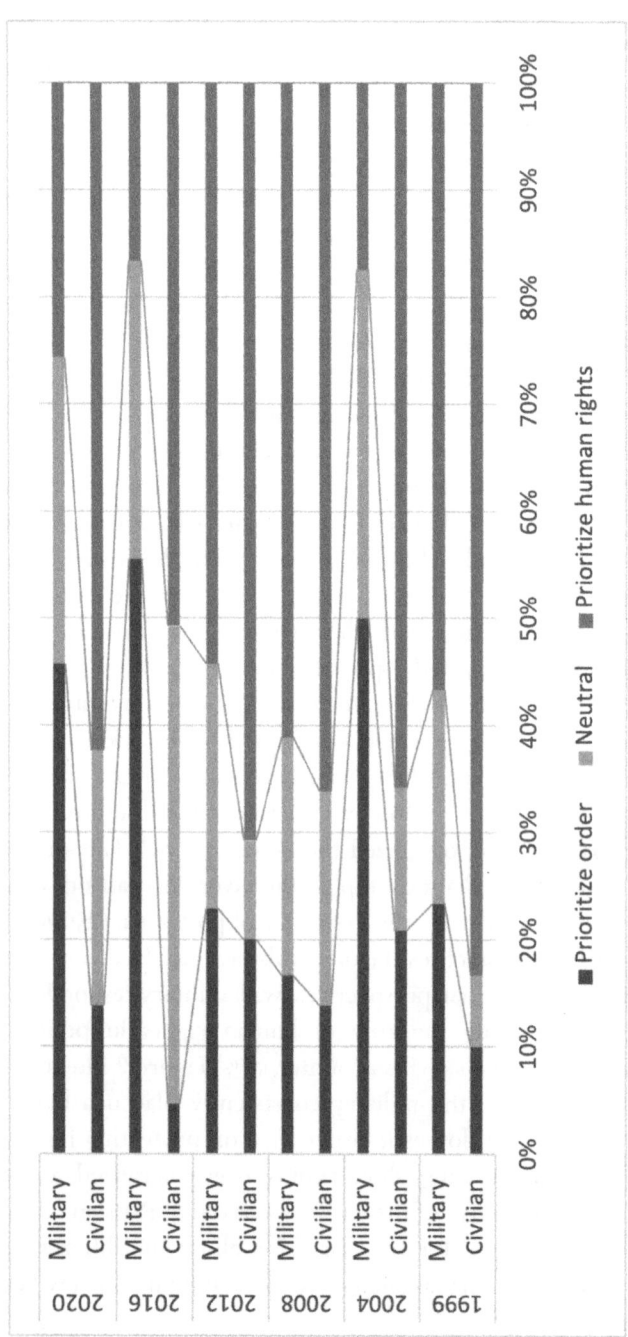

Figure 2: Survey of Russian elites, support for order at any price

Source: William Zimmerman, Sharon Werning Rivera and Kirill Kalinin, "Survey of Russian Elites, Moscow, Russia, 1993–2020," Inter-university Consortium for Political and Social Research, 1 June 2023, https://doi.org/10.3886/ICPSR03724.v8

The shifting social order—characterized by market-driven opportunities, the absence of an official state ideology, a deteriorating welfare system and open borders—also had a profound impact on the military. Recruitment became more challenging as young people increasingly prioritized personal and economic freedoms over state service. As one retired officer reflected: "If you take my generation, we had an ideology ... It was not just about developing the country, but also about upbringing, obedience, loyalty, and so on."[37] Once a pillar of Soviet stability, the military found itself struggling to adapt to a rapidly modernizing society, where state institutions, including the armed forces, were forced to catch up with shifting societal values and expectations.

Rather than focusing on adapting to Russia's evolving society, the interviewed officers emphasized the military's role in instilling traditional gender roles and patriotism in the younger generation. As one officer put it, "I support the restoration of military training in schools, ... these fundamental things are more focused on upbringing than physical training. It makes him stronger, turns him into a fighter, a man." Another respondent echoed these sentiments: "Purposefulness, willpower, determination, command qualities, devotion to ideals, patriotism ... values that must remain unshakable."[38] This belief reinforced the importance of conscription: "Since the army is a powerful educational institution, abolishing the draft would, among other things, weaken the role of patriotic education and civic responsibility."[39]

Some officers even sought to implement these ideological narratives in conflict zones. One respondent described efforts in Chechnya to integrate patriotic values into local communities: "During the May holidays, we started working with them [local Chechens], burying war heroes, participants of the Great Patriotic War. They were very surprised that the school was re-established. They saw that we did not come to rob or oppress them, but, on the contrary, immediately began to help in other ways."[40] Russian military officers generally supported an expanded role for the armed forces beyond their official duties, arguing that military service should serve as a mechanism for properly socializing citizens into a shared set of patriotic norms.

Desire for strong leadership

Russia's administrative weakness and dire economic situation severely hindered the military's ability to adapt to the new circumstances of the 1990s and early 2000s. The military recognized it was unable to guarantee Russia's national security and placed the blame on the civilian-led transition. As one officer recalled:

> While civilian authorities and businessmen were dividing spheres of influence and redesigning everything, the army continued fulfilling its duty—protecting borders, maintaining combat readiness and upholding our nuclear shield. In my personal opinion, the country survived the '90s because of the army. And that army was still the Soviet army.[41]

Military officers felt abandoned by the civilian leadership: "Once again, we trusted all the promises we were given. Once again, we were sidelined. Once again, we were deceived. It was a difficult time." Another noted that "[t]he democrats feared we might rebel, so they stripped us of everything. We were naive, but we didn't realize it."[42] The military's disillusionment with civilian rule reinforced its skepticism toward the post-Soviet transition more broadly. For example, the term "democrats" in this interview—often used interchangeably with "liberals"—served as a slur to describe politicians engaged in corrupt, pro-Western practices while advocating for market reforms under a democratic façade that disregarded ordinary people's needs.

In response to weak civilian leadership, military officers openly resisted orders during the First Chechen War, which was perceived as an unnecessary and illegitimate war against Russia's own citizens.[43] Several high-ranking Russian military officers criticized the lack of preparation and strategic rationale.[44] General Boris Gromov, who commanded Soviet forces during the Afghan withdrawal, denounced the war as "not the army's function" and resigned in 1995, describing the operation as "absolutely unprepared." He later transitioned into politics, serving as governor of Moscow oblast (2000–12). Similarly, General Alexander Lebed, a decorated paratrooper, gained prominence for negotiating the Khasavyurt Accords, signed on 31 August 1996, with Chechen rebel leader Aslan Maskhadov.

The agreement established a ceasefire and mandated the withdrawal of Russian troops from Chechnya, granting the region de facto independence without formal recognition, which undermined Chechnya's independent development and contributed to the resumption of the war in 1999.

Lebed's sharp criticism of Defense Minister Grachev's handling of troop reductions and urban warfare led to his dismissal as the president's National Security Advisor in 1996. He later won the Krasnoyarsk Krai governorship in 1998 and was seen as a potential rival to President Yeltsin. However, Lebed died suddenly in a helicopter crash in 2002, sparking assassination rumors. Officially, the crash was blamed on poor weather. General Eduard Vorobyev also took a firm stance against the war, refusing to lead the 1994 assault on Grozny due to the operation's poor planning, and offered his resignation. Vorobyev later served in the State Duma for the liberal Souz Pravykh Sil (Union of Right Forces, SPS) party (1999–2003).

The military also exerted pressure on Russian foreign policy. A former US navy attaché in Moscow argued that the Russian military played a decisive role in lobbying for the 1999 military operation in Kosovo, an unexpected and controversial Russian troop deployment to Pristina airport in June 1999, immediately after the end of NATO's air campaign against Yugoslavia.[45] General Leonid Ivashov later confirmed that the General Staff, while providing only vague briefings to the president, had secretly planned and executed the operation to seize the airport ahead of British forces, stationed in Kosovo as part of NATO's peacekeeping forces. The plan even included a contingency scenario for military confrontation with NATO. Though Yeltsin later approved the operation, his reaction revealed the extent of military influence: "Well, finally, I knocked them down a peg or two," said Yeltsin. "No, Boris Nikolaevich [Yeltsin], you didn't knock them down—you hit them in the face"—someone in the audience responded.[46]

The military's influence on Russian foreign policy, particularly in the case of Pristina, was distinctly anti-American. During the 1990s, Russian military elites consistently held more negative views of the United States than their civilian counterparts.[47] The former

Soviet military perceived the United States' post-Cold War military activities as illegitimate, provocative and as a threat to Russia's security and status. For example, one of the participants of the 1992 All-Army Officers' Assembly said:

> We see what happened to Iraq when it defied US interests, what happened to Grenada, what happened to Panama, where a legally elected president was extradited and prosecuted. The Americans did not decrease their military presence ... but our fleet, to speak frankly, if provisions continue like this, will be docked.[48]

The All-Army Officers' Assembly was a major gathering of senior and mid-ranking Soviet-trained military officers held in Moscow, during the political and institutional crisis following the collapse of the USSR. It was organized by the newly formed Russian MoD and brought together thousands of officers to address the uncertainty over military command, institutional reform and the political role of the armed forces in the post-Soviet countries.

The assembly vividly demonstrated that the Russian military's foundational beliefs in strong government and national identity had been left unfulfilled in the post-Soviet transition, leaving it politically and institutionally adrift. While civilian elites seized new economic and political opportunities, the military struggled with severe resource shortages and an absence of decisive political leadership. This deepened frustration within the armed forces and fueled resentment toward the dramatic changes reshaping Russia.

Deep core belief convergence under Putin

Under Putin, Russian policies were more closely aligned with the military's expectations of strong government and national identity. Unlike Yeltsin, who blamed military failures and human rights violations on the generals, Putin took personal responsibility for the campaign in Chechnya, shifting accountability to the civilian leadership. This marked a significant change in Russia's civil–military relations, reinforcing the military's perception of a strong, centralized authority.[49]

Putin's hiring practices further blurred the distinction between civilian and military leadership. Frequently emphasizing his background in the security services, he expressed a deep personal connection to service members:

> I don't feel separated from this environment. I've been an officer for almost twenty years, and it's my own environment. I'm very emotional about all the problems that are here as my own. I perceive people from [the security services] in such a way that I feel like a member of this team. I am telling you frankly, and so I am counting very much on information from this environment, to be complete, objective that we will continue to do everything together in order to strengthen the country. And we will not pursue our own exclusively narrow group interests, but we will think the way it is in the officer environment: to think about the fate of the state. If we maintain this approach to the country's problems, it will greatly help us all in strengthening the country, and this, in fact, has always been the goal of any person who makes a conscious choice when becoming an officer.[50]

While some interpreted this as a deliberate militarization of his regime,[51] the influx of former service members into civilian politics was largely the result of Putin's informal, nepotistic hiring patterns rather than a calculated effort to build a police or garrison state.[52] But the result was an increasing convergence of civilian and military elite beliefs, with civilian officials adapting or subordinating their views to align with the military establishment.

Putin actively pursued political objectives long sought by the military, reducing political polarization and stabilizing Russian politics.[53] Many in the military viewed this shift as a long-overdue correction from a period of humiliation and decay, when service members were even discouraged from wearing their uniforms in public due to the risk of street violence: "I did not understand the essence at first, everywhere you were bullied, humiliated. And then suddenly a sharp change, we again remember the veterans, began to honor them. Thank God for waking up, a country without kinship and tribe."[54]

However, Putin's ideological blend of Soviet-era great power nostalgia and Orthodox conservatism, emphasizing traditional values and a strong state, was not seamless but involved trial and error. The interviewed military officers acknowledged a state-driven search for national identity and remained skeptical about its coherence: "They are trying—money, national idea, patriotism. Before, there was no doubt, it was the party line, it was accepted. Now, there's a painful search for a national idea—religion, sport, patriotism."[55] At the same time, civilian interviewees generally saw Putin as building an authoritarian state with a conservative ideology.

The annexation of Crimea in 2014 and the military intervention in Syria in 2015 reinforced Russia's great power identity and further aligned civil–military beliefs. The military perceived these actions as defensive measures against Western encroachment, describing Syria as "fighting in the outer rim," implying a strategy of countering threats before they reached Russian borders. This newfound assertiveness bolstered national pride: "Ten years ago, people were shy to admit they were from Russia abroad. Now, they take pride in their citizenship."[56] Putin's rise gradually reconciled civilian and military deep core beliefs, reinforcing a shared commitment to strong government and a militarized national identity.

However, my civilian respondents recognized the negative effects that military service can have on individuals, including political passivity, aggression, narrow-mindedness, lack of personal freedom and diminished dignity and responsibility. As one noted: "They are unaware of their responsibility, their human dignity. And they do not know how to defend it."[57] This perspective highlights a deep civil–military divide, revealing that civilians and military personnel often see the military's role in shaping Russian society through very different lenses. While many within the armed forces view themselves as key actors in instilling values, discipline and patriotism among Russian citizens, civilian actors may be reluctant to accept the militarization of society and wish to make the military more civilian.

There was skepticism about whether Russia's contemporary military can successfully fulfill its socializing mission. Some interviewees doubted that the institution still instills patriotic or ideological commitment in its recruits. One respondent remarked: "There is no ideology at all. There is only one person in the entire system of military registration and enlistment offices, whom I know personally, who is truly for the homeland, for Christ, ready to lay down his life ... He is the only one in the whole system."[58] This lack of ideological cohesion further challenges the military's ability to serve as a unifying force in Russian society.

Russian policy core beliefs

Policy core beliefs serve as a bridge between deep core beliefs (normative ideas, ideology) and practical decision-making and determine how the fundamental beliefs are translated into specific policy preferences. They guide elite perspectives on the broad policy tools and approaches the government should adopt.[59] These beliefs tend to shift only when policy dysfunction becomes undeniable, though often at a significant cost.

The Russian military is culturally resistant to independent, intrusive assessments and instead relies on formalistic, vetted measurements to provide feedback to leadership. While evaluating combat outcomes and military expenditures is inherently difficult, even peacetime scrutiny is unwelcome. The military sees itself as perpetually preparing for war, and civilian oversight, particularly when driven by efficiency-oriented, evidence-informed methodologies, can create friction. From the military's perspective, such oversight appears to undermine combat readiness, clashing with the traditional military logic of preparing for war.

Changing Russian policy core beliefs is difficult unless actors are confronted with policy shocks that reveal fundamental flaws in their assumptions.[60] Yet without a mutually accepted system of monitoring and learning, these failures have been dismissed as isolated mistakes or random malfunctions, hindering meaningful progress in military reform. But things could be different. Military academies, strategic forums and intrusive monitoring and evaluation mechanisms could promote adaptability and ensure that policy decisions are grounded in reality.[61]

Military intrusion and its end

The Russian government has struggled to maintain national security due to a lack of resources and disorganization within the armed forces. In the post-Soviet period, troops faced severe shortages of fuel, ammunition and delayed payrolls: "As for housing for officers, warrant officers, enlisted men and contract servicemen, they stood on waiting lists for several years, waiting for apartments to be provided."[62] While civilians acknowledged the necessity of a functional military, they did not always share the military's emphasis on national security as the defining element of Russian identity. As one respondent noted: "Obviously, to date, these words [military arguments about patriotism] are manipulation. The last time our homeland was attacked was in 1941. Since then, it was not."[63]

After the Soviet collapse, the military actively voiced its grievances and sought to influence both foreign and domestic policy.[64] Its advocacy reflected a deep-seated belief in the primacy of national security and the need for a strong executive government. Before 2001, defense ministers were military generals, further exacerbating civil–military friction, as their dual role in policymaking and military affairs often came into conflict. For example, General Troshev, who commanded Russia forces in Chechnya between 1995 and 2002, praised Defense Minister Grachev's bureaucratic skill in exploiting legal and financial loopholes to provide additional payments to officers in the mid-1990s, despite civilian leaders demanding budget cuts and reforms.[65]

Putin's agenda and ruling style align closely with the military's expectations regarding national security and executive authority. He has pursued a pragmatic leadership approach domestically, gradually increasing security sector funding while allowing the military autonomy over operational decisions, including tactics, weapons and training.[66] To consolidate his control and assert civilian leadership over the military, he dismissed Defense Minister Marshal Sergeyev and, in 2001, appointed his longtime ally and fellow KGB officer Sergei Ivanov as minister of defense, marking a shift toward intelligence and security professionals in key military leadership positions. Russian national survey data consistently confirm that around 40 per cent of

Russians believe that Putin has primarily represented the interests of the security services throughout his presidency.[67]

Information control

The conduct of the Russian military exemplifies a common principal–agent problem, with lower-ranking officers often being hesitant to tell their commanders the full truth, especially when things are going wrong. At the same time, commanders judge their subordinates using rigid and outdated rules. This gap between what is reported officially and what is really happening on the ground led to the degradation of military readiness and a lack of accountability within the system.

Moreover, challenges in recruitment, retention and promotion have often meant that senior command positions have not always been occupied by the most capable and experienced officers: "Not the most independent, knowledgeable or critical thinkers rise to the highest positions, but those who simply please their superiors. Evaluations, officer meetings—everything is now controlled by commanders, and this does not cultivate personal responsibility among officers."[68] By the late 1990s, less than 30 per cent of the Russian public had faith in the armed forces, reflecting widespread disillusionment with the military leadership.[69] However, some officers stationed at command headquarters failed to recognize these challenges, as one respondent recalled: "Everything seemed to go smoothly. I never panicked, and I didn't see any drastic changes. I worked in the Personnel Department and didn't observe an outflow of officers. It was difficult, with salary delays in some units, but people endured."[70] In reality, the military struggled with chronic retention issues due to inadequate salaries and lack of social protections until Putin's second term from 2004 to 2008.[71]

Similarly, retired officers who entered politics often used their military status to discuss defense issues without necessarily providing factual insights. Some respondents dismissed high-profile veterans-turned-politicians as out of touch: "Shamanov, ... sometimes they say things that make you realize they know nothing about the modern army. Either they ended their careers in the '90s and early

2000s, or they deliberately do not know."[72] However, a military officer expressed a favorable opinion of Colonel General Vladimir Shamanov, claiming that his reputation alone spoke for itself and required no embellishment.[73] Shamanov served in Chechnya under General Troshev, who described him as a very courageous but rude and impatient officer. He commanded the airborne troops and would personally join soldiers during assaults. However, reportedly, his energy often led to unnecessary violence and losses that have earned him a controversial reputation among the Russian media and human rights organizations. Shamanov later ran for political office and served in the civilian government; close to Putin, he is currently a member of parliament.[74]

Additionally, the Russian military often tried to restrict the flow of even basic unauthorized information about the armed forces. For example, the restrictions on mobile phones in the Russian military have long served as a symbolic measure to prevent enlisted personnel, especially conscripts, from contacting their relatives and civilian authorities. The military initially introduced the ban on mobile electronic devices under the guise of counterintelligence regulations. However, the ban was enforced inconsistently, and in 2011 Defense Minister Serdyukov relaxed the rules as part of his campaign to "humanize" service conditions. With advances in technology, phones became a means for soldiers to communicate with military human rights organizations and leak footage of incidents to the media. The early stages of the Ukraine war exposed the risks, as numerous Russian soldiers posted geotagged images with identifiable military symbols, sparking international scandals. In response, smartphones were again banned in 2019,[75] yet their use remains widespread, with only rank-and-file soldiers facing formal prosecution and informal punishment for violations.[76] The ban has minimal counterintelligence implications, as officers continue to use unsecured Western messaging apps, but it effectively reduces independent information leaks, isolating troops from broader society and shielding the military leadership from external scrutiny.[77]

The Russian military became more transparent between 2006 and 2014 following high-profile hazing scandals, when soldiers were starved or beaten,[78] and due to the influence of civilian minister Serdyukov. He personally exposed widespread abuses and inefficiencies within the armed forces and even fired the officers suspected of engaging in these behaviors.[79] The war with Georgia in 2008 shattered any illusions about the Russian military's readiness, forcing a reckoning within its leadership. One civil society member described the dire conditions Russian soldiers faced:

> I went up the mountain [in Georgia], there was a tent with Russian soldiers. Well, there was a unit of contract soldiers, very good men, they were just surviving there. They slept on the floor, cattle conditions, no baths, no toilets. Locals fed them, gave them a chance to wash.[80]

One civilian respondent recalled how Serdyukov confronted officers over reports compiled in *The Black Book*, a compilation of human rights violations within the military collected by the "Soldiers' Mothers of Saint Petersburg," a soldier rights organization:[81]

> If I told Shoigu about it [about crimes and hazing in the military], he wouldn't understand me. But Serdyukov—yes, he was a thief, but more humane. He stormed into the Officers' House, furious, cursing at them, demanding to know how they had let things deteriorate to the point where soldiers' mothers had to write black books about them.[82]

Unlike his military predecessors and immediate successor, Serdyukov did not share the military's institutional beliefs, which enabled him to push for radical reforms (for more details, see Chapter 4). But this also created friction with the officer corps. His autocratic management style and disregard for military traditions generated severe resistance. To mitigate this, Serdyukov appointed former Federal Tax Service employees to key positions in the MoD, overseeing monitoring, housing, education, financial planning and media affairs.[83] His approach exposed the gap between the military's aspirational rhetoric and its actual performance. General Staff Chief Nikolai Makarov admitted the military had failed to modernize its doctrine and capabilities prior to Serdyukov's reform:

> For the past twenty years, we have failed to bring the art of war to a modern level and have continued to live with outdated ideas about the nature of modern warfare ... We were still relying on a mass army and the purchase of obsolete weapons from industry. We overlooked the development of the latest ways and means of warfare. We were in such a state by August 2008 when the Georgian–Ossetian conflict broke out. It pushed us to change a lot of things.[84]

However, many of Serdyukov's reforms were later rolled back in 2013 when Shoigu took over as minister.[85]

Controlling access to military information benefits the armed forces by helping to shape the public narrative about its development. However, this approach does not address underlying structural issues that independent assessment mechanisms could help identify. The military's cultural aversion to external oversight, coupled with a weak internal evaluation system, perpetuates an imperfect equilibrium in Russian civil–military relations. Military and civilian leaders operate with incomplete or distorted information, further widening internal military divisions and civil–military distrust. This self-reinforcing cycle isolates the military from broader society, allowing inefficiencies and institutional blind spots to go unchallenged.

Exclusion of marginals

The Russian military has developed a pattern of institutionally excluding so-called "marginals" rather than addressing systemic issues within its ranks. Military elites and veterans often dismiss incidents of hazing, violence or abuse as isolated cases of individual weakness rather than acknowledging institutional failures. For example, when special operations unit members get severely injured or killed, unit members publicly emphasize their tradition of supporting fallen comrades' families. However, when an injured soldier's mother sought accountability for the death of her son during a mixed martial arts training session, they deflected responsibility, telling her, "[w]e've all been through this, but everyone had different experiences ... your son's body just turned out to be weak."[86] A similarly revealing episode took place in 2019, when Private Ramil Shamsutdinov killed eight fellow soldiers after enduring threats of hazing and sexual violence.[87] The incident sparked national outrage, but rather than addressing the systemic causes, military officials and members of the Russian parliament blamed Shamsutdinov's actions on violent video games and mental health issues. Discussions about institutionalized abuse quickly faded, and the story disappeared from the public agenda.

By tightly controlling information and framing military crimes as exceptional, the Russian military minimizes internal uncertainty and shields commanders from external scrutiny. This selective narrative management allows commanders to reframe incidents to suit their interests while obscuring structural issues. However, this approach deprives both military and civilian leadership of accurate insights into the armed forces' internal dynamics. As one military parliamentarian argued, any external interference in military affairs risks destabilization in the eyes of insiders:

> For a year and a half, we have been interfering in the affairs of the army without end ... In 1916–17, politicians created maternity committees in the army and navy, soldiers' committees—Russia's army collapsed, and under the rubble, the whole of Russia collapsed. Remember your grandparents—what a tragedy this led to.[88]

The parliamentarian was not entirely correct to place the blame for the collapse of the Russian imperial army on the maternity committees. During the First World War, these committees provided welfare support to soldiers' families but also exposed the state's inability to provide the troops with the necessities. In some areas, they became hubs of local activism, with women and educated elites leading relief efforts. Their work highlighted the disconnect between society and the imperial government, fueling criticism and undermining the regime's legitimacy.[89] Notwithstanding the historical inaccuracy of the parliamentarian's statement, it underscores the military's deeply ingrained resistance to civilian oversight, reinforcing its preference for internal autonomy at the expense of transparency and accountability.

At a strategic level, Russian military doctrines—its core politico-military guiding documents—have historically been shaped by perceived threats rather than objective assessments. These doctrines are built around assumptions of the intentions and capabilities of Russia's adversaries—primarily the United States and NATO—as well as the broader political and economic context.[90] Rather than serving as a neutral roadmap for defense planning, Russian military doctrine reflects a subjective interpretation of security threats, reinforced by a biased assessment of Russia's own military and economic capacity.

This approach contributes to flawed decision-making. Russia's strategic politico-military preparedness is based on the correlations of forces and means methodology, which is largely driven by qualitative expert assessments and independent but affiliated military experts. The Russian leadership lacked software, data collection, analysis and monitoring and evaluation capacities as well as specialists capable of conducting multi-method evidence-informed security analysis. Strategic policies were therefore driven by preconceptions rather than evidence-informed evaluations, further entrenching inefficiencies within Russia's defense sector.[91]

Conclusion

During the 1990s, the Russian military struggled to become a more effective fighting force due to a deep cultural divide between civilian and military elites, which rendered the reforms of this period largely futile. When civilian and military coalitions hold divergent deep core beliefs, meaningful defense policymaking and military modernization become impossible. By aligning civilian priorities with military ones, Putin was able to use his national security background to bridge the divide between civilian and military deep core beliefs. His elite hiring decisions ensured that Russia's civilian leadership became increasingly statist and security-oriented. However, while the Kremlin managed to narrow this divide in the 2000s, differences in policy core beliefs continued to obstruct meaningful reform.

The civilian leadership failed to establish functional monitoring and evaluation mechanisms because the military's resistance prevented their institutionalization. While the Russian military supported a strong state with a decisive executive capable of implementing national security policies, it also viewed itself as the primary force for shaping Russian society and resisted external civilian oversight. The military consequently opposed the type of independent review that could introduce public scrutiny or criticism. However, transforming Russian military culture remains a strictly civilian prerogative. As a conservative force, the Russian military maintains the established status quo. However, the civilian government, particularly the president, has the institutional power to disrupt military autonomy by altering the systems of military recruitment, education and welfare, which would affect military culture. While the Russian military has exerted influence over policy, it has never directly challenged or overthrown the civilian government. Why did the civilian government's efforts to reform the military fail? To answer this question, the following chapters examine key policymaking cases and their outcomes.

3

WINDS OF CHANGE?

RUSSIAN MILITARY DEVELOPMENT IN 2000–7

Introduction

On 12 August 2000, the Russian nuclear submarine *Kursk* took part in a large-scale naval exercise, the first since the fall of the Soviet Union. President Putin, inaugurated just three months earlier, was vacationing at the presidential resort in Sochi. Early in the morning, the sailors loaded a dummy torpedo fueled with a highly unstable high-test peroxide. This fuel was designed to propel the Soviet 65-73 torpedoes against US aircraft carrier groups. At 11:29 a.m., the torpedo exploded in the number four torpedo tube, instantly killing the crew of seven in the first combat compartment. Two minutes later, the submarine hit the seabed at a depth of 110 meters, and the second explosion, equivalent to 5 tons of TNT, critically damaged the vessel. Twenty-three out of 118 crew members were trapped in the ninth compartment. For about six hours, they fought for survival, conserving oxygen and hitting the metal hull so that naval acoustic detectors would be able to locate the damaged vessel. Three hours and forty-five minutes after the explosion, twenty-seven-year-old Captain Lieutenant Dmitry Kolesnikov wrote a note to his wife:

Olechka! I love you, don't worry too much. ... There doesn't seem to be a chance; 10–20 per cent. Let's hope that someone will read the list of personnel of the compartments who are in ninth and trying to get out. Hi to everyone, no need to despair. Kolesnikov.

The replacement of one of the emergency oxygen-generating cartridges led to an explosion that ended the lives of the last survivors, including Captain Lieutenant Kolesnikov.[1]

Thirty ships and three submarines had been taking part in the exercise, including the nuclear-powered battle cruiser *Pyotr Velikiy*, whose sensors detected a large explosion. The *Pyotr Velikiy* was even hit by a shockwave that made the battlecruiser shake. Captain Lieutenant Kolesnikov did not know that his fleet commander, Admiral Popov, had reportedly left the exercise area an hour and a half before he wrote his last note. Back on shore, Popov declared the exercise a success without mentioning the first signs of a potentially nuclear catastrophe.

Five days later, on 17 August, President Putin finally cut short his vacation and arrived at the Northern Fleet's Vidyaevo naval base. He seems not to have appreciated the seriousness of the accident and left the navy to deal with it. However, Putin was concerned with how the media covered the incident. Sergei Dorenko, a famous TV host, aired a highly critical show on 2 September criticizing Putin for mishandling the catastrophe and for the disastrous living conditions in the Russian strategic naval base,[2] leading to the sale of the ORT channel to pro-government owners and Dorenko's dismissal.[3]

The *Kursk* catastrophe illuminated the dismal state of the Russian military. The declassified parts of the Russian federal investigation revealed that the Russian navy did not follow the proper protocols, had poorly maintained equipment, underfunded its officers and reported false information. The civilian authorities and President Putin himself were incapable of leading the armed forces in such a state of crisis.

The disaster was caused by many interdependent problems, such as a lack of rescue options, slow decision-making and an unwillingness to accept international help to save the crew.[4] The catastrophe was both a symbol and a symptom of the larger problems in Russian civil–military relations. The military elite's entrenched conservatism, corruption, the armed forces' institutional closeness and civilian officials' and politicians' lack of expertise in defense and security affairs undermined the potential for successful defense reform.

The *Kursk* disaster exposed the poor state of the Russian military, yet the reforms made to improve the situation in the 2000–7 period proved unsuccessful. Instead, the presidential coalition, managed by Defense Minister Ivanov, consolidated control over the armed forces, sidelining the civilian coalition composed of parliamentary democratic parties, liberal politicians and civil society pushing for meaningful change. Senior generals prioritized rearming the troops and improving their social and financial conditions, while civilians unsuccessfully advocated for the organizational reform of the armed forces. Moreover, the defense sector's infrastructure was archaic—something that physically slowed any changes. Minister Ivanov himself was reportedly an indecisive politician who avoided confrontation, took little personal initiative in policymaking and could not overcome resistance from the military coalition, which retained significant institutional autonomy.

Between 2000 and 2007, the Russian defense sector required substantial political, administrative and financial investments that the Kremlin was unwilling or unable to make. During the latter part of this period (2004–7), the presidential coalition continued its attempts to improve the Russian military and provide it with better equipment. However, these efforts proved largely ineffective, despite the appointment of a new prime minister and a new chief of the General Staff. The Kremlin lacked both the institutional capacity and the political will to carry out the necessary reforms, and Putin himself showed little interest in spending his political capital on radical change.

This chapter is structured into two interconnected sections: the first covers Putin's first presidential term from 2000 to 2004, while the second focuses on the dynamics of civil–military relations between 2004 and 2007, before the presidential election of March 2008 when Medvedev was elected president. The first section outlines the key challenges the Kremlin faced in the defense sector at the start of the 2000s and analyzes the composition of the presidential, military and civilian coalitions during Putin's first term. It then explores the competition over defense policy proposals, civilian efforts to reform the recruitment system and the difficulties in addressing problems within the military-industrial complex. The second section discusses the changes in the coalition and examines the implementation of defense policies during the 2004–7 period in Russia's broader politico-economic context. The chapter concludes by identifying the key factors behind the ineffectiveness of defense reforms during this period.

Doomed to fail: the Russian military in the new millennium

When Putin came to power, Russian society was deeply disillusioned with the government. The state was failing to provide basic public services, including pensions, healthcare and regular wages for workers in state-owned enterprises and the military. The 1998 financial crisis had wiped out much of the population's savings. The domestic military-political situation was unstable: there were frequent terrorist attacks in Dagestan and Chechnya, as well as occasional bombings of civilian targets in central Russian cities. To face the challenges of post-Soviet state and economic collapse, Moscow needed an effective military and law enforcement apparatus to reassert internal control. This included ending the conflict in Chechnya, combating rising organized crime and entrenched corruption, addressing the widespread use of illicit substances and ensuring the operational readiness of its nuclear forces, which was critical to maintain the image and deterrent capacity of a former superpower in a period of severe institutional fragility. Most Russians believed the country was heading in the wrong direction, with the political situation often described as "critical or explosive."[5] Faced with widespread dissatisfaction, the new president needed to set out a plan for change. Putin made clear that he aimed to restore a strong state and feared that political unrest could potentially lead to Russia's fragmentation, which he was determined to prevent.[6]

At around 4:00 a.m. on 4 August 1999, the first sabotage-reconnaissance units of Chechen insurgents, led by internationally wanted terrorists Shamil Basayev and Ibn al-Khattab, descended from the high mountains into villages in Dagestan—a Russian region in the North Caucasus, bordering Chechnya.[7] Local police engaged the militants, but by 7 August the main force of around 1,500 to 2,000 Chechen insurgents and mercenaries had crossed into Dagestan. Their objective was to establish an independent Wahhabi state and spread radical Islamist ideology throughout the region. The militants launched a multi-phased offensive, initially seizing villages in the Botlikh and Tsumadin districts, with a second wave of attacks in September targeting the Novolaksky district.[8] The attack proved to be a huge mistake for the militants. It triggered the Second Chechen War, a brief but decisive conflict that resulted in the defeat of the insurgents, the restoration of full federal control over Chechnya and the beginning of a prolonged, low-intensity counterinsurgency campaign.

Combined Russian military and police forces initially struggled to repel the invasion. According to Putin, who served as the head of the FSB back then, Moscow could barely mobilize 65,000 troops out of its 1.4 million service members to counter the Chechen attack.[9] This, along with the *Kursk* disaster, exemplifies the severe challenges facing the Russian military in the early 2000s. They included inadequate equipment, intra-military violence and desertion, which had collectively eroded the military's basic combat effectiveness. The Russian armed forces were a political liability for the Kremlin at the start of the new millennium.

The problems were deeply entrenched. Despite having a comparable number of personnel to the United States, Russia's military budget in 1999 amounted to only 4 per cent of US defense spending.[10] Around 90,000 officers lacked proper housing, and nearly 48 per cent of all service members lived below the poverty line (about US$48 a month in 2000, with housing and food usually provided by the army), leading to dropout rates of up to 50 per cent in cadet schools between 2000 and 2001. Mikhail Kislitsyn, Russia's chief military prosecutor, reported 28,500 violations of soldiers' and officers' rights in 2000 alone,[11] such as a lack of housing and supplies, violation of labor rights and intra-military violence.

Violence and corruption

The military's problems spilled over into the civilian world, where the Kremlin had little power to shape public opinion. The problem of violence within the military resonated within Russian society, with parents afraid to let their kids waste their physical and mental health in the Russian military.[12] According to Defense Minister Ivanov, 531 servicemen died and around 20,000 were injured in the ten months of 2002.[13] In 2002, service members committed 20,400 crimes, including around 4,200 cases of desertion. Some desertion cases escalated into violent incidents, including mass shootings and suicides. For instance, in 2001, a group of soldiers killed a general who had attempted to prevent their escape from the regiment. The following year, two airborne soldiers murdered ten people after illegally abandoning their unit. At least twenty-four similar incidents were reported in 2002.[14]

Theft and embezzlement were particularly widespread within the Russian military, with officers and soldiers illegally selling weapons and often setting weapon depots ablaze to cover their tracks. Between 2000 and 2002, fires destroyed an estimated US$363 million worth of military weaponry, with many of these incidents linked to attempts to conceal weapons smuggling.[15]

Russia's mandatory military service—twelve months of conscription for male citizens aged eighteen to thirty (eighteen to twenty-seven before 2024)—has long been highly unpopular. Many civilian politicians and parents sought to avoid the draft by securing deferrals through university enrollment, offering bribes or citing medical exemptions. Survey estimates indicate that the total value of bribes paid to recruitment officers in Russia surged from US$12 million in 2001 to US$353 million in 2005. Additionally, almost 20 per cent of military cadets dropped out of their studies in 2002, citing financial and family difficulties.[16] Contributing factors included the ongoing counterinsurgency operation in Chechnya and widespread rumors that the government might eliminate education-related deferrals,[17] further discouraging young men from committing to military service.[18]

However, widespread crimes and the poor conditions in the military failed to affect public perception of its readiness to defend the homeland.[19] Surveys indicated that the military consistently shared a high level of legitimacy as a key state institution with other key institutions, including the president, the FSB and the government.[20] For example, opinion polls consistently show that Russians, on average, believe that the military is capable of defending the country in case of military threat. This perception became even stronger during the period of confrontation with the West (see Figure 3). The Russian armed forces, as a state institution, held significant importance for Russian society, with its image mythologized—except for those who have experienced military service firsthand or have relatives with military experience.

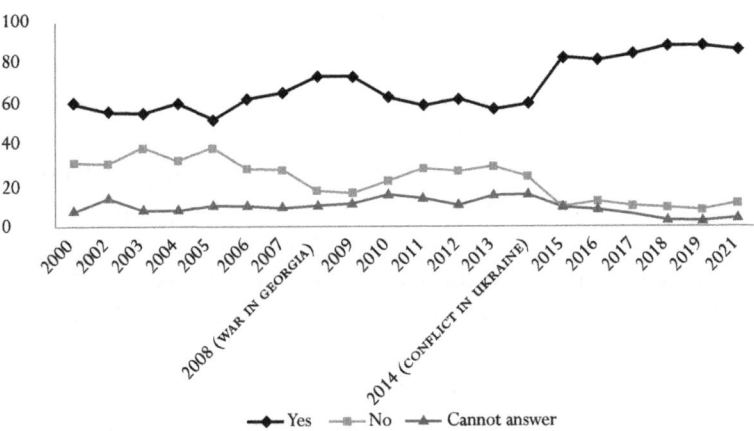

Figure 3: Perception of combat readiness among the Russian public

Source: Levada Center, "Rossiĭskaia armiia" [Russian army]. Question: "Is our army capable of defending Russia in case of a real military threat from other states?"[21]

Struggling defense industry

By the time Putin became president, the military-industrial complex was struggling, consuming limited funds for its physical survival while failing to produce new armaments due to shortages of modern electronics, tools and materials.[22] Putin criticized the defense industry for its outdated structure, slow and inconsistent modernization and reliance on state subsidies at the expense of market efficiency. He emphasized the importance of competition and claimed the state would no longer procure outdated equipment. Technical assets and research and design capabilities were rapidly becoming obsolete due to underinvestment, and Russia's defense factories were struggling with an aging and insufficient workforce.[23]

Structurally, before the reform of the military-industrial complex in 2008, each defense enterprise in Russia was subordinated to one of five defense agencies, depending on the type of products it produced. Regardless of their legal status, the enterprises were de facto controlled by managers who were competing for domestic and export orders. However, funding was insufficient to support all contenders. For example, the Omsk-based Transmash plant produced the T-80 main battle tank, while the Urals-based Uralvagonzavod plant produced the T-72 and T-90 tanks. The ministry's decision to procure this or that type of tank could therefore mean bankruptcy for the factory without orders.[24]

The crisis worsened due to the failure of the implementation of the State Armament Program (GPV) 1996–2005, adopted during the First Chechen War. The program was implemented by only about a fifth of Russia's armaments plants, and, due to the economic crisis, it had effectively ceased to exist by early 2000.[25] Therefore, by the turn of the millennium, the Russian defense industry was in a critical state, verging on collapse. It lacked sufficient funding, and the armed forces stopped receiving even the basic equipment needed to sustain military readiness.

Band of colleagues: Putin's first civil–military coalitions

The successful realization of reforms in Russia in Putin's first two terms largely depended on the appointments to important decision-making positions in the MoD and the military. Three major stakeholder coalitions played a central role in shaping Russian defense policy and civil–military relations—presidential, military and civilian—with the presidential coalition being the most influential.[26]

The presidential coalition revolved around the minister of defense—a political appointee of the president and a key figure in managing civil–military dynamics. The minister holds significant authority over military development, a role that requires both political determination and bureaucratic proficiency. The minister sets the tone for civil–military relations by appointing key deputies and recommending candidates for the position of chief of the General Staff to the president. However, the minister's influence in the military is limited by the need to rely on the chief of the General Staff for senior military appointments. Even Putin is unable to simply appoint the generals he likes as they need to work with the chief of the General Staff, who may have a strong opinion about his favored subordinates.

In 2000–7, the presidential coalition became more stable with the same president and the appointment of a civilian minister of defense. Putin appointed his close friend Sergei Ivanov as defense minister in March 2001, retiring Marshal Igor Sergeyev. Internally, the Kremlin blamed Sergeyev for the early success of the terrorist incursion in Dagestan by claiming that he had inappropriately prioritized a buildup of strategic missile forces at the expense of ground troops, which was considered inappropriate given the domestic security environment.[27]

Ivanov first met Putin during their early careers in the KGB in the 1970s. Ivanov's time in foreign intelligence earned him a position as deputy head of the FSB, where he reported directly to the future president.[28] His career in intelligence was more distinguished than Putin's as he served in "capitalist bloc" countries, including Finland and Kenya, while Putin only served in East Germany (Dresden). For Soviet officers, assignments in capitalist nations were considered highly desirable, offering rare opportunities to gain firsthand experience of life in the West. While foreign assignments exposed officers like Ivanov to higher living standards in the West, the KGB's organizational culture fostered a belief in the superiority of the intelligence services and the Soviet authoritarian system, which later influenced Ivanov's political career.

Ivanov left the intelligence service in 1999 when Putin appointed him secretary of the Security Council, a key constitutional advisory body that supports the president in national security, defense and foreign policy matters.[29] It functions as a de facto executive body to coordinate sensitive operations and unify the political elite; its permanent members include top state and security officials.

Ivanov's friendship with Putin became a defining factor in Russia's civil–military relations:

> Ivanov was a close friend of Putin. He trusted him, and Putin never dismisses his friends. He could have even become his successor as president. Ivanov became a deputy prime minister to prepare for the presidency, but then he made a mistake by claiming he had achieved more in the KGB than Putin.[30]

Putin has always been sensitive about his approval rating, not tolerating personal attacks or attempts to portray him as weak.[31] Before Ivanov made that statement, Putin treated him as a trusted partner, whose ideas became central to defense policy and civil–military dynamics during his tenure as defense minister.

In office, Ivanov became known for his careful, professional demeanor and preference for incremental decision-making over radical action.[32] In 2000, he reportedly stated that Russia needed to demonstrate "reasonable national egoism," ensuring that its neighbors "respect our national interests," particularly on NATO expansion and the protection of ethnic Russians in the former Soviet republics.[33] Ivanov believed that these states' geopolitical choices directly affected Russia's goal of restoring its great power status, which meant that his strong patriotic and nationalist views aligned closely with the military's vision.

However, as a political appointee with no professional military experience, Ivanov became more of a partner to the military bureaucracy than an authoritative figure imposing civilian control. He favored maintaining stable relationships with the generals, avoiding internal conflicts and focusing on coalition-building.[34] As one military journalist noted, "[t]he final decisions always should have been made by Putin, but he delegated them to Ivanov at the time. Ivanov himself was indecisive, analytical; but decisiveness was necessary to carry out reforms back then. For him, the armed forces were an unknown land."³⁵

Ivanov thus came to rely on the military leadership politically, which reinforced the military's belief in its superiority within defense sector development. The chiefs of the General Staff under Ivanov were seasoned, conservative officers who sought to maintain traditional military structures. Without strong civilian oversight from the defense minister, the military remained too insular to be reformed successfully. Rather than finding allies among civilians or at least more progressive military commanders, Ivanov personally opposed parliamentary oversight of military affairs, instead advocating for unilateral presidential control.³⁶ These views resonated with the military's belief in strong political leadership and executive authority, solidifying Ivanov's support among senior officers and military elites. Moreover, Ivanov's close relationship with Putin enhanced the link between the Kremlin and an MoD dominated by uniformed officers, opening the doors for a stronger military influence on the president.³⁷

During Putin's first term, the Kremlin sought to make the military more open and transparent. An interviewed civil society member noted that the MoD published "statistics on incidents and crimes. There was a wave of openness: social councils, human rights councils and interaction between society and the state."³⁸ The drive for greater transparency lay in the Kremlin's desire to seek external expertise from civil society and the academic community to support policymaking. It also helped legitimize the Putin regime by coopting active civil society members into the policymaking process.

A key example of this effort was the 2001 "Civic Forum," where government officials, civil society organizations, academics and businesspeople met to discuss and propose ideas for Russia's development. During the forum, representatives from the federal executive and human rights organizations debated a draft law on alternative civilian service, which would let conscientious objectors fulfil their national service without holding arms, with Putin attending the final session.³⁹ An interviewed civil society member described the process: "Civil society and the government met at twelve sessions, one of which addressed alternative civilian service, with participation from the Ministry of Defense and the Ministry of Labor. Alexander Pochinok, the minister of labor, heard criticism of the draft law and later used that feedback in government meetings."[40]

The introduction of alternative civilian service is one of the key civil–military disputes I describe later in this chapter. The service offers male citizens a non-military option to fulfill their conscription duties, for example in healthcare, education, local government or sometimes in unarmed support roles within the military. It gave an option to replace the standard twenty-four-month military service (twelve months after 2007) with a forty-two-month placement in civilian roles (twenty-one months after 2007). To qualify, applicants must prove that they have conscientious or religious objections to armed service, but in practice the approval process is extremely difficult, and recruitment centers have often rejected such requests.

Before Ivanov's appointment as defense minister, Putin had already begun assigning representatives from the intelligence community to key positions within MoD-affiliated organizations. In November 2000, the government established Rosoboronexport—a monopolist state armament exporter—under the leadership of Andrei Belyaninov, a former intelligence officer. On 1 December 2000, the president also created the Committee for Military-Technical Cooperation with Foreign Countries, and appointed Mikhail Dmitriev—a former head of the SVR's analytical department—as its chief.[41] These appointments enabled the Kremlin to tighten its grip over the arms export industry, with Ivanov's former intelligence colleagues heading major arms export agencies. These strategic moves were designed to ensure that defense spending and arms procurement processes remained as transparent and accessible to the Kremlin as possible.

In addition to the MoD, the civilian government under Mikhail Kasyanov, the politically influential prime minister of the SPS party, sought to improve the management of mandatory service and enhance the transparency of military expenditures. As one interviewee noted, "[t]he changes were specific to finances and draft issues. It was necessary to persuade the generals to make the finances more transparent so that other players could support the conversation about changes in the military."[42] To spearhead this effort, Kasyanov appointed his colleague Lyubov Kudelina, the deputy finance minister, as the head of the Main Financial and Economic Department of the MoD. Kudelina, the first high-ranking woman in the MoD, played a key role in pushing for greater accountability and financial reform within the armed forces:

> The Ministry of Finance saw the budget being overexpanded, and sometimes they had time to react. Hence the Ministry of Finance was always in conflict with the Ministry of Defense. During those months, multiple meetings were held to discuss the draft budget. If there were inadequate expenditures in the final version [those that the Finance Ministry considered inappropriate], then either the president said not to touch, or someone turned a blind eye [as a result of lobbying, corruption or other private factors].[43]

A former high-ranking government official emphasized that the defense budget is a complex document that requires careful explanation for non-specialists to understand. Under Kudelina's leadership, the Ministry of Finance began receiving more detailed budget disclosures from the MoD, but the information needed thorough sorting and analysis, for which the prime minister and his advisors needed military assistance. But there were only a few non-uniformed military experts, limiting the government's ability to navigate and overcome the military's bureaucratic obstacles.[44] Ultimately, simply describing the draft budget in more detail to the prime minister or president was insufficient to establish effective civilian control over defense spending.

All in all, during his first term, President Putin established a ministerial coalition built on personal loyalty. He appointed his close friend Sergei Ivanov as minister of defense, who, in turn, placed former KGB/SVR/FSB officials in key positions within the military-industrial sector. Ivanov, known for his calm and consensus-driven approach, was not the type of minister to push for radical changes without direct orders from Putin. Meanwhile, the civilian side of the government focused on addressing issues related to financial control and conscription but faced significant challenges in building cooperative relations with the military, which remained resistant to outside influence.

Military coalition

Led by the chief of the General Staff, the military coalition consists of senior military officers and their subordinates. This composition is critical, as it directly affects the relationship between the military and the president and plays a key role in shaping the implementation of military policy. Depending on how closely the coalition aligns with the defense minister's agenda, it can either fully support or actively resist the minister's decisions, significantly influencing the success or failure of reforms and strategic initiatives.

As the highest-ranking military officer in the Russian armed forces, the chief of the General Staff not only holds strategic and operational command but also serves as the primary "interpreter" of the military's needs for the civilian leadership. The relationship between the minister of defense and the chief of the General Staff is, therefore, a cornerstone of Russian civil–military relations. The defense minister must balance military requests with civilian policy objectives and budgetary constraints, while the chief of the General Staff is responsible for aligning military requirements with the minister's directives. This dynamic coordination is essential to ensure that both military needs and civilian priorities are effectively integrated into national defense policy.

Anatoly Kvashnin served as chief of the General Staff from 1997 to 2004, a period marked by two major military reforms, the rise of Putin and the Second Chechen War. Kvashnin's military career followed an unusual path for a Russian general, as he graduated with two degrees from a civilian mechanical engineering program and a military program (the Soviet analogue of the US Reserve Officers' Training Corps [ROTC]) from the Kurgan Machine-Building Institute in 1969 before attending the Armored Forces Academy and the Academy of the General Staff. He gained extensive command experience in the Turkestan Military District, which was one of the most challenging assignments in the Soviet Union due to its harsh living conditions. Kvashnin also held key command roles in Chechnya from the start of the first war in 1994 until 1997, taking over after several commanders refused to lead the operation due to the unpreparedness of the troops.[45] His command began with a disastrous assault on Grozny in which dozens of Russian tanks were destroyed or captured in urban combat. Kvashnin was known for his harsh criticism of civilian authorities, particularly for abandoning weapons in Chechnya before the conflict and for signing the Khasavyurt Accords that temporarily paused the hostilities.[46]

Kvashnin was also regarded as an energetic and decisive officer—traits that were rare in the Russian military of the 1990s and that did not always benefit it. In addition to defeats in the First Chechen War, his willingness to execute reform initiatives without careful consideration led to policy reversals.[47] Under his leadership, the late 1990s reforms saw the merger of the Space Forces with the Strategic Missile Forces, the dismantling of Infantry Headquarters and the reduction of strategic missile numbers—all decisions that were later rolled back by the MoD. Kvashnin also approved the 1999 Pristina airport dash in Kosovo. During the early years of Putin's presidency, Kvashnin was responsible for implementing Defense Minister Ivanov's military reforms and developing the federal program for transitioning to an all-volunteer force, a policy program designed to gradually increase the share of volunteer soldiers to 49 per cent by 2007.[48] The chief of the General Staff also attempted, unsuccessfully, to transform the General Staff into a powerful quasi-MoD, further challenging his relationship with the ministry.[49]

Kvashnin was a seasoned combat officer but a limited and narrow-minded political strategist. Serving as chief of the General Staff during the early post-Soviet period required exceptional skill and commitment to bridging the civil–military divide. But he struggled to navigate civilian public affairs and failed to grasp Putin's overarching goal of consolidating power. This disconnect resulted in ineffective military reform and ultimately led to his resignation in 2004.

Civilian coalition

The civilian coalition consisted of actors outside the military chain of command who played an important role in shaping the development of the armed forces for the last time before the Duma elections of late 2003, when independent opposition parties were removed from the parliament. This group included members of parliament, independent experts, executive branch officials interested in a particular policy—on the alternative military service as it concerned labor market policies, for example—civil society activists and other sociopolitical actors concerned with defense policy.

Without a formally defined structure, the civilian coalition often experienced internal disagreements and lacked a unified strategy. All interviewed military officers criticized civilian proposals, describing them as superficial, lacking research and a solid evidence base, illuminating the coalition's limited ability to influence defense reform. The civilian coalition's most active members were two liberal parties, Yabloko and SPS, along with representatives from the Duma's Defense Committee. These two parties were among the few remaining liberal and pro-democracy opposition parties in Russia in the early 2000s. Yabloko, founded in 1993, positioned itself as a centrist, social-liberal party advocating for human rights, democratic governance, market reforms and a peaceful foreign policy. The party was critical of President Putin's consolidation of power, his control over the media and the rollback of democratic reforms. The SPS was a liberal-conservative, pro-market political party active during the late 1990s and early 2000s that represented the interests of the urban middle class, technocrats and economic reformers. SPS advocated for free-market economics, privatization, limited government, political pluralism and Western integration. It was more economically liberal and right-leaning than Yabloko. Both parties failed to cross the 5 per cent threshold required for proportional representation in the 2003 Duma elections and lost their seats.

SPS was founded by prominent center-right politicians, including Boris Nemtsov, Yegor Gaidar, Sergei Kirienko, Irina Khakamada and Anatoly Chubais.[50] With the exception of Khakamada, all had served in President Yeltsin's governments and remained politically active throughout the 1990s. To develop policy proposals related to defense, SPS brought in Makhmut Gareev, a decorated retired deputy chief of the General Staff and Second World War veteran, along with experts from the Academy of Military Sciences, an independent think tank affiliated with the MoD.[51] The party's initiatives were driven by Nemtsov, its charismatic leader. The government cooperated closely with SPS, as confirmed by a senior government official personally involved in the policy process:

> The SPS proposals were discussed in my office in the government, and at meetings of the Council of Ministers [the federal government].[52] The group was not so large as the one about the pension reform,[53] the format was narrower. The SPS invited Colonel General Gareev; he was such a liberal general in reserve, a veteran. He helped to understand the mentality of the military a lot.[54]

Yabloko was led by prominent figures including economist Grigory Yavlinsky and former diplomat and historian Vladimir Lukin. The primary author of its defense reform program was Alexei Arbatov, a well-known expert in international security and disarmament. Arbatov had worked as a civilian researcher since 1976 and served as a member of parliament from 1993 to 2003. His reform proposals emphasized fiscal responsibility, improved budget transparency, a defensive military posture with well-equipped mobile forces, a modernized military-industrial complex and a robust nuclear deterrent.[55]

Before 2003, the State Duma's Defense Committee included influential actors and was led by retired army general Andrei Nikolaev. Nikolaev headed a left-wing patriotic movement affiliated with the Communist Party of Russia. He left the military in 1997 after refusing to carry out President Yeltsin's order to relocate a border control checkpoint between Georgia and Russia further into Russian territory, which would have restricted access to a local village road. Nikolaev invited journalists to the site and publicly criticized the decision, a move that gained him public support but also led to his resignation.[56] Under his leadership, the committee was inherently conservative and generally opposed the progressive military reforms promoted by the liberal parts of the Duma.

However, there were progressively minded individuals within the committee who shared parliamentary information and advocated for reform on behalf of the civilian coalition.[57] Before the widespread availability of the internet, having access to details such as the

Presidential coalition		Military coalition	Civilian coalition	
Prime Minister Mikhail Kasyanov	Defense Minister Ivanov	The General Staff, Gen. Kvashnin	SPS	Yabloko	Defense Committee
Lyubov Kudelina, MoD finances	SVR officials at the armaments export sector		Boris Nemtsov Yegor Gaidar	Grigory Yavlinsky Alexei Arbatov	
	Defense and armaments agencies				
Aleksandr Pochinok, minister of labor		GOU, Main Operational Directorate	GOMU, Main Organizational Mobilization Directorate	Gen. (R) Makhmut Gareev, Academy of Military Sciences Experts		Regional governors
				Experts of the Institute of Transitional Economy		

Figure 4: Coalitions in 2000–3

Defense Committee's meeting schedules, agendas and participants was considered valuable for advancing policy initiatives.

The civilian coalition faced significant challenges in advancing its agenda. The military coalition's veto power was difficult to circumvent, forcing civilians to navigate a fragmented parliament—where the Defense Committee was dominated by conservative former military officers—or the presidential bureaucracy. SPS had a comparative advantage due to its members' personal access to the president, but this access was based on personal connections rather than broad institutional access. The party's representatives were excluded from the initial stages of planning and the formulation of military doctrine, restricting their influence over decision-making.

The first shot at reforming the Russian military: 2000–3

In 2000, Putin delegated an ambitious reform program aimed at transforming the country's stagnant, semi-reformed economy into a more manageable, market-oriented system to German Gref, then Russia's minister of economic development.[58] The reform package included major overhauls to taxation and federal governance, including the creation of seven federal districts,[59] as well as arbitration laws and reforms of key organizations and sectors, such as Gazprom, Russian Railways, the Unified Energy System of Russia (RAO UES), pensions, housing, education, land and labor.[60] Putin publicly supported the need for a balance between market growth and social protection, but the reforms faced resistance from a conservative coalition of public officials and the Communist Party.[61] Moreover, reform proposals addressing political institutions, such as executive–legislative relations, the electoral system and federal relations, were excluded from Gref's final program,[62] reflecting Putin's personal desire to consolidate control over the country, as became evident in later years.

Defense reform was a key component of this broader reform agenda. In 2000, Russia had a huge Soviet-style military that was hard to reform because of its complexity and a network of interconnected problems. According to a former high-ranking official appointed by Putin, the reform was structured around three key "blocks": combat, finances and civilian control.[63] The combat component focused on structural changes to improve combat effectiveness—a domain primarily controlled by the military, although external experts occasionally sought to influence it.[64] The financial component dealt with control over military spending—a responsibility shared by parliament and the presidential coalition and the source of frequent civil–military conflicts. The civilian control component related to parliamentary oversight, non-governmental organizations (NGOs) and citizen participation in military affairs.

The vision for military development under Putin had begun to take shape even before he assumed office. The Russian military doctrine adopted in the spring of 2000 prioritized unifying the command-and-control system, strengthening strategic nuclear forces, maintaining mobilization resources and gradually creating permanent combat-readiness units (see Appendix 3).[65] Numerous civilian demands, including the elimination of hazing, intra-military violence and corruption, as well as improving the living conditions of officers and their families and adopting international norms, were largely ignored. These issues were addressed only to the extent that they aligned with the military's broader doctrinal statements. For example, one of the priorities of military development in the 2000 doctrine was maintaining structures for deploying mobilization resources. Therefore, hazing was a problem insofar as it affected recruitment efforts. However, if recruitment continued at an adequate pace, hazing became a less significant issue in Russian military development.

The military doctrine is a fundamental document in military planning. As one retired major general explained: "The military doctrine forms the foundation for the supreme commander's directive, which includes a list of top-secret plans."[66] The Supreme Commander's Directive is a formal, high-level order issued by the president as supreme commander-in-chief. This directive serves as an instrument for setting strategic military objectives, guiding operational planning or initiating specific military actions or policy shifts.[67] The retired general continued: "[I]t consists of two key components: the mobilization of industry and personnel, and the goals and guidelines for establishing military groupings in areas of potential threat."[68]

Defense Minister Ivanov approved the initial reform plan in 2000 while serving as secretary of the Security Council.[69] Between 2001 and 2003, the civilian coalition tried to influence the reform process, with Yabloko and SPS being the two most active political parties advocating similar ideas. Both parties focused on achieving an all-volunteer force as a key structural reform that could help address financial and combat-related issues. However, they differed in their strategies for implementation. Yabloko proposed a gradual professionalization of specialized units, such as the Strategic Missile Forces, Space Forces, strategic aviation and submarine regiments, airborne forces and special forces. SPS, by contrast, suggested implementing a six-month mandatory military service across the board while staffing permanent-readiness regiments with up to 400,000 all-volunteer soldiers.[70]

Nemtsov and Gaidar participated in a key meeting of the Main Organizational and Mobilization Directorate of the General Staff in November 2001 to discuss the transition to an all-volunteer force. As one senior official in Putin's administration recalled:

> The SPS was the center of ideas, and General Gareev knew how to pitch it all to the generals. The General Staff was the most stubborn, its chief particularly. We spent many hours with him, convincing him that changes were needed. We agreed that the General Staff would accept the proposals, but we would publicly say that it was them who developed these ideas.[71]

The MoD responded to the SPS and Yabloko proposal for an all-volunteer force with a policy proposal that was designed to maintain mandatory conscription while gradually increasing the proportion of volunteer service members within the military. But the document outlined a three-year planning stage, effectively bogging the civilian initiative down in bureaucratic red tape and stalling any meaningful progress.

The military largely dismissed civilian reform proposals, as the military doctrine had defined the primary directions for military development before civilian input was even considered. The doctrine was drafted by an interdepartmental working group comprising military officers and civilian bureaucrats under the Security Council of the Presidential Administration. At the time, future defense minister Sergei Ivanov served as the Security Council's secretary, having held the position since November 1999, while Putin had been serving as prime minister since August 1999, before becoming acting president on 31 December 1999 on Yeltsin's resignation. With the future president and defense minister prioritizing geopolitical and military objectives, civilian influence had already been significantly weakened before the reform process even began. As one military expert noted: "These ideas were not particularly influential because the structure of the armed forces is not formed in a vacuum. Everything is tied to the national defense tasks of a particular state."[72] The core components of the civilian proposals were, therefore, met with skepticism.

The Russian elite believed that an all-volunteer military was unrealistic due to Russia's perceived financial limitations. The main obstacle was the poor state of logistics and material provisions within the military, which lagged far behind Western standards.[73] According to interviewed officers, there was an idealized perception that Western soldiers served standard hours from 9:00 a.m. to 5:00 p.m. and benefited from robust labor protections and social security—conditions deemed unattainable in contemporary Russia. As a military journalist and retired colonel stated: "Even now [in 2021], when the chief of the General Staff has ordered the streamlining of service hours, our officers and volunteer soldiers often stay on base until 9 or 10 p.m. in case they are needed."[74]

At the same time, the MoD continued to prioritize preparations for large-scale war. In Russian defense terminology, regional and large-scale wars are armed conflicts requiring full mobilization of the economy and administrative apparatus and the potential use of nuclear weapons.[75] This understanding influenced Russia's overall military strategy, as different types of warfare necessitate distinct formations, operations, tactics and weaponry. In the end, progressive defense reforms were fundamentally incompatible with the mass mobilization plans and infrastructure designed for large-scale conflicts.[76]

The framing of the conscription issue also differed significantly between civilian reformers and the military. Gaidar, from SPS, frequently described conscription as an unequal and unfair tax on the poorest and most disadvantaged segments of Russian society. He argued that wealthier and middle-class individuals could easily bribe recruitment officers or obtain medical deferrals, disproportionally burdening underprivileged groups with military service. Abolishing the draft, he suggested, would shift this burden away from marginalized groups and allow only those willing to serve to join the military.[77]

However, the military rejected this framing despite acknowledging the poor physical and mental health of many Russian conscripts. For them, the problem was rooted in civilian society's failure to properly prepare young citizens for mandatory military duty. The proposed solutions focused on strengthening recruitment stations, criminalizing draft evasion, reintroducing early military training programs at schools and enhancing sports education.[78] These measures were incompatible with civilian reformers' perspectives, who sought to adapt the military to society and not vice versa, creating a fundamental disagreement and leaving the conscription issue unresolved.

Civil–military war

Despite their ideological similarities, Yabloko did not hesitate to publicly criticize SPS. Arbatov, Yabloko's leading defense expert, reportedly attacked the SPS proposal for six-month mandatory service, arguing that it would quadruple the demand for conscripts, worsening the problem.[79] Yabloko's MPs in the Duma also refused to cooperate with the MoD and criticized the government for undermining meaningful reforms. A former senior Yabloko staffer explained that the party's leadership viewed SPS as a "spoiler party" affiliated with Putin, believing it was designed to split liberal supporters and weaken Yabloko's influence.[80] As a result, despite their shared positions on defense reform, the two parties failed to collaborate, reducing their chances of successfully influencing the president and the military.

A retired colonel also emphasized that the Kremlin viewed members of the Duma as populists who "needed to get elected, while the Kremlin did not."[81] Many shared this opinion as the idea of democracy had been delegitimized in Russia by the implementation of harsh neoliberal economic reforms, which ordinary people often saw as unfair and corrupt. The reformers, who called themselves "democrats," were deemed responsible for the decline in Russian living standards and the rise in poverty. Many Russians accordingly believed that democratically elected politicians were inherently weak, corrupt and insensitive to public needs, in contrast to strong leaders, who were perceived as independent of external influence and pressure. Despite this perception, a civilian interviewee noted that while the Duma committees were generally conservative, "there were democratic deputies, and it was possible to work through them. The committees passed the military budget, and their members were experienced individuals with security clearance."[82] This created limited but valuable opportunities for civilian actors to indirectly influence defense policy.

Ultimately, the military coalition publicly campaigned against the civilian coalition's involvement in the policy process. At the start of the 2000s, Chief of the General Staff Anatoly Kvashnin and Colonel General Yuri Baluyevsky—head of the Main Operations Directorate and Kvashnin's future successor—began working on a new set of military reform proposals. Their efforts focused on revising previous reform plans and adapting them to the political and economic realities of the time. While the chief of the General Staff and senior generals developed the core proposals, the final selection of the policy program rested with a key member of the presidential coalition, Minister of Defense Ivanov.[83]

In 2001, Kvashnin published a paper outlining a five-stage framework for military development that proposed an inflated role for the General Staff in the defense policy process. The first stage involved creating a unified, evidence-based reference system through a comprehensive baseline evaluation. Kvashnin was advocating for a centralized, consistent set of metrics and criteria to evaluate military units across the armed forces. Rather than relying on political considerations, anecdotal evidence or traditional assumptions about military strength, he proposed using quantifiable data and performance indicators, such as combat readiness, manning levels, logistical capacity and training outcomes.

Second, the military had to develop a military-strategic justification for the future structure of the armed forces, covering areas such as military management, mobilization, armament and deployment planning. The third stage required resource and economic justification, aligning military needs with available resources, budgeting and macroeconomic constraints. In the fourth stage, the General Staff would draft detailed programs for force construction and development. Finally, based on these programs, the government would establish the national defense budget, ensuring it reflected the military's strategic priorities and resource needs.[84]

Kvashnin's vision positioned military reform as a military-led process in which civilian experts and public servants would play only a secondary, supporting role. Notably, the General Staff was expected to lead the development of three out of five components of what Kvashnin called the evidence-based reference system. Similarly, the military-strategic justification was designed to be predominantly military-driven, with four out of six criteria falling under military control. The resource-economic justification primarily focused on determining the timeline for implementing changes in the military, with national defense tasks being revised only in cases of "significant resource limitations."[85] Kvashnin's paper made no mention of civil society's involvement in defense affairs, reflecting his public advocacy of a military-driven approach to defense sector development that largely excluded civilian participation.

As a final measure, SPS sought to appeal directly to Putin. In May 2003, Nemtsov and Gaidar requested a meeting with the president, just months before the approval of the final federal targeted program. The meeting proved unsuccessful for the civilian coalition, as the program remained largely unchanged. The program's structure fitted with the overall policy direction that had been determined several years earlier, leaving little room for civilian influence.[86]

Substance of the reforms

Russia's military doctrine, adopted in 2000, set the priorities and goals for Russian military development. The doctrine's provisions materialized in two programmatic documents, approved in early 2001: the "Plan for the Development of the Armed Forces for the 2001–5 Period" and the "State Armament, Military and Special Vehicles Program for the 2001–10 Period."[87] Faced with a highly limited budget, these documents prioritized strategic security, which successfully deterred nuclear conflict but diverted critical resources away from conventional forces.[88] In March 2001, Putin issued an order merging the Privolzhsky Military District with the Ural Military District to create a unified command with sufficient forces in the Central Asia region. He also re-established the General Command of the Ground Forces that had been abolished a few years earlier (discussed above) and separated the Space Forces from the Strategic Missile Forces.[89]

Mixed recruitment system

The competition to eliminate or reduce mandatory military service was so fierce that it even affected Putin. In March 2001, Putin signed a decree to reduce the maximum number of military personnel by 200,000, aiming for a total of one million service members by 2006. He would later reverse this decree. The president viewed the transition to the mixed manning system as a means to realize this objective. In April 2002, during his annual address to the Federal Assembly, a constitutionally mandated presidential speech to both houses of parliament outlining national priorities and key policy directions, Putin mentioned an experiment involving a transition to an all-volunteer force in certain military units, which could allow the Kremlin to "switch to shorter conscription terms."[90] In December 2002, Putin made it clear that conscription would remain a permanent feature of the Russian military, and SPS's proposal of a six-month mandatory service was rejected. Speaking at the Airborne Forces (VDV) Institute in Ryazan, he argued that conscripts were necessary to guard warehouses and serve in logistical and support units.

The military coalition headed by the General Staff agreed to conduct a pilot project for the partial transition to an all-volunteer force in 2002–3 and develop a comprehensive plan by the end of 2003.[91] The plan proved impossible to realize due to inadequate piloting and inflated costs. The military proposed converting the 76th Airborne Division into an all-volunteer unit. However, civilian experts viewed this pilot as an attempt to delay meaningful reform, as the 201st Division in Tajikistan (later a base) had been fully manned with volunteer soldiers since 1992. The division had been preserved through bilateral agreements since the early 1990s to support Tajikistan during the civil war and institutional collapse and to fill the security vacuum along Tajikistan's extensive border with Afghanistan. Russia views this region as an external border with a vital role in protecting Russia and the region from the spread of religious extremism, terrorism and illicit drugs.[92]

The General Staff also drastically increased the costs by proposing that volunteer non-commissioned officers (NCOs) be housed in individual apartments rather than dormitories or barracks. NCOs are a category of military personnel who hold leadership positions without being commissioned officers. They typically rise through the enlisted ranks based on experience, performance and training. NCOs serve as the intermediaries between the officer corps, who make command decisions, and the enlisted ranks, who carry out tasks. Therefore, housing the NCOs in separate apartments was an overstep for both budgetary and command reasons.

Additionally, the MoD insisted on prioritizing a rearmament program alongside the transition, inflating the reform costs by 60 to 70 per cent compared to the civilian coalition's proposals.[93] This approach doomed the program, as a large-scale rearmament effort and generous housing offers were not part of the original agenda, and the government lacked the necessary resources to fund these measures. As expected, the MoD failed to implement the 76th Airborne Division's transition, and, by the end of 2004, the division was once again staffed with conscripts.

Despite the failure of this experiment, the government launched a federal program aimed at transitioning to an all-volunteer force in August 2003.[94] Under the program, which also proved unsuccessful, volunteer soldiers were to be housed in dormitories with up to three other service members rather than in individual apartments. The program's deadline for full implementation was pushed from 2004 to the end of 2007. The program failed to introduce significant changes to combat readiness or establish special training schools for the sergeant corps. These schools were supposed to become a key opportunity for volunteer soldiers to improve their leadership skills and acquire the new technical knowledge necessary to become successful NCOs.

Putin ultimately reversed his previous decision on the reduction of the size of the military, leaving the troop size at 1.1 million service members in 2005 due to the poorly executed plans to increase the number of volunteer soldiers. With recruitment shortfalls, the MoD lacked the capacity to staff a smaller, all-volunteer force as only about a third of the enlisted personnel were volunteers by that time.[95] To ease parents' concerns, Putin prohibited the MoD from deploying conscripts to war zones.

The story of the attempted transition to the all-volunteer force thus ended in Russia before it even began. As of this writing, Russia has not abolished mandatory service.

Western aspirations

At the beginning of his tenure, Putin prioritized cooperation with NATO and other Western states to expand Russia's global influence and secure greater international respect.[96] Despite the crisis in the West–Russia relationship due to NATO's bombing of Belgrade, capital of Yugoslavia, and the subsequent Russian military advance to Pristina (now in Kosovo) in 1999, the president saw Russia's development as directly linked to its geopolitical posture, as noted at the time by a former member of the Russian Security Council who worked closely with Putin. Putin needed stronger integration with the West to improve Russia's economic and international position after almost a decade of post-Soviet degradation. However, this policy was met with resistance from the military coalition.

The translation of pro-Western geopolitical aspirations into policies, particularly when they did not align with defense documents, hindered their realization. For example, the first draft of the federal law on alternative civilian service was originally introduced in 1994 but got stuck at the first reading in the Duma due to the opposition from the military in light of the war in Chechnya. In 1996, Russia joined the Council of Europe, which required that it introduce alternative civilian service for conscripts unwilling to bear arms within three years of Russia's accession. This was delayed until 1999, when Putin, as prime minister, ordered the creation of such a service.

The order created a new episode in the civil–military confrontation, with four competing bills from the more liberal side of the policy spectrum (from human rights defenders) and the more conservative (from the MoD) being submitted to the Duma between late 2001 and early 2002.[97] Alternative civilian service was introduced in a relatively liberal form based on a compromise between the military and parliamentarians.[98] The military attempted to block the proposal but achieved only limited success, as civilian proponents successfully convinced Minister of Labor Alexander Pochinok and other senior government officials of the bill's importance. Pochinok, whose ministry would be responsible for allocating conscientious objectors to enterprises, personally advocated for the proposal. However, the final version of the bill mandated four years of civilian service instead of two, a change that Pochinok unexpectedly approved just days before the law was passed by the Duma and signed by the president.[99]

The establishment of the NATO–Russia Council in 2002 further reflected Putin's ambitions for closer ties with the alliance, despite ongoing tensions over NATO's enlargement policy, which Russia was unwilling to accept.[100] Attempts to replace anti-NATO/US attitudes in the military in the 1990s were unsuccessful. As one retired general recalled, when the Defense Council removed the term "adversary" from the military doctrine in 1993, the change infuriated the military leadership: "How can you say there is no adversary, they said. We explained that now you must think ahead—the old adversary is gone. It is necessary to analyze the current political and military situation and, if needed, develop plans for the targeted use of the armed forces."[101] Therefore, at the operational level, the Russian military continued to prepare for large-scale warfare. But that meant there was a basic tension: the only adversary that could be imagined in such a conflict was NATO.

The military's anti-Americanism also degraded Russia's ability to learn from NATO in its military development. For example, one interviewee recalled that, in the 1990s, General Leontiy Shevtsov had reportedly worked on unifying Russian and NATO field manuals in Bosnia, where Russian peacekeeping troops were stationed as part of the NATO-led Implementation Force. He was allegedly impressed by how NATO forces logistically supported their soldiers, as much of NATO's military efforts were dedicated to logistics and support (intelligence, communication, supplies, transport) and the rest to combat operations; in Russia, the opposite applied. However, Shevtsov was moved to the Internal Ministry after his work with NATO, and his experience was abandoned.[102]

Consolidating defense production and finances

The presidential coalition prioritized consolidating unilateral control over the armed forces and the defense industry. In late 2000, the president approved two strategic documents that focused on the concentration of defense research and industrial capacity: the federal program "Reforming and Developing the Defense-Industrial Complex, 2002–6" and the "Foundations of State Policy on the Development of the Defense-Industrial Complex until 2010 and Beyond."[103] These documents focused on creating modern management and legal frameworks and structurally consolidating the defense industry. The head of the working group on the foundations of state policy emphasized that the future of the military-industrial complex would lie with large, integrated structures such as holdings and corporate groups. He even criticized President Yeltsin's non-interventionist approach, claiming that each factory and design bureau was acting independently due to the absence of effective oversight.[104]

Similarly, in its 2002 defense policy proposal, the Kremlin emphasized that "the main direction of the state policy on military construction for the period until 2005 would be the consolidation of efforts" across various federal and regional government bodies, civil society organizations and citizens to "launch large-scale work to improve the military sphere of the state after 2005." The government's plan for 2006–10 focused on "the formation of a fundamentally new look for the military organization … as well as the consolidation of all layers of Russian society around the national idea of defending the Homeland." This vision emphasized the central role of state-led coordination and national unity in shaping the military's modernization efforts.[105]

In September 2003, Putin issued a decree that strengthened the MoD by centralizing its control over the implementation of military development plans and military-technical cooperation with foreign partners.[106] As part of the administrative reform formally launched in 2003, the MoD gained control over several key services and agencies that were previously under the president's direct authority, including the Federal Service for the Defense Order, the Federal Service for Military-Technological Cooperation, the Federal Service for Technological and Export Control and the Federal Agency for Special Construction.[107] These services were specialized Russian state bodies overseeing different aspects of defense and military-industrial policy. The Federal Service for the Defense Order monitored the implementation and financing of state defense contracts. The Service for Military-Technical Cooperation managed arms exports and defense partnerships abroad, while the Service for Technical and Export Control regulated the transfer of sensitive technologies and ensured compliance with export control laws. Lastly, the Federal Agency for Special Construction, known as Spetsstroy, was responsible for constructing military and strategic infrastructure, including bases, bunkers and secure facilities.

Finally, Prime Minister Mikhail Kasyanov's decision to appoint Lyubov Kudelina as head of the MoD's Main Financial and Economic Department proved strategically beneficial for the presidential coalition.[108] She quickly became an invaluable expert, working closely with the Ministry of Finance to streamline and stabilize the defense budgeting process, making it more efficient.

Outgunning the civilian coalition

In the end, Defense Minister Ivanov declared the end of defense reform at an extended meeting of the MoD on 2 October 2003.[109] In total, the reform had led to a slight reduction in the number of military personnel while centralizing presidential control over the military.[110] The government had achieved neither significant structural changes nor the abolition of mandatory service.

Members of the civilian coalition recognized that the military had "outgunned" them. Putin's priorities centered on consolidating presidential control over the armed forces, ensuring rational defense spending and fulfilling international treaty obligations. The MoD held key bureaucratic positions within the defense sector, while the lack of specialized training for civilians in military affairs further limited civilian influence. Additionally, the Duma's Defense Committee also opposed innovative reforms. Official proposals were developed behind closed doors at private meetings, leaving unauthorized politicians and civilian experts without access to the decision-making process.

The military coalition was unwilling to accept civilian proposals, and the presidential coalition largely dominated the policymaking process, leveraging the defense sector's closed nature to implement its own agenda. The lack of civilian experts in military affairs resulted in many civilian proposals being contradictory or poorly substantiated, making it easy for the MoD to oppose them.[111] Moreover, civilian demands required significant political and administrative resources, including amendments to legislation, such as changes to the military doctrine and armed forces development plans. The president had few incentives to align with the civilians, as his focus was on centralizing control over the military. While this centralization simplified the presidential relationship with the military, it neither reduced corruption nor improved the military's effectiveness on the battlefield.[112]

Importantly, centralization of control over the military-industrial complex was met with unusual resistance from Russia's regional governors. For example, Viktor Ishaev, the governor of the Khabarovsk region, resisted efforts to transfer a controlling stake in the Komsomolsk-on-Amur aviation plant (KnAAPO, located in the Khabarovsk region) to the Sukhoi holding.[113] Governors also insisted on ensuring that a portion of tax revenue of the newly formed defense-industrial holdings would remain in the region, regardless of the location of the holding's headquarters (usually Saint Petersburg or Moscow). Additionally, governors asked for the right for regions to own or manage a minority stake in defense enterprises to enable closer cooperation and a stronger sense of local ownership.[114]

The regional governors' demands proved fruitless. The tax principle was formally acknowledged in the "Foundations of the State Policy of the Russian Federation in the Development of the Defense-Industrial Complex for the Period until 2010 and Beyond," which allowed twenty-seven regions to endorse the document.[115] But no binding federal legislation was introduced to guarantee regional retention of taxes from federal holdings. In practice, tax centralization continued, especially as federal holdings were often registered in Moscow or Saint Petersburg.

Similarly, no policy was adopted to transfer share ownership of military-industrial enterprises to regional governments. For example, 75 per cent of KnAAPO ownership was transferred to the Sukhoi holding, and 25 per cent was restricted to the Russian federal property fund.[116] Federal consolidation under vertically integrated state holdings remained the dominant trend, virtually eliminating formal regional leverage over military-industrial production. Together with the consolidation of control over the military-industrial complex, Khabarovsk and other Russian regions were gradually left without taxes from the military-industrial plants located on their territory.

The low tide of military development: 2004–7

Putin's second presidential term, from 2004 to 2008, marked a shift from a neoliberal economic approach and a pro-Western orientation in response to pro-Western revolutions in Georgia and Ukraine, NATO enlargement in 2004 and stronger centralization of political power in Russia. Concepts such as "sovereign democracy," vertical integration and control over the economy's commanding heights became the defining features of this new approach.[117]

The publicly declared goal of consolidating reform efforts, highlighted earlier in this chapter, translated into the president's unilateral control over defense policy and the civilian coalition's marginalization in civil–military relations. President Putin updated the presidential coalition with a new prime minister who supported the centralization of federal power and a new finance minister who would play a strong role in the subsequent reforms in the 2007–12 period. At the same time, the presidential coalition implemented several key administrative reforms that diminished the military coalition's influence on the Kremlin. Despite this change in approach, the presidential coalition did not become significantly more powerful in civil–military relations, as the MoD continued to be staffed with military personnel and did not improve its oversight mechanisms. Additionally, the new chief of the General Staff, appointed in 2004, was a strong actor who advocated for the military-led development of the defense sector.

The president focused on continued efforts to rearm the military and implement the federal program for the gradual transition to an all-volunteer force (see Appendix 3).[118] The MoD planned to discharge 160,000 service members, reducing the total force to one million by 2005, with a target of 50.7 per cent of enlisted personnel serving on a volunteer basis by 2008. This transition was essential for forming permanent combat-readiness regiments staffed by experienced contract soldiers. Combined with the planned modernization of equipment and armaments, these measures aimed to enhance the operational preparedness of the armed forces. Symbolically, the policy proposal emphasized deeper integration between the military and society through improved pre-military training and patriotic education for sixteen- and seventeen-year-olds, implemented via educational institutions and civil society organizations. None of these policy initiatives were implemented fully or achieved their goals.

Servants of the state: key actors in the 2004–7 period

In 2004, Putin appointed a new prime minister, effectively ending the civilian coalition's access to the president through former prime minister Mikhail Kasyanov. The new head of government, Mikhail Fradkov, was a former diplomat and KGB officer.[119] After the fall of the USSR, Fradkov held various economic positions, serving as an advisor, deputy minister and minister in the Ministry of Foreign Economic Relations and Trade from 1991 to 1997. In May 2000, he became the first deputy head of the Security Council, overseeing economic security. In 2001, he was appointed to head the Federal Tax Policy Service, which was transformed into the Federal Tax Service in 2003. Fradkov served as prime minister from March 2004 to September 2007.

Colleagues describe Fradkov as a careful, calm bureaucrat who was never deeply involved in politics, despite being a member of Putin's United Russia party. Fradkov's appointment ended the era of politically influential prime ministers like Kasyanov.[120] He was well connected, having served as Ivanov's deputy when Ivanov led the Security Council. During his inaugural address to the State Duma, Fradkov emphasized his priorities in the defense sector, including restructuring the military-industrial complex, boosting rearmament and increasing welfare funds for service members.[121] Fradkov chaired a reformist, technocratic government, divided into three functional "layers": ministries responsible for institutional development, federal services acting as enforcement agencies and federal agencies interacting directly with citizens. The power vertical, a system of centralized, top-down authority, in which power flows hierarchically from the presidency, was built on three key pillars: the government under Fradkov, focusing on economic issues; the security sector, managed directly by the president; and the Presidential Administration, led by future president Dmitry Medvedev between October 2003 and November 2005.[122] Fradkov's government mirrored his personality—calm, depoliticized and centered on economic development.

Another key addition to the presidential coalition was the new minister of finance, Alexei Kudrin, a well-known economist and prominent figure in Russia's transition to a market economy. In the late 1980s, Kudrin studied economic reforms at the Institute of Economics of the Soviet Academy of Sciences. He had known Putin since the early 1990s, when both served in the Saint Petersburg city administration. In 1997, Kudrin became the first deputy minister of finance and recommended Putin for the position of chief controller general of the Ministry of Finance.[123] During Kasyanov's tenure as prime minister, Kudrin served as deputy prime minister, focusing on fiscal services, macroeconomic development and financial economic forecasting.[124]

A strong advocate of fiscal discipline, Kudrin played a central role in creating the Russian Stabilization Fund, which helped protect the Russian economy during the 2008 financial crisis.[125] His intellectual prowess and deep understanding of complex financial systems made him a good fit for overseeing the massive and intricate financial flows within the defense sector, ensuring tighter budgetary control and long-term stability.

Military coalition

General Kvashnin stepped down as chief of the General Staff in July 2004. He was replaced by General Yuri Baluyevsky, who served in this position until June 2008. A military officer since 1966, Baluyevsky joined the General Staff during the Soviet era and gained extensive experience serving in key regions, including western parts of the Soviet Union, East Germany, Georgia, Armenia and the North Caucasus. As a senior general, he was known for his strong anti-NATO stance, though he expressed support for economic integration with the EU.[126] As head of the Main Operations Directorate, he played a significant role in planning the 1999 Pristina airport advance.

Baluyevsky represented the last generation of senior post-Soviet military commanders who could openly criticize Kremlin decisions. He initially opposed Putin's idea to leave the Intermediate-Range Nuclear Forces (INF) Treaty—a bilateral arms control agreement signed between the United States and the Soviet Union on 8 December 1987—but later reversed his position.[127] Entering into force on 1 June 1988, the INF Treaty marked a significant step in ending the Cold War arms race. The treaty required that both countries eliminate and permanently forswear all ground-launched ballistic and cruise missiles with ranges between 500 and 5,500 kilometers (310 to 3,420 miles). In the early 2000s, both sides began accusing each other of non-compliance. The United States claimed that Russia had violated the treaty by developing and deploying the 9M729 cruise missile. Russia accused the United States of violating the agreement through missile defense installations in Europe, as the Mk 41 Vertical Launching System used in these systems can also launch Tomahawk cruise missiles, which are prohibited under the treaty (the United States formally suspended its obligations, followed by Russia, in 2019).[128] Baluyevsky, a staunch advocate of nuclear deterrence, viewed the INF as a pillar of global stability, which heavily influenced his perspectives on US missile defense systems in Europe and arms control agreements.

Baluyevsky's tenure as chief of the General Staff highlights the military's slow realization of reform ideas. Many of the changes he supported, such as the transition to brigade-based formations,[129] outsourcing non-military functions and maintaining a 1 million-strong military with a majority of all-volunteer soldiers, were implemented after he left office, during the 2007–11 reform period.[130] Baluyevsky also promoted greater transparency, advocating for the publication of annual reports on the state of Russian military development.[131]

Despite his progressive stance on certain reforms, Baluyevsky was vocally anti-American, viewing the US-led global order as a threat to Russia's national security and stability.[132] His strategic vision extended beyond the military domain as he advocated stabilizing US–Russia relations through trust-building measures in missile defense, space, non-proliferation and counterterrorism. Yet his innovative ideas did not result in significant improvements in combat readiness. Still, under Baluyevsky, the General Staff began developing core concepts for the major military reforms launched in 2008. His experience demonstrates that sectoral expertise alone was insufficient for success under Putin's regime—effective military development also required political and administrative wisdom.

Presidential coalition		Military coalition		Civilian coalition	
Prime Minister Mikhail Fradkov	Defense Minister Ivanov	Gen. Baluyevsky (left in June 2008)		United Russia	Non-parliamentary actors
Alexei Kudrin, minister of finance	SVR officials at the armaments export sector		Chief of armaments, deputy defense minister	Defense Committee	Regional governors
Lyubov Kudelina, MoD finances		GOU, Main Operational Directorate		CPRF (Communists)	

Figure 5: Coalitions in 2004–7

Civilian coalition

In December 2003, the newly elected Duma excluded Yabloko and SPS. Boris Gryzlov, the then speaker of the Duma from Putin's United Russia party, accurately described the new parliament: "The Duma is not a place for discussion."[133] A retired general viewed the shift as a turning point, lamenting that the Duma had become passive and that its Defense Committee was effectively controlled by the MoD:

> We tried to set up this system of control through the Duma. Nemtsov was there,[134] and then Alexander Piskunov[135]—he was a military man, a political officer, but graduated as an engineer. Then they were all kicked out of the Duma. When the leadership is purely military, priorities like maintenance, personnel welfare and housing take a back seat, and maintenance problems accumulate.[136]

With Putin's United Russia securing a constitutional majority,[137] the Duma became a convenient tool for advancing Kremlin-backed policies. General Viktor Zavarzin—a United Russia member known for his role in the 1999 dash to Pristina in Kosovo and later serving as Russia's representative to NATO—was appointed head of the Defense Committee. Zavarzin maintained a low public profile, delivering only a few general speeches and media comments.[138] However, he reported that the committee worked closely with the MoD, confirming expectations that the new Duma would support rather than oversee and check the executive branch.

Tightening the screws: policy changes in 2004–7

Between June 2004 and July 2007, the Russian parliament passed several amendments to the federal law "On Defense," the primary legal framework governing the country's defense sector. Most of these amendments further centralized presidential control. One of the most significant changes occurred in June 2004 as part of the administrative reform bill,[139] which granted the president the legal authority to coordinate federal and regional executive bodies involved in defense; to directly create or disband paramilitary troops and agencies, set their operational tasks and oversee their development; and to establish the procedures for national mobilization. Before the June 2004 amendments, the president already held broad constitutional authority as commander-in-chief, but the legal mechanisms and procedures for exercising direct control were less clearly codified and often delegated through the government or the MoD. Prior to the 2004 amendments, the president's role in coordinating regional executive authorities in defense matters was more implicit or symbolic, with actual coordination typically being mediated by federal agencies or Security Council directives, not directly by presidential orders.

The law also led to a major change in Russian civil–military relations by removing the General Staff from the part of the law concerning the defense minister's control over the armed forces, formally distinguishing the General Staff as a "military agency" from the MoD as a political body. This was a critical but largely overlooked development, as it excluded the General Staff from the political chain of command. This structural shift reduced the military's direct influence on the president while consolidating power under the minister of defense, making him the primary civilian authority in control of the Russian armed forces. While the General Staff remained the leading military agency, its legal power to set priorities for military development was significantly diminished.

But the MoD was slow to fully adopt its new political role, as it was still heavily staffed by military officers and lacked the characteristics of a true civilian ministry with strong audit roles and wide integration of civilian personnel. Additionally, the legal amendments integrated non-miliary security agencies into the defense sector, allowing other security agencies—including the police, the FSB and the Ministry of Emergency Situations—to participate in shaping defense plans, rearmament programs, military-industrial development and the operational preparation of regional territories for defense purposes.

The state's role in key strategic sectors such as oil and gas, aerospace, defense, nuclear energy and shipbuilding was also significantly strengthened during this period. The government established several state-owned corporations, including Rusnano,

Rosatom, Rostec[140] and the United Engine, Aircraft and Shipbuilding Corporations, alongside military-industrial joint-stock companies like Tactical Missiles Corporation and Almaz-Antey.[141] These corporations gained access to state financing with the strategic goal of becoming globally competitive by modernizing their largely outdated industrial infrastructure.[142] One of the corporations' key clients was the Russian MoD, whose rearmament contracts were crucial for keeping many defense factories operational.

Hazing and violence

On 31 December 2005, Private Andrey Sychyov, of the supply battalion at the Chelyabinsk Armor Institute, was preparing to celebrate Russia's most important national holiday, New Year's Eve. Traditionally, soldiers gather in their barracks or canteens to mark the occasion with sweets, juices, fruits and other treats rarely available to them. However, the celebration took a dark turn when Junior Sergeant Alexander Sivyakov, who was illegally intoxicated, became dissatisfied with the conscripts' cleaning efforts after the festive dinner. Enraged, Sivyakov forced the conscripts to squat for hours with their hands tied behind their backs and subjected Sychyov to a brutal beating that lasted over three hours. The base clinic was closed for the holidays, and the private, fearing further torture from the junior sergeant, did not call for help and did not receive medical attention until 4 January, by which time his condition had worsened.[143] The Prosecutor's Office later reported the following: "As a result of this violence, the victim suffered positional compression of the lower limbs and genital organs, which led to the development of gangrenous inflammation."[144] Later in January, Sychyov had both his legs and a finger amputated, and his genitals were surgically removed.

Sychyov's assailant, Junior Sergeant Sivyakov, was stripped of his rank and sentenced to four years in prison. However, no commanding officer faced prosecution or even disciplinary action for failing to prevent the crime committed by their subordinates. Initially unaware of the incident, Defense Minister Ivanov dismissed a journalist's question, stating that nothing serious had happened as otherwise he would have been informed, sparking widespread public outrage. The Sychyov case became a symbol of the pervasive hazing, torture and poor morale within the Russian military. To this day, Russian journalists continue to report on Sychyov's life, a symbol of Russian military violence and failed command.[145]

The military traditionally shifted the blame for this violence onto young conscripts. In June 2003, Chief Military Prosecutor Alexander Savenkov emphasized that eliminating hazing in the Russian armed forces required improving the quality of conscripts. "If we eliminate the conscription of illiterate, poorly educated, underweight and criminal individuals, we will restore the strong and combat-ready armed forces we had fifteen years ago," he stated.[146] This was a typical military response, failing to address the deficiency in military command and instead shifting the blame onto civilians.

Some military respondents also downplayed hazing as a systemic problem, instead viewing it as a natural aspect of male socialization within the armed forces. They argued that physically and emotionally stronger, more experienced soldiers would avoid unpleasant tasks and enforce informal rules to maintain order in the unit. According to this view, if a young soldier struggled to integrate, it was natural for senior soldiers to "teach him lessons." One retired officer's remarks exemplified this mentality, claiming that hazing was inevitable due to the "male nature" of the military, stating that "a sergeant would never clean up the toilet."[147]

Despite differing perspectives on hazing, all interviewees agreed that fatalities were unacceptable, often blaming unit commanders for neglecting their duties and society for producing conscripts they deemed unfit for service. A former civilian official echoed this sentiment:

> The military tended to say that cases of hazing and deaths were isolated incidents, not systemic issues. They claimed that if you made changes, the entire system would collapse, and there would be no army. In reality, no one wanted to do anything—everyone lived within the same system, and that was it.[148]

The persistence of hazing was exacerbated by several structural issues. These included the broader absence of protections for conscripts' rights, dysfunctional educational programs, weak intra-military investigative mechanisms and the poor overall welfare of officers and soldiers. In 2003, General Nikolai Pankov, head of the MoD's Main Directorate of Personnel, admitted that senior officers were not held accountable for promoting junior officers without justification. And there was no alternative selection system to ensure merit-based advancement. This corruption and lack of oversight weakened the quality of command personnel, further contributing to the prevalence of hazing and mistreatment within the armed forces.

In response to the outcry over Private Sychyov, the MoD introduced several measures aimed at promoting transparency and addressing public concerns. These included allowing parents to conduct scheduled inspections, publicizing the contact information of regiment commanders and the deputies responsible for soldier welfare and establishing the Social Council of the MoD,[149] which served as a platform for engaging with former military elites, influential opinion leaders and media representatives. The council was established as an advisory body to promote civilian oversight and public engagement in military affairs. These initiatives were intended to demonstrate the MoD's openness and willingness to consider alternative perspectives. However, in practice, the military coalition staffed the Social Council with pro-Kremlin figures such as patriotic singers, veterans, civil society activists and businesspeople, limiting its effectiveness as an independent oversight body.

Defense industry

Between 2004 and 2007, the government introduced three key amendments to the federal law "On Defense," further centralizing control over defense policy. The amendments allowed the federal government to monitor the implementation of the state rearmament program and granted the president unilateral authority to determine the number of civilian employees in defense bodies, as well as the list of organizations supporting defense and security efforts with civilian personnel. In 2005, the MoD introduced a centralized procurement system led by the chief of armaments, who also served as deputy defense minister. Instead of fifty-two separate military directorates that could independently procure weapons and equipment, only one central authority remained.[150]

Another amendment established the Federal Service on Defense Order, a dedicated agency responsible for monitoring defense procurements within the defense industry on behalf of its primary client, the MoD. The service's main task was to ensure that delivered armaments met the requirements specified in defense contracts, including adherence to state standards and the specific needs of individual military clients, such as branches of the armed forces and special units. From 2004 to 2006, the new service was led by Andrei Belyaninov, a former KGB colleague of Putin who had previously served as director of Rosoboronexport, the state monopoly in control of defense exports.[151] In 2007, Belyaninov was moved to the Federal Customs Service and replaced by First Deputy General Sergei Maev, a veteran armaments officer from the Soviet and Russian armed forces.[152]

To address production problems in the defense industry, the Russian government relied on the implementation of the Federal Target Program "Reforming and Developing the Defense-Industrial Complex." The program aimed to create an efficient structure of defense enterprises, increase the use of production capacity involved in military manufacturing, improve the structure of defense exports by raising the share of innovative products and increase the state's ownership in the capital of core companies within key integrated structures to a controlling stake.[153]

Lastly, in 2006 the federal government established the Military-Industrial Commission of the Russian federal government. The idea had originally come from regional governors, such as Viktor Ishaev of Khabarovsk, who had proposed the creation of such a body several years earlier. The regional governors suggested they be included among its members to help oversee the reform of the military-industrial complex. Their aim was to provide the president with an alternative source of information on defense and industrial policy beyond the federal ministries.[154] Ultimately, the commission included ministers, senior federal officials, staff from the Presidential

Administration and representatives of federal agencies, but regional governors were not invited.

Defense policy in 2000–7

Between 2000 and 2007, the Kremlin tasked the military with reforming the enlistment system, improving financial transparency and addressing social security and payment issues. The president aimed to enhance his control over the armed forces while ensuring compliance with international security agreements and treaties. Meanwhile, civilian leaders prioritized transitioning to an all-volunteer force and resolving issues of hazing and intra-military violence. However, these efforts largely failed, highlighting the deep-rooted problems within the military and civil–military relations.

The reform efforts failed to produce meaningful change due to structural inefficiencies, poor discipline, overlapping bureaucratic interests and the Kremlin's exclusion of external oversight from the defense sector. Army General Anatoly Kulikov noted that despite a few positive developments, the armed forces remained burdened by a cumbersome structure with redundant units and personnel. Discipline and combat readiness were so poor that executing combat orders often required major effort.[155] Kulikov attributed much of the dysfunction to the overlapping responsibilities and vested interests of various government groups, which led to the inefficient allocation of limited state resources. This problem was further compounded by the Kremlin's strategy of sidelining the Duma and civil society from defense management, limiting external oversight and meaningful reform.

Defense Minister Ivanov played a decisive role in the outcomes of the reform. "For Ivanov, the armed forces were terra incognita. He tried to understand them, but the General Staff never fully accepted him as one of their own. He remained on the sidelines, more of an observer than a leader."[156] If Putin had intended to implement meaningful military reforms, then appointing Ivanov as defense minister was a strategic misstep. Ivanov was too lenient and non-intrusive at a time when the MoD needed a strong, assertive leader capable of commanding the military and enforcing necessary changes.

However, Ivanov appeared well suited to advance Putin's broader vision for the development of the defense sector. While maintaining a non-confrontational posture, he avoided unnecessary conflict with military and defense-industrial elites, enabling the Kremlin to gradually centralize control over these constituencies. Although significant military reform did not materialize during his tenure, Ivanov effectively fulfilled his role as the president's representative within the military establishment and as an executor of Putin's grand vision of constructing a new power vertical in the country, including in Russian civil–military relations.

Failed personnel and defense industry policies

The implementation of nearly all major reforms in the 2000–7 period proved unsuccessful, including the special federal program for transitioning to an all-volunteer force, the rearmament initiative and the delayed establishment of the alternative civilian service.

The transition to the all-volunteer force fell short of its targets. By 1 January 2008, the Russian military had around 100,000 volunteer soldiers, with over 20 per cent of positions remaining vacant, or around 30 per cent of the plan. The fear of hazing in the military reduced both the quantity and quality of available conscripts, straining the armed forces and creating long-term challenges for military readiness and effectiveness.[157] To meet recruitment targets, the MoD reportedly pressured conscripts into signing contracts at the end of their mandatory military service term, automatically categorizing them as "volunteers."[158] Unsurprisingly, this proved counterproductive: Chief Military Prosecutor Sergei Fridinsky reported that more than 7,000 "volunteer" soldiers had deserted in 2008, many of whom had been conscripts coerced into signing contracts.[159] This problem resurfaced during the Russo-Ukrainian War fifteen years later. Russian military commanders either forced conscripts to sign contracts or forged them outright. These soldiers often deserted the battlefield or became casualties during their first combat engagements. The consistent inability to solve critical policy problems is a typical trait of Russian civil–military relations.

During the brief conflict with Georgia in 2008, the Russian military made the illegal decision to deploy troops with 30 per cent of their ranks filled by conscripts. Chief of the Ground Forces General Alexei Maslov admitted that volunteer soldiers were not significantly better prepared or more combat-ready than conscripts. Their training was repetitive and failed to develop advanced skills, and high turnover rates led to trained soldiers leaving the military prematurely. This problem was further exacerbated by inexperienced junior officers and sergeants who lacked adequate command and leadership capabilities.[160]

Between 2000 and 2008, Russia allocated around 10 per cent of its total government expenditure to the military, with spending rising from US$23.8 billion in 2000 to US$46.9 billion in 2008 (constant 2023 US$).[161] Despite this increase, the rearmament program failed to introduce substantial new equipment. The 2005 (1996–2005) and 2015 (2006–15) rearmament programs fell short of their goals. GPV-2005 was implemented during a period of deep defense budget cuts and an overall unfavorable macroeconomic environment, including the 1998 financial crisis. Similarly, nearly every year of GPV-2015 was affected by surging military equipment prices, often far outpacing inflation, leading to persistent delays in delivery.[162] Instead, the rearmament program focused on maintaining aging vehicles and armaments inherited from the Soviet Union, whose operational lifespan was gradually running out.

The military-industrial complex faced a systemic crisis due to aging equipment and personnel. In 2006, according to Russian government officials at that time, over 80 per cent of the fixed assets at Russian defense enterprises had been fully depreciated. Their production relied on technologies developed before 1993, and workers in the military-industrial complex were on average now around fifty years old. Most investment in asset renewal came from the enterprises themselves, with the state contributing less than 15 per cent. Overall funding amounted to less than 20 per cent of what was needed to keep the enterprises from decay. Capacity utilization at defense enterprises remained below 30 per cent, with the state defense order comprising only 25 to 30 per cent of their total workload.[163] That is why the MoD faced rising armament costs driven by increasing prices for materials and spare parts.[164]

Addressing this issue required a dedicated and comprehensive policy program. However, neither the newly stablished Federal Service on Defense Order nor the federal government could produce such a program, as it would require the modernization of outdated factory equipment, improvements in management practices and an upgrade in the quality of the workforce. These issues proved too complex to address within the program's timeframe and were only seriously tackled in the 2008–21 period (see next chapter), when the government launched more comprehensive military-industrial reforms.

The creation of the alternative civilian service initially showed promise but later became bogged down in the reform of the Ministry of Labor. The government restructured the Ministry of Labor, which was responsible for the allocation of jobs to conscientious objectors, separating the Federal Service of Labor and Employment (Rostrud) and transferring its regional branches to the control of regional governments. Local employment offices also became administratively independent from the federal Ministry of Labor, which slowed the reform's implementation at the local level.[165] The MoD, through local enlistment offices, also contributed to delays by slowing the approval of requests for alternative service, thereby pushing applicants into military service.

Consequently, the original vision of alternative civilian service being equivalent to military service gradually faded, instead becoming a heavily bureaucratized option primarily viewed as a concession to "pacifists" rather than a viable, equal alternative to conscription. This undermined its broader acceptance and effectiveness as part of Russia's defense reform efforts.

Blind oversight

During the 2000–7 period, the Kremlin had weak monitoring capabilities over the defense sector. Oversight primarily depended on appointing former KGB and military officers to senior positions in the MoD and the defense industry. Key roles—including the minister of defense, the heads of the Federal Service for Military-Technological Cooperation, the Federal Service for Technological and Export Control, the Federal Service on Defense Order, Rosoboronexport, the Federal Agency for Special Construction and the Defense Committee of the Duma—were filled by individuals from Putin's professional network or the military, limiting external oversight and independent accountability.

The Kremlin was also reluctant to hold senior military leadership accountable for public failures in defense reform. Major incidents such as the sinking of the *Kursk*, the failed transition to an all-volunteer force and widespread hazing did not lead to the dismissal of top commanders or thorough investigations into their roles. Instead, responsibility was often shifted to low-ranking clerks and officers as in the case of Sychev, while senior members of the military coalition were shielded from criminal prosecution.

In 2008, the Kremlin implemented the planned transition to a one-year military service. However, it did not reform the country's outdated military recruitment stations, the shortcomings of which became painfully evident during the partial military mobilization announced by Putin in September 2022. Recruiters routinely disregarded medical or family exemptions and sent draftees directly to frontline units with little to no preparation.

But there were some signs of progress. The MoD began paying wages regularly to officers and soldiers, developed more stable material and logistical support and identified a "potential adversary" in the armed forces of the United States and NATO following the waves of NATO enlargement. Yet wages remained low—and certainly insufficient to make military service attractive. Additionally, the MoD faced military resistance to the implementation of an officer attestation program—a regular evaluation or special exam for all officers—and had to drop this idea even though it required no legal changes, only the minister's administrative approval.[166]

The centralization of control over the military coincided with a significant reduction in parliamentary oversight. The defense budget remained largely classified, which benefited both the MoD and the president: the MoD could hide spending discrepancies, and the president was shielded from accountability for any funding misallocation.[167] Meanwhile, the Presidential Administration strengthened its control over key oversight bodies. In 2004, the power to appoint the chairman of the Accounts Chamber, Russia's supreme audit body, was transferred from the Duma, which was already dominated by Putin's ruling party, to the president.[168] In the end, the so-called "consolidation of efforts" among government bodies became a consolidation of presidential power, dismantling what little independent oversight remained in Russia's defense sector.

Civil–military relations and defense reform in 2000–7

The military reforms introduced during Putin's first two terms underline the close relationship between civil–military relations and defense policy. Key elements of Russian civil–military relations during this period matched with increasingly centralized, authoritarian development in the post-Soviet era. On the one hand, Russia's military culture favored strong, non-democratic civilian control, while, on the other, the Russian Constitution and key federal defense laws granted the president unchecked authority over the armed forces. Although Russia's political elites generally showed little interest in military development, the civilian coalition members who did advocate for reform—such as SPS and Yabloko representatives, as well as Prime Minister Kasyanov—had effectively been removed from the political system by 2004. The combination of domestic political development under Putin and the military's entrenched views on defense sector development and Russian statehood created an imperfect equilibrium in civil–military relations that undermined the potential of the reforms during this period.

Until 2008, external factors further diminished the urgency for reforming the armed forces. Russia's strong economic growth during the early 2000s, its deepening integration with the West and the consolidation of Putin's presidential coalition contributed to an atmosphere where structural changes could be delayed. The military also maintained a high level of public support, despite widespread issues with hazing, violence and corruption. The perceived success of the Second Chechen War reinforced this "imperfect equilibrium" in which the military remained underdeveloped but there was little pressure from within the political or military establishment to alter the status quo.

In the 2000–7 period, the high degree of civil–military consensus required for policy change made significant reforms difficult. The military retained many institutional prerogatives that let it slow or block the reform. The General Staff, as an influential politico-military body, maintained direct access to the president and exerted near-total control over military expertise, monitoring and education. Despite the president's growing domination of the Russian political system, the military as a special executive body retained a certain degree of regulatory autonomy. This autonomy limited civilian influence and shaped the president's approach to reform. Rather than pursuing the necessary radical structural changes, the president focused on consolidating his control over the military.

Despite the chief of the General Staff's efforts to enhance the military's role in policymaking, the Kremlin held firm, resisting any meaningful power-sharing. Civil society and opposition demands, particularly for the transition to an all-volunteer force, were similarly dismissed. Although civilian actors were formally included in the policy process, their influence was minimal, and the final decisions remained conservative, largely ignoring key civilian reform proposals.

In 2001, Putin publicly commented that

> there was one problem that really could not but lead to sad thoughts: it was very difficult to fight against the Russian bureaucracy. It was difficult to work out solutions, it was difficult to get them to the implementers [make public officials implement them], and it was even more difficult to ensure their implementation.[169]

However, instead of addressing this bureaucratic inefficiency, Putin increasingly relied on public servants, including the entrenched military bureaucracy. Together with a tendency to depoliticize policies, this empowered military coalitions to advocate for their desired outcomes and against unwelcome proposals. For example, the Kremlin consistently resisted holding the military accountable for a systemic problem with military discipline. One major reason for this reluctance lay in the structure of civil–military relations, which hindered effective monitoring of soldiers' behavior and shielded military commanders from repercussions for failing to implement government policy.

Addressing these highly complex issues required the involvement of multiple stakeholders, many of whom were closely connected to Putin. In the case of the *Kursk* submarine disaster, for instance, responsibility extended beyond senior generals and navy officers to figures like Putin and then-defense minister Igor Sergeyev. Central command had failed to pay salaries for months and neglected key safety exercises, while navy officers had been forced to take second jobs as taxi drivers to support their families. Similarly, problems within the defense industry implicated a wide range of actors, from defense enterprise managers to ministers of finance and defense. In such a deeply interconnected policy environment, administrative accountability quickly turned into a political issue. Holding any one individual legally accountable risked triggering investigations, unwanted public scrutiny and the potential revision of policy programs. Many actors used blame-shifting as a strategy to cover themselves—Admiral Popov (then Northern Fleet commander), for example, pushed a conspiracy theory that the *Kursk* submarine had sunk after being hit by a NATO espionage vessel.[170]

A less obvious but critical factor contributing to deficiencies in Russia's civil–military monitoring arrangements was the lack of civilian expertise in defense affairs. This knowledge gap disempowered independent politicians and civil society members from effectively scrutinizing military policies. Managing the defense sector requires specialized knowledge, which was largely inaccessible to civilians and even to some defense ministers. Russia did not offer educational programs in military affairs for civilians or politicians, leaving military academies—whose cadets incurred service obligations upon graduation—as the primary gateway to such knowledge. Civilian policy proposals often lacked proper adaptation to the complex, multilayered military context.

Access to decision-making venues, such as the State Duma, was a clear prerequisite for delivering expertise to policymakers, but the gradual erosion of Russia's democratic institutions limited these opportunities. The Kremlin made little effort to bridge the civil–military gap as maintaining this divide was beneficial for consolidating unilateral presidential control over the defense sector. Without mechanisms to foster civilian expertise and participation, the defense sector remained insulated from meaningful external oversight or reform.

Conclusion

The defense reforms of 2000–7 fundamentally reshaped Russian civil–military relations, but their results were mixed. On one hand, they reinforced presidential control over the armed forces, consolidating centralized decision-making. This period of centralization reduced resistance to civilian oversight and laid the groundwork for the more ambitious reforms implemented between 2008 and 2011. On the other hand, these changes curtailed opportunities for institutionalized dialogue on military development, sidelining diverse perspectives on defense policy.

The framing of military reform as a purely technological or administrative challenge rather than a political one further limited its effectiveness. The reforms focused on structural efficiency and modernization but failed to address deeper institutional and cultural obstacles within the armed forces. In Putin's Russia, military reform became an extension of domestic politics. Its direction, limitations and ultimate shortcomings were shaped by the dynamics of an increasingly authoritarian regime that prioritized control over genuine military effectiveness, preventing the Kremlin from successfully transforming the armed forces.

4

FROM COMBAT EFFECTIVENESS TO OVERSIGHT OVERLOAD

RUSSIA'S MILITARY DEVELOPMENT IN 2007–21

Introduction

On a hot summer night on 7 August 2008, the Russian 58th Army, stationed near the Roki Tunnel in Russia's North Ossetian republic, was in a state of high alert. Tensions had been escalating over the previous two months as Georgian forces and Moscow-supported South Ossetian separatists engaged in sporadic exchanges of fire. By early August, Georgian forces in nearby villages were reporting intensified shelling by South Ossetian militants.[1]

Just before midnight, Georgian forces launched an artillery barrage on Tskhinvali, the capital of the breakaway region of South Ossetia. Within hours, the Georgian 2nd, 3rd and 4th infantry brigades, supported by tank units, launched a ground offensive to regain control of the area. Their key objective was to secure the bridge near the Roki Tunnel and block Russian reinforcements. However, Lieutenant General Anatoly Khrulyov swiftly mobilized his 58th Army, passing through the strategic tunnel between Russia's Republic of North Ossetia and Georgia's breakaway South Ossetia region faster than the Georgian forces could reach it. By 10:00 a.m. the next morning, aircraft of the Russian 4th Air Army were launching airstrikes on Georgian positions, including the city of Gori.² By the end of the day, Russian tanks had encircled Tskhinvali, trapping the Georgian forces that had just entered the city and forcing them to retreat. On 12 August, Russian president Dmitry Medvedev declared a ceasefire, but Russian forces pressed further, advancing to the village of Igoeti—just 40 kilometers from the Georgian capital, Tbilisi—before finally halting their offensive.³

This five-day war strengthened Russian positions in the Georgian separatist regions of South Ossetia and Abkhazia. But the conflict also revealed a debilitating set of problems in the Russian military, which had engaged a numerically smaller and poorly organized Georgian military. During the conflict, Russian forces lost three tanks, fourteen IFVs, four armored personnel carriers and eight aircraft, including one Tu-22M3 strategic bomber on a reconnaissance mission. More than thirty Russian trucks and two helicopters were damaged or destroyed.⁴ Many of these vehicles were destroyed by friendly fire and road accidents rather than enemy engagement.⁵ Domestically, the Russo-Georgian War was a turning point for Russian civil–military relations and defense sector development. As General Makarov, the new chief of the General Staff, put it in December 2008:

> It is impossible not to see a certain gap between theory and practice, a discrepancy between the words about the need to teach troops what is necessary in war and the real state of affairs. On this basis, the operational and combat training of the armed forces must be brought to a qualitatively new level.⁶

The 2007–21 period was decisive for Russia's civil–military relations and military development. At the beginning of this period, the Russian armed forces greatly increased their combat effectiveness. The key changes in the Russian military happened during the 2007–12 reform, when the MoD implemented radical structural changes. This is surprising because, in general, politicians and analysts often describe reforms during Medvedev's presidency as a façade and imitation—modernization without structural changes, "a mixture of fake reforms and half-measures."⁷

This chapter explains why this defense reform was by no means an imitation but should instead be seen as a challenging attempt to re-create Russia's armed forces that started to bear fruit from 2014 onward, when the military became more effective, agile and respected by society.[8] The subsequent annexation of Crimea in 2014, the war in Eastern Ukraine and the intervention in Syria proved that the Russian military had again become a powerful foreign policy instrument. Russia's illegal actions in Ukraine and its intervention in Syria were condemned by the West, worsening Russian relations with Europe and the United States. The presidential coalition reformed civil–military relations by moving them toward stronger conformity with presidential demands and imposing intrusive oversight mechanisms.

However, initially, and despite Russia's poor performance in the war with Georgia illuminating the deep scale of the military's problems, the implementation of the reform did not go according to plan. The opposition inside the military and presidential coalitions slowed or outright cancelled key changes, such as the procurement of Western equipment, the transition to a predominantly all-volunteer force, the introduction of the military police and the military education reform.

This chapter starts with an overview of the policymaking context, followed by an analysis of the composition of the presidential, military and civilian coalitions during this period. It then explores why certain reforms succeeded while others failed. The chapter is divided into two sections: the first covers the reforms designed and implemented under Serdyukov between 2007 and 2012, while the second examines the changes introduced under Shoigu between 2012 and 2021.

Meeting Russia's military needs

On 10 February 2007, eighteen months before the Russo-Georgian War, President Putin delivered a speech at the Munich Security Conference that marked a major turning point in Russia's defense and foreign policy agenda.[9] In the address, Putin accused NATO of encroaching on Russian security by expanding into former Warsaw Pact countries and criticized member states for breaching the Treaty on Conventional Armed Forces in Europe.[10] Domestically, elites interpreted NATO expansion as a signal that the West was no longer interested in accommodating Russia's national interests.[11] Just five days later, on 15 February 2007, Putin appointed Anatoly Serdyukov as defense minister.

According to one individual who worked with Putin during his first term, the president's growing distrust of the West stemmed from his belief that Western governments would never fully accept the legitimacy of Russia's increasingly authoritarian system. Unlike China, whose authoritarianism was tolerated, Russia's human rights violations and democratic backsliding drew consistent Western criticism:

> After 2004, the transformation began: the redistribution of property, presidential control over parties, elections—it became impossible to get elected as an independent candidate. In 2004, after [the terrorist attack on a school in Beslan], he [Putin] said we were surrounded by terrorists and the Arabs.[12] In 2007, he said that the West was the enemy. The West did not want to accept his regime; [they] demanded human rights. He wanted his Russia to be accepted as it is, like China has been, but it was impossible.[13]

The 2004 Beslan school hostage crisis, in which Chechen terrorists attacked a school in North Ossetia, resulting in over 300 deaths and more than 500 injuries, intensified Putin's narrative of external threats. He framed the tragedy as part of a broader plot by an "outside force" intent on destabilizing Russia and undermining its nuclear deterrence.[14] "Our country—once with the most powerful system of defense of its external borders—found itself unprotected overnight, neither from the West nor from the East," Putin warned.[15] However, he did not explain how domestic Islamist terrorism was linked to this "outside force," or why he perceived Russia to be vulnerable specifically to threats from the West.

The core concepts behind Russia's military reform in the 2007–12 period were developed several years before the reform was officially launched. According to a former parliamentarian, elites had been discussing this reform program since 2004. However, its implementation was repeatedly delayed, as resources for it were redirected toward addressing domestic welfare issues.[16] This turned out to be a departure from previous reform attempts, which had taken place in a relatively cooperative geopolitical environment. By July 2007, Russia had suspended its obligations under the Treaty on Conventional Armed Forces in Europe, citing self-defense against NATO's eastward enlargement.[17] This shift in rhetoric aligned with internal assessments of the military's problems and the ongoing planning for comprehensive reforms. An interviewed military expert noted that, by May 2008, he was already actively involved in drafting a large-scale reform program.[18]

Coalition dynamics in 2007–21

The defense minister's relationship with the military predetermined the degree of military autonomy and how intrusively the military was supervised.[19] Between 2007 and 2012, the military had little autonomy, with the minister of defense closely monitoring and controlling its actions. Minister Serdyukov appointed numerous civilian officials to senior positions within the MoD, many of whom actively imposed their directives without any deference to established military hierarchies or traditions. After 2012, the new minister, Sergei Shoigu, delegated most tasks to the military, thus increasing its autonomy, and refrained from personal involvement in daily oversight or discipline. He relied on military-led centralized data flows with frequent reporting to military commanders and their headquarters. However, these technical solutions were of limited effectiveness, and the military learned how to dodge unwarranted oversight.

Coalition of the willing: key actors in the 2007–12 period

In May 2008, Putin stepped down as president to assume the role of prime minister under a new, younger and reportedly more reform-minded president: Dmitry Medvedev. Putin had endorsed Medvedev's candidacy, having previously established a long and stable working relationship with him. Medvedev had worked with Putin since their time in Saint Petersburg in the early 1990s and became the Presidential Administration's deputy chief of staff under Putin in 2000. Journalists often described their relationship as professional and friendly, with Medvedev's loyal and dutiful approach aligning well with Putin's preference for dependable senior officials. They formed an alliance later called the "tandemocracy."[20] Even though Medvedev would formally be the commander-in-chief and head of state for four years, Putin retained significant formal and informal influence over Russia's policies and governance.

A former law lecturer at Saint Petersburg State University, Medvedev gained substantial administrative and political experience while working within Putin's circle of government managers during Putin's early career in city administration. He later became an expert on Putin's Commission on External Relations within the city administration, beginning his cooptation into the Kremlin's inner circle. Medvedev followed Putin to the federal level, joining his Presidential Administration as deputy head as well as serving on the board of directors of Gazprom, Russia's state-controlled gas monopoly, from 2000 to 2008.[21] In 2005, Putin appointed him to oversee four major "national projects" aimed at reforming healthcare, education, agriculture and housing. By November of that year, Medvedev had risen to the position of deputy prime minister.[22]

Medvedev's approach to government appeared to mark a departure from Putin's increasingly conservative policies. He campaigned on four "I's": institutions, infrastructure, innovations and investment.[23] Even though he mostly focused on the technological meaning of "innovations," he often mentioned that "humanistic" values were important for Russia's development. Medvedev's openness to the West, a preference for Russia being more tightly integrated into international structures and progressive socio-cultural positions found supporters among Moscow's liberal elites. But his approach was misunderstood by more traditional, conservative groups, particularly in the military. While Russia's elites agreed change was needed, they disagreed on what changes exactly, with market liberals and state interventionists taking opposing stances.[24] The former advocated socio-economic modernization, democratic social transition and market-led innovation and considered Medvedev's presidency a chance to build a new Russia with a democratic political system and economic growth. The interventionists, by contrast, focused on narrow technological change and active state policies to reindustrialize the country and make it more efficient.

"The suit jacket"—a civilian in charge of the Russian MoD

The presidential coalition prioritized appointing a defense minister who would align with reform objectives and act as an effective policymaker. This person was Anatoly Serdyukov, appointed in February 2007 while Putin was still president. Serdyukov's appointment symbolized the Kremlin's shift toward prioritizing loyalty and administrative competence over experience in the security services. In 2008, President Medvedev retained Serdyukov as head of the MoD. Under the "tandemocracy," the military was formally subordinate to President Medvedev and Defense Minister Serdyukov. However, in practice, the military continued to orient itself toward Putin, who, as prime minister, retained significant informal influence and held the formal right to "propose" ministerial appointments, including that of the defense minister.

Serdyukov had no personal connections to the military, which turned out to be an advantage for Putin. At the time, President Medvedev was the official commander-in-chief, and the army no longer reported directly to Putin. Because Serdyukov was not part of the military's old networks, he could not use the armed forces to strengthen President Medvedev's position.[25] Serdyukov was a trusted appointee of Putin, and many key figures in the military-industrial complex had established working relationships with the former president. Other major security agencies, including the FSB and the police, were also led by officers who had originally been appointed by Putin, keeping his informal influence in civil–military relations.

Serdyukov's rise began in 2000 with his marriage to Yulia Pohlebenina, the daughter of Viktor Zubkov, a personal assistant of Putin from their time in Saint Petersburg.[26] From 2000 to 2007, Serdyukov steadily advanced within the Federal Tax Service, first in Saint Petersburg and then in Moscow, becoming its head in 2004.[27] His loyalty and effectiveness were demonstrated during the high-profile legal case against Yukos—the private oil company owned by now-exiled oligarch Mikhail Khodorkovsky. The company was dismantled following tax evasion charges.[28] The European Court of Human Rights ruled that Russian authorities acted unfairly in their handling of the tax case against Yukos, providing the company with insufficient time to prepare an adequate defense.[29] This demonstrated to Putin that Serdyukov was both reliable and capable of executing sensitive tasks in line with the Kremlin's strategic goals.[30] Serdyukov was also known for his ability to centralize tax administration and effectively combat tax-evasion schemes.[31] "He was absolutely loyal, [and] had no political [or] administrative ambitions"—this was how a former State Duma member described Serdyukov.[32] Putin demonstrated his support for Serdyukov in September 2007 when Serdyukov's father-in-law, Viktor Zubkov, was appointed prime minister. According to Russian law, public officials are prohibited from having close relatives in subordinate positions, leading Serdyukov to submit a letter of resignation. However, Putin rejected his resignation.[33] Serdyukov's loyalty to Putin and dedication to administrative efficiency became key assets in his career advancement.

But Serdyukov's appointment as defense minister came as a shock, even within military circles. An insider journalist noted that "an hour before the Defense Ministry's Collegium,[34] General Baluyevsky [the chief of the General Staff] started receiving congratulations for his appointment—typical of Putin's style." Putin presented Serdyukov as a seasoned financial auditor who could ensure the "rational spending of the [state] budget's money."[35] But Serdyukov's abrasive personality quickly created friction with the officer corps. "At first, Serdyukov was very rude and treated the military poorly," recalled one respondent. "He thought he could wave his hands and everything would fall into place."[36] However, Serdyukov gradually adapted and began to understand the complex, interdependent nature of the military system. Although he toned down his confrontational approach, he continued to enforce discipline.

Nevertheless, Serdyukov was a poor cultural fit for the military elite, who were unaccustomed to civilian officials dictating orders, particularly if they were women with no military background: "The women from the Federal Tax Service believed they would run the armed forces. They enjoyed ordering generals around."[37] Most of these appointees were women without a military education.[38] This shift forced military generals to report to civilian administrators overseeing logistical and support operations, many of whom had no military experience.

Moreover, the minister disrupted traditional norms by demanding results without regard for rank or status, which clashed with the military's deeply hierarchical culture. Many Russian generals, often older and accustomed to desk roles, were unprepared for Serdyukov's insistence on physical fitness. He pushed them to meet minimum physical requirements, which all military officers were technically supposed to maintain. As a response to his insistence on meeting formal requirements, Serdyukov quickly earned several derogatory nicknames among the military elite, including "the suit jacket" (*pidzhak*) in reference to his limited military background, with only minimal ROTC experience during his student years. Another nickname was "the footstool" (*taburetkin*), a jab at his involvement in the furniture business during the 1990s before entering public service. A retired general and scholar who supported Serdyukov and worked with the MoD during his tenure remarked that "Anatoly Eduardovich had carte blanche. It was crucial that he was a civilian. No military officer would have undertaken such a transformation due to professional psychological biases. They would have understood too many nuances, anticipated potential fallout and sought incremental steps instead."[39] From the outset, these civil–military relationships were fraught with tension, as the officers viewed the civilians as outsiders, while the civilian officials often looked down on their military counterparts, for example by making senior generals wait for hours before admitting them to the minister's office—which would have been unthinkable under previous defense ministers.

The presidential coalition also included former defense minister Sergei Ivanov, who at the time served as deputy prime minister overseeing the military-industrial complex. But Ivanov's close ties with the defense industry and his cautious personality slowed the pace of reforms. As a result, in December 2011, he was reassigned as head of the Presidential Administration. Medvedev replaced him with Dmitry Rogozin, a former Russian representative to NATO, deputy speaker of the Duma and leader of the nationalist/far-right party Rodina (Homeland).[40] Rogozin had no experience in defense production but wrote a dissertation titled "The Russian Question and Its Influence on National and International Security" and had authored several nationalist and anti-Western publications.[41] His appointment surprised many as he had no established connections with the military-industrial complex.[42] Instead, it was a political move, placing a vocal, far-right patriot in charge of modernizing the defense sector and coordinating its relationship with the MoD.

Another key player in the presidential coalition was the minister of finance, as the Finance Ministry controlled budgetary and fiscal policy, making its approval essential for any expansion of the military budget. Alexei Kudrin held this position between 2000 and 2011. Kudrin and Putin had known each other since their days in the Saint Petersburg Mayor's Office in the 1990s, working together in the Committee for External Economic Relations. From 2006 until his resignation, he also sat on the government's Military-Industrial Commission, playing a crucial role in the financial aspects of military reform. This role led to tensions between the minister of finance and the president due to disagreements over increased spending on the military. Kudrin strongly opposed the proposed increase in military spending, arguing it would jeopardize other development programs and strain Russia's budget, but Medvedev dismissed these concerns, stating that raising taxes was an option. In a final exchange, he told Kudrin to focus on delivering the government's instructions rather than questioning them.[43] After this public spat with Medvedev, Kudrin was forced to resign; he was succeeded by Anton Siluanov, an experienced economist who had served as Kudrin's deputy for six years.[44] His appointment signaled continuity in fiscal policy, but, unlike Kudrin, Siluanov was apolitical and lacked a personal connection with Putin.

The structure of the presidential coalition in the 2007–12 reform period was more complex and civilian than in previous years. With Medvedev as president and Putin as prime minister, the power vertical was split into a tandem system. Serdyukov benefited from double support: from Putin, who originally appointed him, and from Medvedev, to whom he was formally accountable.[45]

Military coalition

In June 2008, President Medvedev replaced Yuri Baluyevsky as chief of the General Staff with General Nikolai Makarov, a change that had been anticipated for months.[46] Baluyevsky was known for his resistance to radical reforms and had openly criticized several key decisions by Serdyukov and even Putin, including the withdrawal from the INF Treaty and the relocation of the naval headquarters from Moscow to Saint Petersburg.[47] Makarov, on the other hand, was seen as a loyal and compliant figure. Before he became chief of the General Staff, he headed the General Staff's armament directorate, a position that enhanced his understanding of the equipment and the armed forces' regional structure. Military experts emphasized that Makarov's calm, unambitious nature made him the ideal candidate to execute the reform agenda: "If there was Baluyevsky or a man like Makhmut Gareev, that would be the end."[48]

General Makarov had a long career as an infantry officer in the Soviet and Russian armed forces, earning the rank of general in 1989. Following the collapse of the Soviet Union, he commanded the staff of peacekeeping forces in Tajikistan. In 2005, as commander of the Siberian Military District, Makarov supported greater parental involvement through parents' committees within military regiments and even held an online meeting to address public concerns—an unusual initiative for a senior officer at the time.[49] As chief of the General Staff, he embraced modernization and reform, advocating for the import of foreign armaments to localize the production of advanced technologies in Russia. Makarov openly criticized the Russian military-industrial complex, complaining about its inability to produce cost-effective equipment with adequate crew protection from mines and shrapnel.[50] He also played an active role on the international stage. He frequently visited EU and NATO member states to build trust, negotiate international armament agreements and vocalize Russia's opposition to NATO's missile defense system in Europe.[51]

General Makarov quickly became known as the executor of Serdyukov's sweeping defense reforms. Throughout his term, Makarov maintained a low media profile, rarely offering independent statements or opinions in the media. His public comments mirrored Serdyukov's views, and he consistently upheld the ministry's decisions even when they triggered opposition from senior officers.[52] A military journalist criticized this dynamic, suggesting that Makarov's failure to push back against Serdyukov's radicalism contributed to tensions within the military:

> Chief of the General Staff Makarov bore gigantic responsibility. Medvedev had poor control over the Ministry of Defense, and Serdyukov was given the reform at his mercy [had full control over the reform]. Makarov should have explained it [military topics] better to Serdyukov, but he made ridiculous statements sometimes, which surprised everyone.[53]

Makarov's loyalty and commitment to reform earned him the presidential coalition's favor. Makarov's tenure emphasized the consolidation of centralized control over the military, where obedience to civilian leadership took precedence over traditional military autonomy.

The military coalition also lost influence due to Serdyukov's sweeping personnel changes. In just two and a half years following Serdyukov's appointment, the MoD, the chief of the General Staff, branch commands and regional commands underwent the most significant shake-up since Stalin's pre-war purges, with only six out of fifty senior officials retaining their positions.[54] Early on, Colonel General Anatoly Mazurkevich—chief of the Main Directorate for International Affairs—and Army General Alexei Moskovsky—deputy minister and chief of armaments—were removed from their positions. Their departures were followed by the retirement of Commander in Chief of the Air Force General Vladimir Mikhailov and Colonel General Boris Chelstov, chief of the Air Force Supreme Headquarters. The navy was not spared either, as Admiral Vladimir Masorin was sent into retirement; he was succeeded by Admiral Vladimir Vysotsky.[55]

The generals lacked any organized political force, giving them no real chance to stop a minister and a chief of the General Staff who had full presidential and prime ministerial backing. This enabled the presidential coalition to implement its reform ideas with little consideration of military opinion. However, while no one expected active military protests, the accumulated dissatisfaction with how the reform was being conducted and the initially destructive results eventually reached a level that made supporting reform politically burdensome for both Putin and Medvedev. Upon his return to power, Putin ousted Makarov just nine months after the general had announced that the structural transformation of the Russian military was complete, paving the way for the next phase—a full-scale rearmament program.[56] This program, which was much more popular among the military as it aimed at equipping the newly restructured forces, was implemented under his successor, General Valery Gerasimov.

Civilian coalition

The rise of Medvedev brought a greater appearance of civil society involvement in policymaking, though with limited real influence and tangible outcomes. The most influential civilian body was the Council for Foreign and Defense Policy, a think tank whose members contributed to policy program development. The State Duma remained largely passive, with Viktor Zavarzin of United Russia chairing the Defense Committee until December 2011—a figure who ensured broad compliance with MoD demands. While some individual Duma deputies and members of the Communist faction criticized Defense Minister Serdyukov, their public opposition rarely translated into action: "The Duma played no role whatsoever. The pro-government majority supported all government decisions. Many deputies criticized in public but then voted as expected."[57]

The civilian coalition also included former military officers dismissed during the reform who opposed Serdyukov's policies and political parties/movements that channeled this frustration. Some had not received apartments promised by the MoD after years of service, while others became politically active post-retirement, disagreeing with the minister's approach and Medvedev's oversight. These groups frequently voiced their discontent in the media and organized protests across Russia. For instance, in November 2010, the Union of Airborne Veterans, joined by nationalists and Communists, held a rally in Moscow demanding Serdyukov's resignation and the cancellation of the reform.[58] The protest followed a public conflict after Serdyukov's visit to an airborne training center in September 2010, where he angrily berated officers for building a church rather than renovating the canteen and barracks.[59] Another protest occurred in Chelyabinsk, where veterans demonstrated against the closure of a regional military automobile institute. Organized by the liberal "Right Cause" party, the rally was attended by several hundred people.[60]

Serdyukov also mobilized the Russian defense industry against the MoD by adopting hardline negotiation tactics and demanding price cuts. In some cases, this halted defense orders and left factories without critical income.[61] The conflict escalated in 2011 after the MoD approved a new rearmament program worth RUB19 trillion (US$630 billion in 2011 or about US$853 billion in 2023), the largest defense budget allocation in post-Soviet Russia.[62] The unprecedented financial scale raised tensions, as the MoD's strict demands for cost efficiency and quality clashed with the inefficiencies of the aging, infrastructure-heavy military-industrial complex. Organizational challenges within the defense procurement system, combined with the substantial rewards tied to lucrative contracts, further intensified the conflict between the MoD and defense manufacturers, making the industrial sector a key player in the reform process.

The new-look Russian military

The 2007–12 military reform, which Serdyukov referred to as "The New Look" in October 2008, signaled a significant shift away from the outdated principles that had long shaped Russian defense strategy.[63] As Chief of the General Staff Makarov acknowledged, the Russian military had spent decades lagging behind global advances in military technology and strategy. While other nations had developed precision weaponry, space-based systems and real-time command networks, Russia remained trapped in the paradigms of mass mobilization and obsolete weaponry from the Soviet era. Key signals of transformation—such as the 1991 Gulf War and the 2003 Iraq War, where coalition forces executed network-centric operations

FROM COMBAT EFFECTIVENESS TO OVERSIGHT OVERLOAD

Presidential coalition	Military coalition	United Russia	Civilian coalition CPRF (Communists)	Non-parliamentary actors
President Dmitry Medvedev				
Prime Minister Vladimir Putin		Defense Committee head Gen. (R) Viktor Zavarzin (before December 2011)	Defense Committee head Admiral (R) Vladimir Komoyedov (before September 2016)	Council on Foreign and Defense Policy
Defense Minister Anatoly Serdyukov				Vitaly Shlykov
Alexei Kudrin, minister of finance (before September 2011)	Gen. Baluyevsky (June 2008) Gen. Makarov (June 2008–November 2012)			
Former Tax Service officials and civilian contractors			Retired military officers	
Anton Siluanov, minister of finance (from September 2011)	GOU, Main Operational Directorate		Defense industry	
Social Council of the MoD	GOMU Main Organizational Mobilizational Directorate			
Sergei Ivanov (before December 2011), Dmitry Rogozin (after December 2011), deputy prime minister for the military-industrial complex				
Vera Chistova, deputy minister of defense for financial affairs (April 2009–November 2010)				
Tatiana Shevtsova, deputy minister of defense for financial affairs (from August 2010)				

Figure 6: Coalitions in 2007–12

with extensive use of advanced information and communication technologies to link forces, sensors, decision-makers and weapons systems into a unified network—were largely ignored by the Russian military. These shortcomings had become evident during the Russo-Georgian War in August 2008. As Makarov noted, the conflict was a wake-up call, forcing the military leadership to overhaul the armed forces' structure.[64] What followed was a period of rapid and radical transformation aimed at modernizing the military's composition, command structure and technological base.

What's old is new again: reform ideas

Makarov was correct in his criticism of the Russian military's outdated development. However, he was not entirely right in his criticism of the Russian military's science and defense policy analysis. The ideas for the reform, although officially launched after the Georgian war, had been in development for years. As early as 1996–8, the Council on Defense—an advisory body under President Yeltsin—proposed key changes that Serdyukov and Makarov would later adopt.[65] By 2004, think tanks and the General Staff had produced a series of policy proposals, including contributions from Vitaliy Shlykov, a former Main Intelligence Directorate (GRU) officer and founding member of the Council on Foreign and Defense Policy (SVOP). Shlykov, a former Soviet intelligence operative specializing in foreign military development who had been imprisoned for two years in Switzerland during the 1980s, became a respected public defense expert in post-Soviet Russia. He was a vocal supporter of the reform and remained so until his death in 2011.[66]

The SVOP's proposals received attention from General Anatoly Kvashnin, chief of the General Staff from 1997 to 2004. "He underlined our proposals with red and blue pencils: blue for agreement, red for disagreement," one expert recalled. Despite this interest, the MoD rejected the final report, and some of its recommendations were labeled provocative.[67] Still, in 2005, Chief of the General Staff Baluyevsky acknowledged that future reforms would emphasize a more flexible, battalion-based structure, with private organizations taking over non-military duties such as barrack maintenance, catering and cleaning.[68] These ideas, dismissed or postponed for years, ultimately formed the core of Serdyukov's defense reform three years later. For example, in December 2007, the MoD established the experimental Eastern Regional Command, which served as a precursor to the military district reform that would decentralize command-and-control functions to the district (regional command) headquarters. However, the experiment was deemed unsuccessful and cancelled in May 2008, shortly before Baluyevsky's resignation as chief of the General Staff. Even though the experiment failed, it revealed important problems in how Russia's military was commanded. It showed that combining different regional military functions into a single regional structure created confusion and made coordination more difficult. These lessons proved valuable during the later stages of reform.[69]

The war with Georgia exposed critical flaws, including an outdated command-and-control system, poor coordination and deployment failures.[70] "The armed forces showed an inability to mobilize and respond quickly and effectively. This war revealed the shortcomings of the army," noted a retired major general and former General Staff officer.[71] Even pro-government media criticized the outdated weaponry, subpar communication systems and insufficient professional enlisted personnel, as well as the illegal deployment of conscripts to the battlefield.[72] A military journalist claimed that one officer called rocket artillery using his satellite phone because there was no reliable military communication system.[73] The use of conscripts in combat, despite official denials, further highlighted the gap between public declarations of military readiness and battlefield realities. These failures also reflected the ineffectiveness of prior rearmament efforts led by Minister Ivanov and two successive chiefs of the General Staff.

The war exposed the disconnect between patriotic government rhetoric and operational outcomes, ultimately altering the reform program's scope and priorities.[74] Shortly after the conflict, Putin and Medvedev convened a Security Council meeting to address the shortcomings of the Russian armed forces. During the meeting, they ordered significant improvements in performance and combat readiness, officially launching the long-anticipated military overhaul.[75]

In October 2008, Serdyukov publicly presented the first plan for the reform, setting the stage for the most radical transformation of the Russian military since the Soviet era.

A radical reform package

Serdyukov's reforms were comprehensive, involving multiple policies implemented in separate phases (see Appendix 3). First, the MoD aimed to downsize the officer corps by dismissing thousands of officers while shifting recruitment efforts toward professional soldiers and sergeants. Second, the MoD sought to dismantle the so-called "cadre compounds"—understaffed military bases intended to replenish forces and serve as a second line of defense in the event of full-scale war. These compounds were largely ineffective, consisting of a small contingent of officers and conscripts responsible for maintaining outdated military equipment for potential future mobilization. Third, Serdyukov initiated a transition to a brigade-based military structure to enhance mobility and responsiveness. The MoD also restructured military education by consolidating and downsizing military academies to improve efficiency. Finally, these structural reforms were accompanied by a large-scale rearmament program, which Serdyukov launched before his resignation, aiming to modernize the Russian armed forces.

Staff cuts

The disbandment of units and the restructuring of the military around a new framework centered on sergeants and junior commanders led to the mass firing of thousands of officers.[76] As a retired major general described the process, the MoD's Main Personnel Directorate issued quotas to regional commands, instructing them to dismiss a specific percentage of staff at each rank. But this reduction was carried out without sufficient consideration for functional needs, resulting in an inadequate and overstretched command-and-control structure. Young officers frequently declined promotions, knowing that their salaries would remain stagnant while their workloads would increase significantly. Paradoxically, some junior officers were demoted to sergeants at the start of the process, but the MoD still failed to meet its targets for the recruitment of sergeants.[77] On the operational side, combat exercises were intensified, and military salaries were gradually increased, though the added workload for active officers began immediately, generating dissatisfaction.[78]

The staff reduction also hit the MoD and the General Staff, drastically downsizing and decentralizing their functions to the newly established Joint Strategic Commands, the highest-level regional military headquarters created to streamline command and control by integrating different branches of the military within each military district under a single unified leadership. The reform slashed the MoD's central structure almost fivefold, from 51,000 to 13,400 personnel, with around 3,000 positions earmarked for civilian staff by 2012.[79] The reform also reduced the size and scope of the GRU within the General Staff.[80] Lastly, non-combat support services, such as food supplies and cleaning, were outsourced to private contractors.[81] As a result, thousands of officers, including colonels and generals, were dismissed; they went on to form a vocal group of retired officers (*otstavniki*) who became some of Serdyukov's most prominent public critics.

Serdyukov and Makarov adopted a strict stance against hazing and violent behavior, making it a priority to enforce discipline and accountability within the armed forces. Human rights organizations noted a significant improvement in the MoD's openness and responsiveness to their requests for soldier protection.[82] And commanders were increasingly held accountable and dismissed for cases of hazing. However, some officers challenged their dismissals in court, using disciplinary procedures to protect themselves from forced retirement.[83] Despite legal obstacles requiring formal disciplinary or court orders to dismiss officers for negligence in handling hazing incidents, Serdyukov's policies had a tangible impact, with a reduction of reported cases of violence and hazing. For example, the number of convictions under Articles 334, 335 and 336 of the Criminal Code—violations of military conduct rules, insulting a serviceman and violent actions against a superior— dropped from 2,169 in 2008 to 1,351 in 2012, with further yearly declines thereafter. Similarly, convictions under Article 286—abuse of authority, which can include violence in the armed forces—fell from 2,294 in 2009 to 1,682 in 2012, also continuing to decrease over time.[84]

To legitimize his reforms in the eyes of the public, Serdyukov leaned heavily on the MoD's Social Council and an active public relations campaign. The MoD sought to suppress public criticism by organizing meetings and conferences for experts and State Duma members.[85] Although these groups lacked access to the formal decision-making process, they were influential opinion-makers. "We raised the issue in the Security Committee of the State Duma, but to silence our complaints, Serdyukov orchestrated a grand presentation at the ministry, involving a joint meeting of the Security and Defense Committees, complete with a movie, glossy folders and a lavish banquet," a former State Duma member recalled. While the Duma had limited power to directly influence the defense reform, its members could draw public attention and engage in naming and blaming, undermining the legitimacy of the reform and its architects. To counteract this, Serdyukov's MoD cleverly manipulated information, selectively presenting positive outcomes and showcasing progress to an audience largely unversed in military matters, thus diverting criticism and mitigating opposition.

District and structural changes

The MoD restructured six former military districts into four joint strategic commands, decentralizing operational command from Moscow to the military district level. A member of the Military-Industrial Commission described the reform as creating the "complete subordination of all forces to commanders of unified strategic commands (military districts)," leading to a redistribution of authority and diminishing the influence of service chiefs,[86] who were stripped of operational command. Their roles were redefined to focus on training, doctrine and procurement, not operational command.[87] At the same time, a shift in the financial structure centralized the allocation of budgetary expenditures and took away the powers of the military district commanders to control their budgets.[88]

One of the key reform objectives was to replace the ground forces' five-tier structure (military district—army—corps—division—regiment) with a streamlined three-tier system (operational command—brigade—battalion). However, the reform met resistance from both the VDV and the Strategic Missile Forces. The VDV successfully cancelled the planned disbandment of its divisions shortly before General Vladimir Shamanov—a renowned commander from the Chechen Wars—was appointed its chief.[89] Shamanov was a significant figure in Russia's civil–military relations, having left active service in 2000 to become governor of the Ulyanovsk region and later serving as an advisor to Prime Minister Fradkov and head of the Main Directorate of Combat Training and Service under Defense Minister Serdyukov from 2007 to 2009. Shamanov argued that the VDV was already combat-ready and did not require structural reform.[90] Leveraging his dual identity as both a decorated warrior and a prominent public official, Shamanov successfully blocked the planned restructuring of the VDV.

In 2009, Serdyukov unsuccessfully attempted to establish a fully functional military police service within the armed forces, a move intended to strengthen the MoD's oversight over troops. The proposed military police would have taken over law enforcement and investigative functions from the Federal Prosecutor's Office, the Investigative Committee (SKR) and the FSB[91] and would have reported directly to the deputy defense minister.[92] However, the initiative met significant resistance from other security services within the presidential coalition, complicating its implementation.[93] For example, the FSB opposed the plan because it threatened to interfere with its counterintelligence operations in the military.[94] As a result, the military police was only established in 2014, with limited authority and no independent investigative power. "The primary [authority of] investigation remained under the control of unit commanders, undermining the fairness of these investigations," noted one expert.[95] The failure highlighted the role of other security agencies as veto players in Russian civil–military relations, particularly when their official prerogatives were at risk. When federal ministries or agencies submit bill proposals, they are subject to mandatory legal reviews by other government bodies, such as the Ministry of

Justice, the Presidential Administration and the government's Legal Department. While the FSB, the SKR and the Federal Prosecutor's Office are not part of the formal legal vetting process, they may be consulted if a draft bill affects their mandate. They may submit formal objections or recommendations at this stage. In the defense reform case, they served as key channels for blocking or delaying unwanted policy initiatives.

A more successful story of reform was the development of the Special Operations Forces Command (KSSO). KSSO forces were intended to become an elite, independent component of the Russian armed forces, designed to carry out special missions both inside and outside of Russia, and are often compared to the US Joint Special Operations Command or the British Special Air Service. Similar to other initiatives, the initial idea to create such a force dates to the early 2000s, when Colonel Vladimir Kvachkov proposed a special operations command under the General Staff.[96] However, the institutional change only took place in 2009, when Chief of the General Staff Makarov established the Directorate of Special Operations based on the GRU unit (nicknamed Senezh) near Lake Senezh in Solnechnogorsk (around 50 kilometers northwest of Moscow). These service members had extensive combat experience in Chechnya, where they received their nickname "sunflowers" (*podsolnukhi*), either for the color of their bandanas or because their base was located close to the "Podsolnechnaya" (Sunflower) train station. Colonel Oleg Martyanov—Afghan War veteran, ex-spetsnaz (special forces) and GRU officer—was appointed as the first head of the directorate.[97] A second Special Operations Center (nicknamed Kubinka) was later created in Kubinka-2, near Moscow.[98] Kubinka's approach emphasized individual training and elite physical conditioning, inspired by FSB Alpha (an elite Russian counterterrorism and hostage rescue unit) standards. Former Alpha commander General-Lieutenant Alexander Miroshnichenko reportedly oversaw Kubinka's creation and sought to shape the new command based solely on FSB standards and manuals, while Senezh commanders insisted on preserving their established military doctrine.[99] On 1 April 2012, Makarov officially renamed the Directorate of Special Operations as the Special Operations Forces

Command. The successful establishment of the KSSO exemplifies a targeted restructuring of Russia's elite forces, backed by the chief of the General Staff and two influential security institutions—the General Staff's military intelligence and the FSB's special forces.

Rearmament program

The implementation of the State Rearmament Program 2020 (GPV-2020) was highly unconventional for Russia. Originally launched in 2010 with a budget of RUB20 trillion (US$660 billion at 2010 exchange rates), it aimed to modernize Russia's military with large-scale procurements, including 400 intercontinental ballistic missiles, fifty surface warships, twenty-eight submarines, 600 aircraft and 2,300 tanks.[100] However, the MoD was dissatisfied at the high costs and poor quality of domestically produced equipment and opted to procure foreign components and incentivize foreign companies to localize their production within Russia. This led to the purchase of Mistral-class amphibious assault ships from France, Italian vehicles and small arms and advanced equipment for IT, communication, intelligence and special operations from other countries.[101] The deals with France and Italy reflected positive diplomatic relations between Putin and European leaders such as Nicolas Sarkozy and Silvio Berlusconi.[102] However, tensions emerged in 2011 when Putin announced his decision to return for a third presidential term from 2012, straining relations with Western nations. Following the annexation of Crimea in 2014, major foreign defense agreements were halted. The German defense firm Rheinmetall was among the last companies to suspend its cooperation with Russia by cancelling the contract for building a special-operations training center in Mulino, Nizhny Novgorod region.[103]

Serdyukov also launched extensive audits of the financial compliance and effectiveness of key directorates within the MoD and the General Staff. These inspections were conducted by civilian officials with no prior military experience, many of whom had worked with Serdyukov in the Federal Tax Service, including Sergei Khursevich and former TNK-BP[104] finance vice-president Mikhail Motorin. This approach led to significant operational changes and the exposure of corrupt networks, resulting in numerous dismissals and even a suicide.[105] Despite strong military opposition, Serdyukov's anti-corruption efforts brought financial discipline to the ministry and earned positive public feedback.[106]

The MoD also reshaped its approach to the defense industry by centralizing financial audits and adopting a more confrontational stance. Serdyukov and Makarov openly criticized defense manufacturers' inability to deliver modern weaponry within the required timelines.[107] However, the defense industry was not just a military supplier: it was also a major employer, with millions depending on its operations. For example, Uralvagonzavod, Russia's primary tank production facility, struggled to meet the MoD's modernization demands, yet shutting it down was not an option due to the economic reliance of cities like Tomsk, Nizhny Tagil and Chelyabinsk on its workforce. As a result, industrial directors, city mayors and regional governors actively lobbied for government contracts while simultaneously seeking Serdyukov's removal.[108] The conflict escalated to the highest levels of government, involving powerful figures such as Sergei Chemezov, a former KGB general and head of Rostec (previously Rostekhnologii), Russia's state defense conglomerate. Chemezov, a longtime associate of Putin from their time in socialist Germany during the 1980s, had political influence and was instrumental in defending the interests of the military-industrial complex against the MoD's new policies.[109]

The rearmament program also sparked a conflict with the Ministry of Finance, ultimately leading to the resignation of Finance Minister Alexei Kudrin. Kudrin argued for a reduction in the program due to financial constraints, but the program was a core pillar of the military reform. Its main architect was General Vladimir Popovkin, head of the MoD's armament office. A military journalist familiar with Popovkin described the sequence of events:

> Medvedev signed it [the rearmament program] on 31 December 2010. Kudrin was informed about the decision later, although he expected to hold several meetings to advocate for a US$200 billion reduction. He called Popovkin and asked one question: "Vladimir, wherefore?" Popovkin replied, "The Supreme

Commander made the decision—Putin suggested, I agreed, and Medvedev signed."[110]

While there is no public record of this exchange, the broader conflict between Kudrin and Medvedev was well known throughout the reform period.

Kudrin had long criticized Medvedev's government for its interventionist economic policies and what he viewed as irresponsible fiscal spending. Although Kudrin successfully cut several billion rubles from the rearmament program, this was insufficient to address his concerns. Following another round of public criticism, Medvedev forced Kudrin to resign in September 2011.[111] The spat was public and recorded by the media:

> DM [Dmitry Medvedev]—Here is Alexei Leonidovich Kudrin [AK], who is present here, and he has shared the joyful news that he does not plan to work in the new government, and that he has serious practical disagreements with the current president, particularly regarding spending, including on the military. You have only one option, and you know what it is—to resign. Are you going to write your resignation letter?
>
> AK—Dmitry Anatolyevich [Medvedev], I do indeed have disagreements with you, but I will make a decision in response to your proposal after consulting with the Prime Minister [Putin].
>
> DM—You can consult with whoever you like. But as long as I am president, I make these decisions myself.
>
> ...
>
> DM—Alexei Leonidovich, why aren't you going to call Putin?
>
> AK—I'll call him later.
>
> DM—Go call him now. I'm waiting for your answer.
>
> AK—At this meeting, I'm the only representative of the Finance Ministry, and the draft of the protocol decision is incomplete. I have serious objections to it.
>
> DM—Fine. Submit your objections, and then go make the call.[112]

Kudrin's departure exposed underlying fractures within the presidential coalition, driven partly by the radical nature of the defense reforms. However, the coalition managed to navigate the challenge by replacing Kudrin with Anton Siluanov, a more cooperative civil servant from Kudrin's own team.

Military education

Another key focus of the reform was a radical overhaul of Russia's military education system. Initially, the MoD aimed to complete the first phase of this restructuring by 2013, with improvements scheduled for completion by 2020.[113] The plan involved consolidating sixty-five existing military educational institutions into just ten universities.[114] This plan faced significant resistance as it directly affected military professors, cadets and their families across Russia, from Saint Petersburg to Vladivostok.[115] Experts widely agreed that the reforms were necessary due to ongoing issues, including outdated teaching practices and academic misconduct, such as professors plagiarizing translations of foreign military literature.[116] Cadets were also frequently taken away from their studies for non-academic tasks, like prolonged preparations for the annual Victory Day parade (Russia holds an annual military parade on 9 May to commemorate the victory over Nazi Germany).

The MoD actively worked to suppress any criticism from the State Duma regarding the closure of military institutions. One former parliamentarian recalled a meeting about the disbandment of the Kolomensky High Artillery Command School, where the MoD presented a list of criteria for its evaluation. The ministry invited State Duma members to identify any criteria that could justify saving the school, promising to support them if they succeeded. However, the evaluation criteria were designed in such a restrictive way that it was virtually impossible to save the school.[117]

Many of these institutions were located in prime urban areas, where their buildings and surrounding land held immense real estate value, thus making them especially vulnerable to corruption, particularly in Moscow and other major cities.[118] This meant that businessmen and government officials who could "persuade" the government to sell these land plots at below market value stood to make windfall profits by reselling the land to developers.

Relocating faculty, staff and their families from large cities to smaller towns presented additional challenges as they simply did not want to move from large urban centers to remote towns. Critics accused the MoD of "giving away" military educational institutions with a long history and deep-rooted traditions in Russia, further fueling public discontent with the reform.[119] In the end, the ousting of Serdyukov in 2012 halted the unpopular reform, leaving Russia's military education system largely unchanged.

Reform results

Serdyukov's military reform was, at best, only partly successful. Despite remaining in office from 2007 to 2012, several key initiatives, including the establishment of the military police, the development of a professional sergeant corps and structural reorganization, proved unsustainable and met significant resistance. The creation of the military police was blocked by opposition from law enforcement agencies, which feared losing their authority over military investigations.[120] The attempted reform of military education sparked a public backlash, as the drastic reduction and consolidation of institutions attracted negative attention from the State Duma. In response, the MoD attempted to mitigate criticism through public hearings and conferences, but the reform was ultimately reversed only after Serdyukov's dismissal.[121]

Similarly, many military officers expressed deep frustration with Serdyukov's perceived disregard for military traditions and values, and his confrontational style of communication with senior officers was repeatedly cited as a source of resentment among the armed forces. A public outcry forced the MoD to reinstate several historically significant military divisions, including the Tamanskaya and Kantemirovskaya, two decorated divisions famous for their performance in the Second World War and for participating in Yeltsin's crackdown on the parliament in 1993.[122]

Structural reforms were further hindered by bureaucratic inefficiency, resistance from key military branches and the inability to meet reform deadlines.[123] Overall, the reform process revealed three primary mechanisms for blocking policies: personal access to Putin, opposition from other security agencies and ministerial dismissal. By contrast, public protests, appeals from the Duma and broader political opposition had little tangible impact, despite their symbolic significance.

Back to imperfect equilibrium: military development, 2012–21

In the early hours of 27 February 2014, around 120 armed men in full combat gear and without insignia seized the buildings of the Crimean parliament and government in Ukraine. By 28 February, additional forces had blockaded Simferopol Airport, the Belbek military airfield, Ukrainian military installations and Crimea's air navigation control center. Roadblocks were set up, isolating Crimea from mainland Ukraine, while unidentified military vehicles appeared in Balaklava and Feodosia. Ukrainian military personnel at several bases quickly pledged allegiance to the "people of Crimea."[124] Over the next few days, elite units secured strategic locations across the peninsula. By the evening of 2 March, and without a single shot fired, the invading forces had taken over the headquarters of Ukraine's Azov-Black Sea Regional Administration and the Simferopol Border Guard Detachment.[125]

The soldiers involved in the operation belonged to the 16th Special Purpose Brigade, the 76th Air Assault Division and the 45th Separate Airborne Regiment, along with Special Operations Forces of the Russian armed forces—later known as the "Polite People" or "Little Green Men." Despite being armed, Ukrainian troops were caught off guard and received no clear instructions from Kyiv, leaving them paralyzed in the face of the swift and coordinated Russian operation. Ukraine lost the Crimean Peninsula, and military analysts around the world discovered something new—a reformed, more agile and better commanded Russian military.[126]

The military on display in the annexation of Crimea was the product of the 2007–12 reform and the subsequent rearmament program, which improved the Russian armed forces' readiness, equipment and materiel. After nearly two decades of stagnation and decay, Russia's military once again appeared to be a formidable, intimidating force.

But this public image proved more robust than the armed forces' actual combat readiness. Despite notable military achievements in Crimea and Eastern Ukraine, the preservation of the Assad regime in Syria, large-scale military exercises and politically advantageous interventions in Nagorno-Karabakh and Kazakhstan, the pace of military development began to slow. By the end of the 2012–21 period, the Russian armed forces had once again entered a phase of semi-stagnation, struggling to meet key performance indicators or even sustain the progress achieved.

In February 2010, amid Serdyukov's reform efforts, President Medvedev adopted a new military doctrine, signaling a shift in Russia's strategic priorities.[127] The timing was clearly deliberate, as it coincided with the start of the Munich Security Conference. In the new doctrine, NATO enlargement and US missile defense systems were officially designated as threats to Russian security for the first time since the collapse of the Soviet Union. The document outlined Russia's commitment to maintaining permanent combat-ready forces capable of responding to military aggression, restoring peace under UN mandates and defending Russian allies and citizens abroad, such as those Russia claimed were in Crimea. The Kremlin no longer saw centralization of control as necessary but instead tasked the government and military with achieving concrete improvements in combat readiness.

Two years later, Putin's return to power marked the definitive end of Russia's democratic prospects. In the defense sector, Putin replaced Serdyukov, halted many of his controversial reforms and continued to implement the largest chunk of the GPV-2020, a large-scale investment program focused on modernizing military equipment and armaments (launched a year earlier, in 2011). Serdyukov's removal came amid a major corruption scandal involving the Oboronservis company, established by the MoD in 2008 with the aim of centralizing and managing military maintenance, construction, catering, real estate and logistics, so that the military could focus on combat readiness and operations. The SKR opened a criminal case into fraud and embezzlement related to the sale of military property by Oboronservis at prices far below market value. The scandal focused on officials appointed by Defense Minister Serdyukov, including his close associate Yevgeniya Vasilyeva, who was later convicted. President Putin stated that Serdyukov was dismissed to ensure the investigation's objectivity.[128]

In practice, this meant that the disruptive and painful reforms came to a halt, while the defense sector benefited from substantial financial investments. The Russian military finally obtained what it had long desired—modern equipment and increased financial incentives—without having to endure further intensive and destabilizing structural overhauls. The key person behind these changes was Sergei Shoigu, Putin's longtime ally.

Coalitions: Sergei Shoigu, 2012–21

In November 2012, six months after taking office for his third term, President Putin appointed Shoigu as Russia's new defense minister. One of the country's most popular politicians, Shoigu was tasked with reversing Serdyukov's intrusive plans and often antagonistic approach. Unlike his predecessor, who alienated the military establishment, Shoigu emphasized the armed forces' collective expertise, describing the military as a strong community with significant "intellectual potential" that he intended to harness fully.[129] His leadership style balanced Ivanov's caution with Serdyukov's more radical approach.

Shoigu had built his reputation as Russia's longest-serving minister of emergency situations (1991–2012), a role in which he gained public admiration for overseeing disaster relief efforts and maintaining high visibility in the media.[130] He was also a founding member of United Russia, the Kremlin's ruling party, and had briefly served as governor of the Moscow region.[131] As a former member of the Defense Council remarked,

> Shoigu, when he headed the Ministry of Emergency Situations, was a PR man. He built the ministry with experienced generals, but he himself was working on its public image. He is a talented leader, he can build a team, and he tries to study when he does not know something.[132]

Shoigu's approach was markedly different from that of his predecessors—he delegated military operations to the military and provided strong institutional backing for his ministry within the government.

Shoigu continued his strong emphasis on public relations and shaping public perception in his role as defense minister. Under his leadership, the MoD expanded its media influence by revitalizing the "Zvezda" military television channel, strengthening its presence on social media and establishing or reforming international military forums. He also promoted high school military education through the expansion of the Suvorov and Kadetsky academies (MoD-led schools for boys with an emphasis on military skills) and fostered military socialization programs, most notably the patriotic youth movement "YunArmiya" (Young Army). His daughter, Ksenia Shoigu, even joined this effort and started organizing large-scale sports and cultural events featuring active military participation.[133] One of the most striking examples of this effort was the construction of the Main Cathedral of the Armed Forces, a project that symbolically merges Soviet military traditions with contemporary Russian neoconservative and nationalist themes. This initiative reflected Shoigu's vision of integrating military heritage with state ideology through religious and historical symbolism.[134]

The combination of strategic public relations and Russian foreign policy's increasing militarization led to unprecedented public approval of the armed forces. Under Shoigu's leadership, independent criticism of the MoD was increasingly discouraged, with some journalists facing professional repercussions for voicing dissent—one was even dismissed early in Shoigu's tenure for harshly criticizing the ministry.[135]

Military coalition in 2012–21

As minister of defense, Shoigu appeared to reconsider the radical reforms of his predecessor, but, in practice, he reviewed the most problematic parts of the reform and kept the overall direction unchanged. Rather than challenging the fundamental framework established under Serdyukov, Shoigu reintegrated the military leadership into key decision-making positions, effectively remilitarizing the MoD by appointing senior generals to critical roles. This approach minimized conflicts, but it ultimately slowed the pace of change in the military.

Shoigu's most consequential decision was the appointment of General Valery Gerasimov as chief of the General Staff in November 2012.[136] According to a member of the Expert Council of the Military-Industrial Commission, "Shoigu delegated the reform to CGS [Chief of the General Staff] Gerasimov, with General Bulgakov handling logistics and a group from the General Staff Academy supporting them. As minister, Shoigu took over finances, resources, construction and the state defense order."[137] Gerasimov, who had served as deputy chief of the General Staff under Makarov since 2010, was entrusted with stabilizing relations with the military-industrial complex and accelerating rearmament efforts.[138] He also focused on improving inter-service coordination and civil–military cooperation, as well as expanding the General Staff's role as the central authority for managing defense and security coordination across federal and regional agencies.[139]

General Gerasimov gained significant recognition in the West following his 2013 speech at the Academy of Military Sciences in Moscow.[140] This address was later mischaracterized as expounding the "Gerasimov Doctrine," a term coined by Western analysts to describe Russia's blend of military and non-military tactics in modern warfare. However, in reality, the speech was a theoretical summary of Russian and Western military strategies rather than a groundbreaking new doctrine. While his speech gained notoriety, Gerasimov's real achievements lay in his leadership and contributions to military operations.

A highly skilled and experienced officer, Gerasimov was born in Kazan (800 kilometers to the east of Moscow) and graduated from three military academies, including two armored forces institutions and the General Staff Academy. His career spanned multiple postings across the former Soviet Union and Warsaw Pact, including overseeing the withdrawal of Russian forces from Estonia. He played an important role in the Chechen Wars, initially serving under the renowned VDV general Vladimir Shamanov in the 58th Army before taking over its command in 2001.[141] Gerasimov has cited the legendary eighteenth-century Russian general Alexander Suvorov as a key influence on his military thinking.[142] He prefers a data-driven approach to military development, emphasizing strategic forecasting and dynamic responses to evolving threats.[143] Yet this overreliance on data hindered Russian military development under his tenure. The poor quality of monitoring mechanisms led to what statisticians refer to as "garbage in, garbage out," that is, behind the polished charts and impressive figures lay flawed, biased and unreliable data, compounded by systemic issues in data collection and accuracy. This failure rested personally on Gerasimov as the chief of the General Staff, whose primary responsibility was to provide the defense minister with accurate assessments of the armed forces' condition.

From 2012, the relationship between Shoigu and Gerasimov became a defining feature of Russian civil–military relations. The military was tasked with enhancing combat readiness within the strategic framework set by the MoD, while the ministry itself was responsible for securing resources and maintaining cohesion with other government bodies. This arrangement was supported by a favorable political environment. In 2010, Medvedev prioritized military development by approving the GPV-2020 rearmament program, effectively changing a relatively stable parameter that had previously conditioned civil–military relations. Then, Putin and his government supported significant financial investment in the military through the approved program. This combination created a stable relationship between the military and the presidential coalition.

The civilian coalition in 2012–21

Under Shoigu, the civilian coalition, which had previously played a more active role in defense policymaking, became increasingly shallow as Putin's return to power in 2012 marked a period of authoritarian consolidation. The erosion of political freedoms limited civilian oversight, while the MoD's growing budget ensured financial benefits for military veterans and the defense industry, further aligning their interests with the state.

The annexation of Crimea in 2014 and the subsequent war in Eastern Ukraine created a wave of patriotic fervor that further entrenched the military's position within the ruling coalition. Nationalist rhetoric dominated the public discourse, making any criticism of the armed forces or defense policies politically risky, as well as triggering the rallying-around-the-flag effect supporting Putin's popularity.[144] The military was portrayed as a victorious force reclaiming "lost territories," rendering opposition voices nearly irrelevant in civil–military relations. Duma deputies stopped scrutinizing the MoD's policies, and legal changes banning honest debate and the collection of military data followed suit.

Several legal challenges restricted independent access to the armed forces. In 2019, the Duma passed a law banning soldiers from using smartphones and laptops while on duty. The legislation prohibited military personnel from taking photos, recording videos, accessing the internet or discussing military matters with journalists. The move followed incidents where Russian service members' social media posts exposed the country's military involvement in Eastern Ukraine and Syria. In practice, this reduced one of the few remaining feedback mechanisms through which soldiers could complain about service conditions or leak illegal behavior to the press.[145] In July 2021, the FSB published a draft order supplementing the 2020 law on foreign agents, significantly expanding the scope of restricted information related to national security. The law allowed any individual engaged in collecting military-related data that foreign entities could use against Russia to be designated as a "foreign agent."[146] Designated NGOs had to submit detailed financial reports and were subject to unannounced inspections by the Ministry of Justice and prosecutors, often leading to harassment or disruption of their work. In Russian, the term "foreign agent" carries strong connotations of espionage and betrayal, delegitimizing the organization.[147]

In practice, the amendment endangered those attempting to provide independent analysis of the defense sector in Russia. It also sharply reduced the response rate to my interview requests by clouding all defense-related topics with an atmosphere of suspicion. As a result, Russian civil–military relations became increasingly monolithic, with few external checks on defense policies and decision-making. Information about the armed forces is now insulated from outside eyes. The resulting breakdown of Russian monitoring mechanisms ultimately undermined the effectiveness of Russia military development under Shoigu.

The only group of civilian actors that remained relatively influential were representatives of the military-industrial complex. This group was dominated by several state-owned corporations, including Rostec, Almaz-Antey, the United Aircraft Corporation, the United Shipbuilding Corporation and the Tactical Missiles Corporation.[148] These companies accounted for about 70 per cent of the funds allocated under the GPV-2020 rearmament program.[149] In 2020, Prime Minister Mikhail Mishustin declared the defense sector a top priority, with former president Medvedev overseeing military production in his new Security Council role. However, Western sanctions and inefficiencies in Russia's military industries degraded the producers' performance under Shoigu's leadership. Western sanctions have hindered Russia's efforts to modernize the GLONASS navigation system and advanced communications equipment. The entire industry lost access to European and US manufacturing equipment, while, financially, the sector remained deeply unprofitable, owing 700 billion rubles by 2019 and requiring repeated government bailouts.[150]

Restoring the Russian military: military development under Shoigu

After a period of disequilibrium in Russian civil–military relations, with frequent scandals, protests and internal resistance, Putin and Shoigu restored a temporary, mutually satisfactory equilibrium. Shoigu achieved this through extensive rearmament efforts, remilitarization of the MoD, successful military intervention in Syria and skillful media campaigns that bolstered the armed forces' public image. Unlike his predecessor, who frequently made the MoD engage in public discussions, Shoigu also shifted decision-making behind closed doors.[151]

Within his first three months in office, Shoigu halted the planned closure of 300 garrisons, reinstated the rank of warrant officers, which Serdyukov had tried to replace with NCOs such as sergeants,

IMPERFECT EQUILIBRIUM

Presidential coalition	Military coalition	Civilian coalition
President Vladimir Putin	Chief of the General Staff Gen. Gerasimov	Representatives of the military-industrial complex
Defense Minister Sergei Shoigu	GOU Main Operational Directorate	
Prime Minister Dmitry Medvedev	GOMU Main Organizational Mobilizational Directorate	
Anton Siluanov, minister of finance (from September 2011)		
Tatiana Shevtsova, deputy minister of defense for finance		
Dmitry Rogozin, deputy prime minister for military-industrial complex		
Yury Borisov, deputy minister of defense for armaments		
Nikolai Pankov, state secretary, deputy minister of defense		

Figure 7: Coalitions in 2012–21

and expanded the size of central military commands.[152] Most notably, he stopped the military education reform, including the relocation of academies, a month after Serdyukov's resignation. This reform had sought to integrate Russia's military education system with the civilian system by restructuring degree programs into bachelor's, master's and specialist tracks. Shoigu instead scrapped the unification of military academies and returned oversight of education to the branch commands, a move widely welcomed by the military establishment.[153] Under Shoigu, a military police force was introduced but with reduced functions.[154]

Three months into Shoigu's tenure, Putin delivered his annual address at the Collegium of the MoD, outlining his vision for strengthening Russia's military capabilities. The president urged caution in revising Serdyukov's policies too hastily, signaling a degree of continuity in military policy.[155] He also emphasized the need for coordinated efforts between the MoD, the Russian defense industry and the General Staff to develop a fully combat-ready force. Among his key directives were the full staffing of military units by the end of the year, the completion of permanent-readiness units across all strategic directions (e.g., Western/European, Eastern/Chinese, Southwestern/Caucasus) and resolving the housing shortage for active-duty officers. He reaffirmed the priority of the rearmament program, setting an ambitious goal for 70 to 100 per cent of the military's equipment to be modernized by 2019, a goal that was never achieved in practice.[156]

Shoigu's plan

Shoigu established permanent combat readiness as the core objective of his leadership.[157] He formalized this goal through the introduction of the "Defense Plan," a structured policy framework with measurable targets and deadlines (see Appendix 3). Publicly available data indicate that the MoD prioritized investment expansion—focusing on construction, rearmament and personnel—while avoiding further structural reforms. A key objective was to ensure that all units were fully staffed with 425,000 all-volunteer personnel. The MoD also aimed to strengthen intra-military cohesion and improve coordination with other government agencies by establishing a centralized coordination center called the National Defense Management Center (NDMC). To reinforce combat readiness, the ministry introduced quantitative benchmarks for training and operational preparedness, attempting to move toward performance-based military assessment from a more patronage-based or bureaucratic form of assessment. The ministry also accelerated efforts to develop network-centric warfare capabilities, focusing on automated command-and-control systems, secure communication networks and real-time data-sharing infrastructure.[158] This required significant investments in digital technologies, including tactical computing, as well as encrypted and stable communications. However, these technological advances required new skill sets for military personnel, requiring close collaboration between the MoD, civilian contractors, military academies and the military-industrial complex.[159]

At the end of 2019, Putin revised targets, emphasizing technological modernization and combat readiness.[160] He reaffirmed the longstanding goal of equipping 70 per cent of the armed forces with modern weapons and technology, now setting the deadline for the end of 2020. Putin acknowledged that the ground forces were lagging in rearmament efforts and required further investment to reach the desired standards. This goal was not achieved before the full-scale invasion of Ukraine in 2022.

Rearming the military

The rearmament program was a source of continuous tension in the 2012–21 period. The program was affected by external events, namely the annexation of Crimea, Western sanctions and a fall in energy prices. It also caused conflicts in the government, which Putin had to personally resolve.

The GPV-2020 program was originally launched in 2010, but the largest share of the planned procurements happened under Shoigu's leadership, and the results were unsatisfactory.[161] The program was based on several unrealistic and unrealized assumptions. To finance GPV-2020, the Russian government initially relied on a hybrid funding model combining budget allocations with state-backed bank loans. But Western financial sanctions rendered this model unsustainable. Russian banks had originally expected to secure low-cost refinancing from Western institutions but found themselves cut off from foreign capital markets. The government was forced to step in, assuming responsibility for RUB1.2 trillion in defense sector loans.[162] The program's financing assumed that Russian GDP would grow in line with the target of 4 per cent annually, but this was never achieved. Financial strains worsened in 2014 due to the oil price shock and sanctions following the annexation of Crimea, which disrupted import substitution efforts—replacing imports with locally produced goods—and delayed key projects such as the fifth-generation fighter jet (designed to minimize radar detection), the Armata armored platform (for tanks and IFVs) and various naval programs.[163] This created conflict in the presidential coalition, as the MoD had to argue for the financial commitments with economic policymakers, who advocated for a reduced rearmament budget. These disagreements had to be settled through quarterly meetings of the Military-Industrial Commission with Putin's direct involvement. However, billions of rubles in planned expenditures of the GPV-2020 program were postponed to a later period.[164]

Unsatisfied with the program's implementation, the government adopted a revised GPV-2027 program in December 2017. The program was delayed by a year due to the poor economic outlook and challenges with the implementation of the previous program. The original plan was to approve the next armament program in 2016. GPV-2027 allocated around RUB19 trillion (US$306 billion at 2018 exchange rates) with an additional RUB1 trillion earmarked for upgrading storage infrastructure.[165] While the program's nominal budget was similar to GPV-2020, inflation and the currency exchange collapse reduced its real value. GPV-2027 re-directed greater emphasis to ground forces. These forces received a larger share of funds, aiming to close modernization gaps and maintain land-based supremacy against Western states. This included acquiring advanced tanks like the Armata system, reinforcing artillery and tactical missile systems and upgrading legacy platforms, such as the T-80 and T-90 tanks.[166] Ultimately, the full-scale invasion of Ukraine put an end to GPV-2027.

Coordination of the military

One of the most significant developments under Shoigu's leadership was the establishment of the NDMC in 2014. Its goal was to centralize information streams and provide real-time situational monitoring and assessment of politico-military developments to the military command. The NDMC reportedly receives continuous updates on all military activities, including combat operations, emergency responses and training exercises, coordinating overarching support for deployed troops and developing potential responses for senior command. In addition to its operational role, the NDMC oversees military development projects, managing logistics, infrastructure construction and the performance of the military-industrial complex.[167]

The NDMC strengthened the MoD's position in civil–military relations by improving its vertical (ministry–industry) and horizontal (intra-governmental) coordination powers. It was envisioned as a cross-agency coordination hub, integrating seventy-three executive bodies across all eighty-five federal regions, as well as 1,320 state corporations and military-industrial enterprises. The structure was meant to function as a networked system, with the NDMC at the center of a web-like defense architecture. However, in practice, operational control remained firmly in the hands of the General Staff and district commanders, while the NDMC streamlined intra-military coordination and enhanced civil–military cooperation.[168] According to the MoD, by 2016 the NDMC was overseeing 6,500 events daily, reducing decision-making time and improving response efficiency across Russia's armed forces.[169] To extend its reach, the MoD established Regional Defense Management Centers within the district headquarters.

However, despite the creation of the NDMC, persistent interoperability issues within Russia's information systems have undermined the effectiveness of these reforms. Various government agencies continued to operate on standalone information systems that lacked seamless integration, making cross-agency coordination inefficient and fragmented. For example, the evaluation of the unified information space within the Aerospace Forces identified three key issues: an outdated legal framework hindering digital modernization, a lack of fully functioning coordinating bodies for IT management and fragmented automation tools with inconsistent data collection and communication protocols.[170] Two Russian military colonels criticized the poor interoperability of these systems, arguing that Russia's centralized, "star-like" military information structure limited cross-agency coordination and hindered digital command and control. They warned that the federal government's neglect of these issues weakened Russia's ability to conduct network-centric warfare, as became evident during the full-scale invasion of Ukraine.[171]

The Wagner anomaly

In April 2012, then-prime minister Putin publicly endorsed the establishment of private military companies (PMCs), highlighting their potential as tools of influence that could advance Russian national interests abroad without direct state involvement.[172] Over the next decade, the Wagner Group evolved from a covert PMC into a formidable paramilitary force,[173] operating on behalf of the Russian government with no regard for international treaties or human rights obligations, as well as internal military regulations. This was a source of tension in Russia's civil–military relations, prompting efforts by the official military to assert control over a formally illegal paramilitary group. The Wagner Group's informality irritated the military, which was accustomed to formal rules and a strict command line.

The Wagner Group's origins are linked to the military reform in the previous period. Russian investigative journalists reported that the South African mercenary and owner of "Executive Outcomes," Eeben Barlow, had explained how PMCs operate to Russian generals during a closed-door session at the Saint Petersburg International Economic Forum in 2010.[174] The idea of creating a force of retired but experienced soldiers had already been discussed within the General Staff for about a year, with Chief of the General Staff Makarov supporting the initiative but with no formal endorsement. His successor, General Gerasimov, reportedly secured presidential approval after assuming office in 2012.[175] Putin asked his acquaintance and catering businessman Yevgeny Prigozhin to handle the financial and logistical management of the new enterprise. Prigozhin's business expanded into large-scale government contracts, including military base services, with part of the funds reportedly redirected to finance the new force.[176]

Over the next decade, Russian PMCs, particularly Wagner, operated in a legally ambiguous space—denied by the state yet integrated into its military infrastructure. Wagner shared bases with the Russian military, used Russian transport and medical services and was described by the US as a proxy force of the Russian MoD.[177] Between 2014 and 2022, Wagner and smaller Russian PMCs extended their presence beyond Ukraine into Syria, Libya, the Central African Republic and Mali. In Africa, Wagner provided security services to governments in exchange for lucrative resource contracts, funneling profits back to Russian companies. This model allowed Russia to expand its geopolitical influence while avoiding official military involvement.[178]

However, the military coalition was never satisfied with the rise of the paramilitary force. The PMCs operated outside of the Russian military's established norms and procedures, with the Wagner Group receiving heavy equipment, including tanks and artillery pieces, from military stockpiles. Prigozhin criticized the Russian military's operations in Syria, arguing that they were outdated and inefficient. In turn, Shoigu disapproved of Prigozhin's military catering contracts allegedly due to the poor quality of the services provided by his companies. Prigozhin refuted these accusations.[179] In 2018, he had reportedly lost a share of Defense Ministry contracts, possibly due to his strained relationship with Shoigu.[180]

The biggest crisis in Wagner's relationship with Russia's military occurred in February 2018 over the Battle of Deir ez-Zor in Syria. Shortly before the battle, a Prigozhin-linked company signed a deal with the Syrian government, agreeing to secure oil fields from opposition forces in exchange for a 25 per cent share of extracted oil and gas. Wagner fighters then attacked a Kurdish gas facility that hosted US military personnel. In response, US commanders contacted a Russian military representative in Deir ez-Zor to verify whether Russia knew about the operation. After the Russian contact insisted that Moscow had no ground forces in the area, the US air force launched a devastating counterstrike involving F-15E fighter jets, MQ-9 Reaper drones, AC-130 gunships, AH-64 Apache attack helicopters and B-52 strategic bombers, killing and injuring hundreds of Russian mercenaries.[181] The Wagner Group's defeat became a watershed moment, prompting Russian lawmakers to propose regulating PMCs. But the Kremlin never approved the idea.[182]

Moscow may have been better off accepting the Duma's proposal, as the same Wagner forces, after months of public conflict between Prigozhin and the MoD, launched a mutiny in June 2023 amid the full-scale invasion of Ukraine. They seized the Southern Military District headquarters in Rostov-on-Don and advanced toward Moscow, before Prigozhin abruptly called off the rebellion. Two months later, a plane carrying Prigozhin and Wagner's key military commanders exploded midair, eliminating the group's leadership.

The mutiny was the outcome of an experimental anomaly the Kremlin had created itself. The Wagner saga became a defining lesson in Russian civil–military relations—despite its inefficiencies, the Russian military possesses one critical trait that alternative forces lack: unwavering obedience to the president and civilian command. Under Shoigu, the MoD worked to strengthen this trait by trying to enhance monitoring mechanisms in the Russian military.

Monitoring and internal learning

Shoigu's approach to military oversight is an example of the military's continuous adaptability to the presidential coalition's demands and the deficiencies of narrow-minded technological solutions to systemic problems in civil–military relations. Shoigu relied heavily on quantitative assessments, rapid exercises and technological monitoring. He focused on installing CCTV surveillance and sensors across military facilities, vessels, unmanned aerial vehicles (UAVs) and aircraft to enhance direct oversight. He introduced "photo-reports"—usually, a series of photos showing the task's execution and its outcome, which is then shared with the commanders. For example, if a commander wanted to make sure that equipment was stored and tested, he would order junior officers to take pictures of how the soldiers were testing and storing the equipment. This system functioned as a "police patrol" mechanism: very costly, generating lots of paperwork and, crucially, inefficient.[183] Over time, the military learned how to overcome this intrusion, and the photo-reports simply became a formality to satisfy the commanders. As a military journalist and a civil society member claimed, access to the military became much more formal and closed than had previously been the case.[184] Independent oversight became largely impossible, even for pro-government journalists.

In 2016, the MoD implemented an aggressive financial oversight mechanism to enhance transparency and prevent misuse of state funds, which required all transactions involving government-transferred funds to be categorized in detail. If a contract included multiple items, each had to be classified, and spending on each category became entirely transparent to government auditors. A member of the MoD's Social Council described the process: "Shoigu found financial wolfhounds controlling financial bodies. There is his deputy for financial affairs, also the Accounts Chamber. They all control every penny spent."[185] The new system enabled the MoD to introduce quarterly pre-payments to defense contractors, contingent on the successful completion of specific project milestones, as well as granting the government the authority to block any financial transactions that deviated from registered purposes, a measure officially aimed at curbing fraud and embezzlement. In 2018, to further tighten control, Shoigu introduced Order no. 554, requiring detailed financial reporting from state defense order contractors, including monthly electronic reports and itemized cost breakdowns.[186] However, price disputes between the MoD and defense industry enterprises persisted despite the minister's efforts to mediate. In 2019, the MoD asked the Federal Antimonopoly Service to investigate forty-six defense industry enterprises for delayed submission of the pricing documents necessary for arms procurement contracts.[187] The delay in document submission slowed contract negotiations.

Shoigu also intensified combat-readiness exercises, which became a central tool for assessing the military's operational efficiency. In 2014, for the first time in post-Soviet history, Putin issued an unannounced mobilization order, directing troops to move to designated locations and prepare for combat. These drills not only involved military units but also rail transport, aviation, police forces and regional authorities, testing the broader logistical and coordination capabilities of Russia's defense infrastructure. The initial results were disappointing: only 57 per cent of participating troops received a "good" mark of four out of five, exposing weaknesses in the military's ability to deploy quickly and efficiently.[188]

These large-scale exercises revealed critical bottlenecks in the command-and-control structure, highlighting delays in decision-making and logistical shortcomings. The findings led to further adjustments in troop deployment procedures and reinforced the need for streamlined coordination between military and civilian agencies. Over time, the exercises became routine, serving both as a training mechanism and a means to demonstrate military strength to external audiences. While they improved mobilization speed, their effectiveness in preparing forces for sustained, large-scale combat remained uncertain.

At the end of September 2015, Russia officially launched its military campaign in Syria, deploying the air force, navy, select infantry units and special operations forces following Bashar al-Assad's request for Russian help to fight the jihadists and the Syrian opposition. Russian advisors played a crucial role in training and supporting Syrian government troops, directly influencing the effectiveness of their operations. The operation served as a testing ground for Russia's military capabilities, providing an opportunity to evaluate combat readiness, logistics and new military hardware under real battlefield conditions. Syria became particularly valuable for assessing the performance of newly developed vehicles, aircraft and weaponry.[189] Combat lessons from Syria were systematically integrated into military training and doctrine.

As a member of the MoD's Social Council noted:

> Our officers are fighters; they are priceless. That makes them very much like veterans of Afghanistan and World War II. We gained a vast number of officers with combat experience in Syria. We turned the fight against terrorists into a serious examination of

military equipment, even involving civil engineers and weapons designers. Ten percent of the weapons tested were abandoned after Syria.[190]

All senior Russian military commanders underwent at least one tour in Syria, accelerating the pace of military development.

But the lessons in Syria were of limited applicability to other contexts. The Russian contingent faced adversaries with no air defense capabilities, while ground operations were supported by the Syrian military, Russian mercenaries, military police and special forces. As a result, the lessons drawn from the Syrian campaign were not directly transferable to the war in Ukraine, where the operational environment was far more restrictive than elsewhere due to the large number of air defense systems, US intelligence support and a better armed and trained Ukrainian military. This was seldom discussed in public, creating an idealized and unrealistic perception of the Russian military's performance.

Reform results

The 2012–21 period saw the re-militarization of Russia. The structural and organizational changes initiated by Defense Minister Serdyukov laid the foundation for further military development under his successor, Shoigu, who opted for intrusive oversight mechanisms to control the military, conducting snap exercises, requiring photo and video reporting and measuring performance through key performance indicators. The creation of the NDMC, huge financial investments in equipment and infrastructure and the promotion of quicker military decision-making helped the MoD achieve better military readiness.

The development of several critical areas lagged behind, however, such as personnel recruitment and retention, the full realization of the rearmament program and military education. The chronic manning issue was symptomatic of deeper structural problems: the MoD struggled to enlist sufficient numbers of soldiers, and those who did join often left after short periods.[191] The challenges of military development were particularly evident in the GPV-2020 rearmament program, which failed to meet several key interim targets.[192] Industrial limitations prevented the full use of funds allocated to the navy, while the ground forces faced significant shortfalls.

In 2017, Chief of the General Staff Gerasimov reported that the operational readiness of ground forces equipment had improved to 98 per cent over five years, with the share of modern weapons rising from 15 per cent to almost 45 per cent and the air force reaching almost 63 per cent. He also claimed that UAV integration had enhanced reconnaissance effectiveness fifteenfold and that modern command systems covered 60 per cent of operational centers, enabling real-time data analysis and decision-making.[193] However, questions remained over the accuracy of the MoD's assessments and the methodologies used for data collection. For example, the military's target of achieving 70 per cent "modern equipment" by the end of 2020 was never achieved; despite public claims of success, the MoD struggled to meet this goal. By December 2021, Shoigu stated that 71 per cent of the armed forces' equipment had reached modern standards, but this was a figure that included both newly built and refurbished weaponry.[194]

One of the most critical bottlenecks was the state of military education. Shoigu received praise for stopping the necessary but poorly designed reform of military higher education under his predecessor. But, in the end, the military higher education system remained outdated and controlled by service headquarters, leading to weak integration and poor-quality standards across the armed forces. Senior officers often secured teaching or research positions simply because they were close to retirement or had personal connections with the military leadership. Teaching methods were antiquated, relying on rote memorization of lecture slides rather than practical training. There was also no independent assessment of faculty or cadets, as the military struggled with a shortage of junior officers and admitted anyone who met minimal fitness requirements.

Once cadets became officers, they encountered similar or even worse training conditions in active units. The system relied on the competence and commitment of individual commanders, who had to organize training, secure necessary equipment and ensure their soldiers' wellbeing. For some commanders, it was easier to falsify training reports and manipulate control exercises than engage in meaningful combat training, as red tape and bureaucratic hurdles made proper implementation difficult. Corruption further eroded the system, with poorly prepared officers shifting blame onto more dedicated colleagues when training exercises yielded poor results on paper.[195]

In the end, the Russian armed forces approached 2022 in a state of stagnation. Despite several major improvements in the military and the delivery of modern equipment, the Kremlin had failed to resolve several blind spots in Russian military development. As deserters' and soldiers' family members' leaked accounts of the first phase of the war against Ukraine began to emerge, it was clear there was widespread chaos and a lack of discipline on the battlefield. Troops described looting, drinking and an absence of command. Some soldiers abandoned their posts and returned to their home bases without permission. Morale dropped sharply, and cases of outright refusal to fight became common, with entire units laying down their arms and leaving Ukraine.[196]

Conclusion

The influence of coalitions on Russia's military reforms depended on their administrative power in civil–military relations. Military bureaucracy and the Ministry of Finance used official meetings and other procedural events, as well as their personal status and connections, to influence the policy process. At the same time, the MoD struggled with information asymmetries, which it attempted to remedy with enhanced monitoring mechanisms.

During Serdyukov's reform, active and retired officers criticized the changes in the media or brought them to the attention of deputies in the Duma. The strongest opposition came from the defense industry, which was supported by regional governors, city mayors and Putin's inner circle. The FSB and other law enforcement services used formal procedures for giving feedback on the bills and Security Council meetings to oppose the introduction of the military police and other parts of the reform program.

FROM COMBAT EFFECTIVENESS TO OVERSIGHT OVERLOAD

In 2007–12, the presidential coalition of reformers, consisting of top-brass actors and ideological supporters of the minister in the Social Council, was too small for such radical changes. The partial success of the reform was largely caused by Serdyukov's commitment to change and the power of the minister of defense in Russian civil–military relations. Except for the president, the minister was still the main decision-maker in the military. President Medvedev did not interfere in the reform process, and Serdyukov assigned an obedient but administratively savvy chief of the General Staff, General Makarov, who willingly executed the MoD's decisions.

Serdyukov's successor, Shoigu, changed the relationship with the military. He delegated development powers to the General Staff, while the MoD was focused on managing large financial investments and improving oversight mechanisms. However, Shoigu chose an expensive, police-style system of oversight, which the military tolerates so long as service members recognize the president's orders as legitimate and find that complying with them brings more benefits than costs. Therefore, the two weak pillars of the new system are the availability of finances and constructive relationships between the chief of the General Staff and the minister of defense. Conceptually, these two factors belong to the presidential coalition's beliefs and resources of the security coalition framework. Indeed, after the 2000–12 reforms, the degree of civil–military consensus needed for policy change decreased because of the empowered presidential coalition and decreased monitoring costs due to technological advances.

Yet as public reports on the manning of units and hiring of all-volunteer soldiers show, intrusive oversight cannot easily solve internal military problems. Despite better salaries and service conditions, the military was struggling to fill positions and increase the size of the all-volunteer force. The MoD was noticeably silent on the causes of this problem, typically referring to a lack of patriotism and the need for military education aimed at young people—the same argument the military had been making since the Soviet period.

5

RUSSIAN CIVIL–MILITARY RELATIONS AND THE FULL-SCALE INVASION OF UKRAINE

Introduction

The consequences of Russia's full-scale invasion of Ukraine for Russia and its civil–military relations are so profound that they will shape the future development of the Russian military for years to come. While the war shocked many observers, it did not come as a surprise to me. I had been closely following the gradual convergence of political and military developments in Russia that pointed toward the escalation. Traveling to Russia in the spring of 2021 felt surreal. On the surface, life appeared normal—blossoming trees, relaxed conversations and people making long-term plans as the COVID-19 pandemic faded. Yet, from my desk, I tracked intensifying military movements, unprecedented Kremlin rhetoric toward Ukraine and the tightening grip of domestic repression.

Many analysts and government officials struggled to predict the attack and explain Russia's subsequent wartime performance. The prevailing view was that the costs of any invasion would be prohibitively high and therefore deter the Kremlin from acting.[1] This argument assumed that Russia's leadership had access to accurate information and would rationally assess the costs of an invasion.[2]

Nevertheless, Russia proceeded with the military operation. At the time, numerous experts anticipated a rapid Russian advance, expecting Ukraine's defenses to crumble and Kyiv to fall swiftly. This, too, proved mistaken.

Politicians and government officials made similar analytical mistakes. The EU's foreign policy chief, Josep Borrell, admitted that he did not believe US Secretary of State Antony Blinken when he warned, just two days before the invasion, that Russia would launch a full-scale attack.[3] In the United Kingdom, the outgoing chief of the Defence Staff publicly stated in November 2021 that he did not expect a large-scale invasion, arguing instead that Russia would rely on hybrid tactics, including disinformation, to avoid direct military confrontation.[4] Although the Biden administration was among the most vocal in warning of Russia's plans, its policy response remained inconsistent. Key officials were divided over strategic priorities—especially whether to focus on China or on Russia, the scope of arms transfers to Ukraine and the feasibility of diplomacy with President Putin.[5] This book helps explain why such a disconnect in both analytical and political communities was possible.[6]

Preparing for the invasion

Using the ACF approach in my daily work, I closely monitored Russia's constitutional and legal changes, the increasing centralization of civilian control over the military, foreign policy ambitions and sustained investments in the defense sector. These developments convinced me that the Kremlin was deliberately shaping the long-term parameters, contextual conditions, opportunity structures and constraints (see Appendix 2) in preparation for an invasion. In less than a year, the domestic space for opposition politics had sharply contracted, while Russia's military posture and foreign policy rhetoric grew markedly more aggressive. I became convinced that the Kremlin would not tolerate an independent Ukraine with a capable military integrating into European and NATO structures. The Russian leadership viewed a large democratic neighbor like Ukraine as an existential threat both to the Russian political regime and to Russia's broader geopolitical position on NATO enlargement and pro-Western revolutions in the former Soviet bloc.

Preparations for the invasion intensified two years in advance. In the summer of 2020, the Kremlin won a referendum on constitutional changes, including a provision that allowed Putin to remain in power until 2036. Along with resetting presidential terms, the referendum included around 200 mostly declarative amendments, such as guaranteed minimum pensions, a ban on same-sex marriage and an affirmation of the Russian people's belief in God. It also proposed a provision to prevent the cession of any Russian territory, including Crimea and other disputed or unrecognized Russian-controlled territories.[7] The amendments sent a signal that President Putin will not leave office until he dies.

In December 2020, six months after the constitutional amendments, Putin signed a set of laws designed to reduce potential information threats and the potential of public mobilization that significantly expanded the state's repressive powers. The laws allowed individuals to be deemed "foreign agents" for receiving alleged support from foreigners, with harsh penalties, increased censorship and fines on social media platforms; the legislation also allows the state to block websites that "discriminate" against Russian media, as well as banning the leaking of security officials' personal data and further restricting public protests.[8] By 2021, nearly all major independent media outlets reporting on military issues, such as corruption, violence and casualties in Syria and Ukraine, had been labeled "foreign agents" or "undesirable organizations," designations that effectively ban them from operating legally within Russia.

I vividly remember the atmosphere of suspicion and fear spreading across Moscow. My final fieldwork in Russia took place in the spring of 2021 when a potential interviewee who had initially agreed to speak with me about Shoigu's defense reforms failed to appear at our agreed meeting point in Moscow. He then stopped responding to my calls, which was a completely new experience for me. A few months before that, in January 2021, Russian opposition leader Alexei Navalny was arrested upon returning from Germany, where he had received treatment after being poisoned with the military-grade nerve agent Novichok.[9] Navalny received a prison sentence that would ultimately prove fatal—he died in prison in February 2024—and over 11,000 Russians were detained at the protests and events against his imprisonment.[10] In June, his organizations were declared extremist, effectively equating them with terrorist organizations and banning their associates from running for office.[11]

Destroying the structure of Navalny's organizations—he had offices across all major Russian regions—weakened the Russian opposition's mobilization potential and that of anyone who disagreed with the Russian government. Doing so made sense for the Kremlin if it wanted to send a message to the public that nobody should dissent during the war. As of December 2021, just two months before the full-scale invasion, only 3 per cent of Russian survey respondents were certain that the conflict would escalate into a full-fledged war between Ukraine and Russia, while 36 per cent considered it "quite likely."[12] Relatedly, elite support for the unification of Russia and Ukraine had been steadily declining since 1995, when 65 per cent of respondents favored merging the two countries. By 2020, this support had dropped to just 5 per cent, while support for the two countries remaining independent had reached an all-time high of 67 per cent.[13] Neither the Russian public nor the Russian elites were enthusiastic about launching a full-scale invasion against Ukraine. Limiting the opportunities for unrest was therefore a necessary safety mechanism for Moscow.

In early 2021, I was watching closely as Russia began a major military buildup near Ukraine's borders under the guise of military drills. By mid-April, over 100,000 troops with heavy equipment were positioned in Crimea and Eastern Ukraine. Simultaneously, Russia imposed temporary restrictions on foreign naval vessels in parts of the Black Sea and Kerch Strait, limiting Ukraine's access to key ports.[14] Combined with escalating political repression and media restrictions, the military buildup was the clearest sign that Russia was preparing for more than just the drills.

In July 2021, President Putin published a lengthy essay in Russian, Ukrainian and English outlining his view of Russia and Ukraine's shared historical destiny.[15] Putin's vision was unmistakably imperialistic, denying Ukraine the right to an independent path of development and asserting that Ukrainians are essentially indistinguishable from Russians.[16] Putin's essay is best understood as a political manifesto, designed to legitimize any course of action aimed at bringing Ukraine back under Russian control. The essay thus provided an ideological frame that could be adopted by other political and administrative leaders.

Events in November–December 2021 finally convinced me that Putin would issue an order to prepare for the full-scale invasion. Russia resumed troop buildups near Ukraine in November 2021, with satellite images confirming deployments in Crimea, western Russia and Belarus. By December, over 100,000 troops were positioned near the border with Ukraine.[17] Alongside military pressure, Moscow intensified its information warfare, spreading claims about a potential Ukrainian operation in Eastern Ukraine.[18] Moreover, someone I met during one of my fieldworks told me that in the winter of 2021–2 some Russian defense factories, where their relatives worked, had been ordered to operate on a three-shift, 24/7 schedule.

The Kremlin also issued an ultimatum to NATO and the United States, calling for a halt to NATO expansion and a commitment that it would not deploy troops or weapons in member states that joined after May 1997. It also sought to ban NATO military activity in Ukraine, Eastern Europe, the Caucasus and Central Asia, along with provisions for renewed consultation mechanisms, and demanded that Washington ban intermediate-range missile deployments in Europe, restrict bomber and warship operations near Russian territory and confine nuclear weapons to national soil.[19] Needless to say, NATO and the United States rejected the ultimatum.

Full-scale civil–military disaster

Despite clear signs of an impending attack, many Russian citizens and even stationed service members remained unaware of the upcoming disaster due to the highly centralized nature of Russia's civil–military relations. Civilians were not interested in the military, while the military was trained to obey orders, including unexpected ones. Misled by official narratives of routine drills, Russian troops were unprepared for combat. Poorly guarded military equipment and idle, frustrated soldiers stuck in the February mud exemplified the disconnect between strategic decision-making and operational reality.[20] It was another symptom of the long-term problems in Russian civil–military relations.

Russia's leadership appears to have underestimated the complexity of invading Europe's second-largest country, misjudging both Ukraine's resistance and their own military's capabilities. With a landmass and population roughly one and a half times that of Iraq in 2003, Ukraine faced a Russian force of at most 200,000 troops—slightly larger than the 170,000-strong US-led coalition in Iraq.[21] Unlike the coalition's single-axis advance (along one route) from Kuwait, which was supported by 863 aircraft in the first month, Russia attempted to advance along five separate axes without securing air superiority.[22]

Moscow's invasion strategy was reportedly based on flawed intelligence assessments. The Kremlin seemingly planned a rapid assault on Kyiv, expecting local defections and infiltrated agents to facilitate control over political and administrative bodies.[23] This assumption led to tactical miscalculations, such as deploying National Guard riot control units with shields and light weapons in unarmored vans during the initial advance. Ukrainian forces discovered parade uniforms in abandoned Russian tanks, while elite paratroopers suffered heavy casualties due to inadequate reconnaissance and fire support.[24]

Although the Russian government has yet to publicly acknowledge the failures of the initial invasion, some Russian military officers have done so in leading Russian-language military journals. One officer conceded that the intelligence assessments of Ukraine's sociopolitical situation were deeply flawed:

> Instead of flowers and bread, as we expected, local residents of Russian-speaking areas met the rear columns of our troops with civil resistance. Additionally, information about the morale and psychological state of the Ukrainian armed forces proved to be incorrect. The supposed expectations of their unpreparedness for armed resistance and mass surrender were unjustified.[25]

These strategic miscalculations, coupled with unresolved issues in command structure, coordination and supply chains, demonstrated that the Russian military's longstanding inefficiencies had not been fully addressed.

In principle, sound civil–military relations do not stop civilian leaders making flawed decisions, but the military leadership must provide their counterparts with objective, thorough assessments.[26] In the case of the assault on Ukraine, it remains unclear whether the military provided strategic advice or, if it did, whether Putin considered it at all. What is clear, however, is that Russian troops were kept out of the information loop, while commanders fed senior leadership exaggerated assessments of their combat readiness. Equipment functionality, troop morale, logistical preparedness—none of it was truthfully reported. The MoD built its invasion plans on flawed intelligence and self-serving evaluations, leading to a catastrophic miscalculation at the highest level.

Amid early battlefield failures, untrained, disoriented and poorly commanded Russian troops—stunned by the strength of the resistance and heavy casualties—perpetrated war crimes, and it is unlikely the perpetrators will ever face justice. Indeed, the Kremlin has already rewarded the implicated units with honorary "Guard" titles, a designation awarded to formations that have demonstrated exceptional combat performance, discipline and valor.

In Russia's military culture, unwavering obedience to orders is paramount and prized over acting according to international legal norms. Notably, General Sergei Surovikin—who commanded Russian forces in Ukraine—previously led an airborne unit that killed three civilians during the 1991 Soviet coup attempt. At that point a captain, Surovikin was absolved of any wrongdoing and swiftly promoted. Decades later, Putin awarded him the title "Hero of Russia" for his role in Syria before entrusting him with leading the war in Ukraine.

Yet notwithstanding its systemic failures and significant combat losses, Russia managed to wage a large-scale conventional war against a nation of 40 million with a fully mobilized male population, backed by extensive Western military aid. Russian forces inflicted substantial casualties and damage on Ukraine, highlighting that, despite strategic and logistical shortcomings, the military reforms initiated in 2008 had improved Russia's warfighting capabilities. However, these reforms prioritized effectiveness and adaptability over accountability, leaving the armed forces largely unresponsive to both civilian oversight and broader government control. The war has thus exposed deep flaws in Russia's civil–military structures, which are now undergoing forced adaptation.

Wartime civil–military changes

The full-scale invasion of Ukraine has transformed Russian civil–military relations, introducing multiple regulatory changes, shifting the economy toward wartime production and prompting mass mobilization, including the forced retention of enlisted personnel and officers. The Russian military has also operated alongside PMCs, which exist in a state of legal ambiguity, with some of their fighters recruited from prisons. As Putin seeks victory in Ukraine, Russia's civil–military equilibrium is undergoing a drastic shift.[27]

Changes in the coalitions

The war with Ukraine became a driver in the renewal of the presidential, military and civilian coalitions in the 2022–5 period. The political logic behind this was to punish those deemed responsible for Russia's battlefield failures while offering war participants the prospect of postwar integration into the Russian elite. But this process has not unfolded smoothly, with resistance from the Russian bureaucracy and state enterprise managers.

In an address to the Federal Assembly in February 2024, Putin proclaimed that war veterans were now Russia's national elite, contrasting them with the enriched elites of the 1990s. The address was likely to have been well received by my interviewees, who used similar words to describe the Russian elites of the 1990s (see Chapter 2). He also launched the Time of Heroes program to integrate veterans into leadership roles in public administration, education, business and state-owned enterprises. The program offers mentorship, education and career opportunities for war veterans and thus represents a symbolic attempt to renew the civilian coalition.[28] Despite the rhetoric, polling indicated limited public support for veterans as political candidates, with only older voters valuing combat experience in politicians.[29]

The Time of Heroes program has faced resistance from established elites. Most veteran appointments have been symbolic or marginal, focusing on patriotic education and war-related affairs with little real authority. For example, regions like Saratov and Yakutia created deputy roles for patriotic work across local education departments and district administrations.[30] Rosatom established similar low-influence posts, with official duties again including veteran affairs and patriotic education, but in practice these offices have no staff or any real authority.[31] Putin has appointed only two acting governors with war-related backgrounds, both of whom are career bureaucrats with limited frontline experience.[32] As of the summer of 2025, Putin's appeal for the selection of the new war elite served mainly symbolic purposes, reinforcing the loyalty of the war veterans without significantly altering the civil–military coalition.

A turning point in Russian civil–military relations occurred during the Prigozhin mutiny of July 2023, which reinforced presidential control over the military and triggered a series of replacements in the military. The full-scale invasion gave Prigozhin thousands of experienced fighters, national prominence and millions in cash to pursue his political ambitions. However, he operated outside of Russia's formal institutional framework, in contrast to the regular military. While he possessed personal political influence through his ties to members of the presidential coalition, he held no official position within Russia's governing structures, making his growing power structurally incompatible with the existing political order. This created an imbalance between Wagner's lethal power and Prigozhin's lack of institutional political authority.

The military coalition refused to support Prigozhin, despite PMC Wagner's historic connections to Russian military intelligence.[33] Prigozhin even kidnapped senior commanders, the first deputy head of military intelligence General Vladimir Alekseev and Deputy Defense Minister Yunus-bek Yevkurov, which illustrated his outsider status.[34] The mutiny temporarily weakened Putin, but Prigozhin's apparent assassination two months later and the subsequent absorption of Wagner units into official military structures ultimately reinforced presidential control. Throughout the rebellion, Putin retained authority over the regular armed forces and the political establishment, resolved the crisis through negotiation, eliminated the key challenger and implemented institutional safeguards to prevent a similar situation occurring in the future. The mutiny thus strengthened presidential control over the armed forces and other security institutions involved in the war against Ukraine.

The lasting impact of Prigozhin's mutiny, combined with persistent battlefield setbacks, triggered a change in the MoD. In May 2024, Putin dismissed Defense Minister Shoigu and appointed Andrei Belousov in his place, which was followed by a wave of dismissals and arrests within the MoD leadership.

Unlike Shoigu, Belousov comes from a prominent family of Soviet economists and has built a long career in economic policymaking. Since the 1990s, he has held senior positions in government, including as Putin's economic advisor, and played a key role in developing strategic economic programs. He reportedly coordinated military logistics between the Presidential Administration, the MoD, Wagner PMC and other state agencies and oversaw the development of unmanned systems while serving as first deputy prime minister.[35]

The military's quiet acceptance of a civilian defense minister marked a break from the post-Soviet history of Russian civil–military relations. While earlier civilian ministers were often met with skepticism or ridicule due to the entrenched belief that only career military officers should lead the MoD, the war with Ukraine undermined this norm and helped legitimize civilian leadership in defense policy. For the first time in Russian civil–military relations, a minister of defense is being judged by his performance and not his military rank.

Belousov's appointment triggered a major reshuffle within the MoD. Several senior officials and high-ranking officers were dismissed or arrested on charges of bribery, fraud and corruption, and numerous officials responsible for defense procurement, logistics, communications and property management were either removed from office or placed under criminal investigation.[36] The wave of arrests continued through late 2024 and early 2025, with Russian authorities implicating at least thirty-four mid-level officials, generals and contractors, surpassing the number of individuals prosecuted during the Serdyukov corruption scandal.

The Kremlin used this purge to reassert presidential control over the MoD's intergovernmental coordination and financial management through the departures of some long-serving officials managing these sectors. One of them, State Secretary Nikolai Pankov, a career FSB officer, had overseen military personnel policy since 2005 under three different defense ministers.[37] He was replaced by Anna Tsivileva, head of the Defenders of the Fatherland Foundation (see below) and reportedly Putin's relative, despite her lack of military experience. Her appointment coincided with the rise of her husband, Sergei Tsivilev, who became minister of energy in May 2024 after serving as governor of the Kemerovo region.[38]

Former deputy finance minister Leonid Gornin replaced Tatiana Shevtsova, who had been transferred to the MoD in 2010 from the Federal Tax Service by Defense Minister Serdyukov (see Chapter 4). Shevtsova oversaw the ministry's finances and budgetary operations, remaining in her position seven years after Serdyukov was implicated in corruption scandals. Gornin previously served as deputy and assistant to Finance Minister Anton Siluanov (also see Chapter 4), so his appointment reinforced the Finance Ministry's oversight of the defense budget and procurement system, with the potential to streamline investment and financial control procedures.[39] In parallel, Pavel Fradkov, son of former prime minister and SVR director Mikhail Fradkov and a former official in the Presidential Administration (see Chapter 3), assumed responsibility for managing military property.[40]

Legal changes

Between 2022 and 2025, the Russian government introduced a series of legislative changes to protect the military from criticism and prevent military and social dissent. From the outset of the war, the Kremlin through the federal government and the Duma began tightening information control. Roskomnadzor, the official media regulator, required all media reports on the war, officially referred to as the "special military operation," to only use information from government sources. In March 2022, the Duma introduced a new article into the Criminal Code that criminalized public statements deemed to "discredit the armed forces." Penalties include imprisonment of up to seven years, fines of up to 1 million rubles, loss of citizenship and revocation of military or civil ranks.[41]

In July 2022, Putin's United Russia party deputies affiliated with the security services introduced further amendments to the Criminal Code. A new article criminalized collaboration with foreign entities deemed hostile to Russian security, with prison terms of three to eight years and fines of up to RUB1 million (about US$12,000 in 2025).[42]

These legislative measures had several cumulative effects. First, they prevented any civilian or institutional actor from questioning the Kremlin's military decisions. Second, they criminalized dissenting views on the war, thereby reinforcing the legitimacy of both the armed forces and the presidential narrative. Third, by forcing the Duma—particularly nominally civilian representatives—to serve the interests of the security and military blocs, the Kremlin blurred the line between civilian and military coalitions. In the first few months of the war, Moscow virtually forced all coalitions to become united and work for the war effort.

These changes proved essential in late September 2022, when Moscow announced a partial military mobilization. Around 300,000 Russian reservists were called up to replenish the forces fighting in Ukraine.[43] In response, over 2,000 anti-mobilization protesters were arrested, while hundreds of thousands of people fled the country.[44] Just a few days after the mobilization was announced, I happened to be on a train from Russia to Europe. My carriage was filled with young men, many of whom were leaving the country for the first time.

The mobilized men faced disorganized recruitment procedures, a lack of basic equipment, minimal training and poor command structures. Many were deployed to the frontlines within days of being summoned and killed shortly thereafter. Nonetheless, the mobilization helped stabilize the front and played a key role in halting the Ukrainian counter-offensive the following year.

Although it became a watershed moment in Russian society, the mobilization did not significantly alter civil–military relations. Years of systematic efforts to eliminate the civilian coalition from the defense sector had succeeded: at this critical juncture in the war, no political actor could articulate the widespread fear and anger triggered by the mobilization. Those who attempted to do so were swiftly arrested. While the centralization of Russian civil–military relations had harmed defense reforms in the past, it proved effective in 2022 because it created a system where many people found it more reasonable to help mobilized men by donating equipment, medical supplies and vehicles than to protest against the government. Supporting the troops became a way to reduce their risk of being seriously injured or dying, even if people disagreed with the war itself.

However, repression was not the only tool used to support the Russian war effort, as the Russian government also expanded welfare provisions for war participants and their families. Beginning in 2022, the presidential coalition introduced guaranteed university and vocational admissions for veterans and their children, as well as special quotas for families of killed soldiers.[45] In 2024, subsidized mortgage rates of 2 per cent were extended to veterans nationwide, young military families were granted priority access to housing aid and spouses of discharged service members received preferential employment rights, job security and retraining support.[46]

Yet most welfare initiatives not initiated by the presidential coalition faced resistance in the Duma. Numerous bills, such as one-time housing payments for disabled veterans, insurance for siblings of fallen soldiers and free travel or education benefits, were rejected or withdrawn between 2022 and 2025.[47] These proposals, largely driven by parties other than United Russia, reflected attempts by civilian coalition members to capitalize politically on the expansion of the welfare agenda.

During the war, the Russian government introduced harsh new penalties for military insubordination. Amendments to the Criminal Code imposed prison terms ranging from two to fifteen years for offenses such as disobeying orders, desertion, attacking commanders, evading service, destroying military property and voluntarily surrendering. Refusal to participate in combat operations under mobilization now results in up to ten years' imprisonment. As of August 2024, commanders had the unilateral authority to arrest service members for serious disciplinary violations.[48] These measures acted as a deterrent to insubordination by sharply raising the costs of disobedience as well as strengthening military cohesion by expanding the authority of unit commanders over the disciplinary measures against their subordinates.

Institutional changes

The war has led to major institutional shifts in Russian civil–military relations. In 2023, President Putin established the Defenders of the Fatherland Foundation to align presidential policy with the needs of war veterans and their families. He also expanded presidential authority by ordering the integration of volunteer formations into the MoD and the National Guard. Simultaneously, the Kremlin initiated the economic mobilization that allowed the military to have a stronger influence on the civilian industrial output, such as through labor rights restrictions, mandatory fulfillment of defense contracts and expanded state control over wartime production.

The Defenders of the Fatherland Foundation, headed by Anna Tsivileva, coordinates medical, legal and psychological support for veterans and their families while also promoting pro-war narratives and historical memory projects among children and in the media. It links presidential directives to the practical needs of beneficiaries and the bureaucracy tasked with implementation.[49] Tsivileva's appointment as the state secretary of the MoD officially strengthened her role as a key representative of the MoD among other civilian bodies.

After early battlefield losses, Moscow launched large-scale recruitment in mid-2022, accepting volunteers into its forces and deploying PMCs. This proliferation of loosely coordinated units created serious challenges for Russian civil–military relations. Many volunteers were not formally subordinate to the MoD, undermining command unity, and they likely held similar policy beliefs, as many of the mercenaries had prior experience in Russian security institutions. However, operating outside the formal coordination system and depending on informal resource channels, these units weakened the unity of command and introduced risks to Russia's political stability.[50] For example, Wagner's leader Prigozhin publicly threatened to withdraw from Ukraine in the spring of 2023 unless his demands were met.[51]

The Kremlin responded by amending the federal defense law in November 2022 to allow volunteer formations to be formally incorporated into the MoD and National Guard. In June 2023, the MoD required all volunteer units to sign contracts with the ministry.[52] This move prompted Prigozhin's rebellion and ultimately led to the end of Wagner as a PMC. Other volunteer units reportedly complied with the new regulations and were absorbed into state structures.[53]

After the mutiny, Wagner fighters were integrated into MoD and National Guard units, with the largest faction being redeployed to Africa as the newly created "African Corps";[54] others joined regular military formations fighting in Ukraine. Estimates suggest that up to a few thousand ex-Wagner fighters have been absorbed across different structures.[55] This integration preserved combat capacity while dismantling Wagner's independent command, reducing the mutiny's long-term operational impact and reinforcing centralized state control.

The presidential coalition initiated legal changes to enable economic mobilization to support the war effort. In July 2022, it allowed the activation of industrial reserve capacities, use of state material reserves and modification of labor laws—including extended working hours and reduced annual leave.[56]

Defense production demands surged following the partial mobilization of September 2022. To address supply shortfalls, the federal government relaxed the regulations on military procurements. It authorized advance payments of at least 80 per cent on defense contracts, simplified inter-firm transfers and allowed sole-supplier contracts. By December 2024, companies receiving state defense subsidies were shielded from forced debt collection until the end of 2027. An automated price-monitoring system, managed by the Federal Treasury, was also introduced to improve oversight and reduce monitoring costs in the military-industrial complex.

To prevent workforce shortages, the government subsidized salary costs for military-industrial complex firms hiring workers from other regions and introduced subsidized housing and mortgage programs for their employees in the Far East and Arctic in 2023. New hires from universities gained access to free retraining and conscription deferments. In February 2025, a draft law proposed allowing young military-industrial complex workers to replace military service with factory-based civilian service.[57]

Between September 2022 and March 2023, the presidential coalition introduced punitive and protective measures to secure the state defense order. These included criminal liability for disrupting defense production and state-appointed external management for underperforming defense firms. Additionally, large military-industrial complex firms were classified as economically significant organizations (EZOs). EZOs receive legal immunity from transparency rules, enjoy simplified domestification rules (transfer of the legal body from abroad) and are legally able to strip shareholders from "unfriendly" countries of their rights through Russian court proceedings.[58]

Expectations for the future

Successful military reforms in Russia depend on a strong presidential coalition capable of uniting key actors and mobilizing political will for policy change, as well as on the integration of non-military experts into defense policymaking (see Conclusion for more). Such political will has historically emerged only in conjunction with an assertive foreign policy that increased the Kremlin's interest in military modernization.

All of these factors are present in Russia at the time of writing in 2025. Russia is set on an anti-Western confrontational path, with the government focused on defeating Ukraine's armed forces. The flow of information, including open-source, from the frontline facilitates the development of reform proposals as it is harder for the military to hide or frame its failures. The civilian government has also gained a lot of experience in civil–military coordination, especially in boosting military-industrial output to replenish equipment lost on the battlefield.

However, as I have sought to demonstrate, meaningful military reform requires alignment between the president, the defense minister and the chief of the General Staff, forming a crucial decision-making team. The defense minister has to navigate bureaucratic resistance while securing resources and policy changes, and the chief of the General Staff is responsible for translating political objectives into military action. Without this coordinated leadership, reform efforts are unlikely to succeed. Although Putin replaced Defense Minister Shoigu with Belousov in 2024, he has yet to appoint a new chief of the General Staff. General Gerasimov, who has served in the role for over a decade, symbolizes all the problems the Russian military has accumulated or has been unable to solve. However, he has delivered strategic results for the Kremlin, including the annexation of Crimea, operations in Syria, interventions in Eastern Ukraine and short-lived missions in Nagorno-Karabakh and Kazakhstan. While these were politically problematic, they were military achievements for which Gerasimov was directly responsible. Additionally, Gerasimov played a key role in politicizing military intelligence, transforming it into an aggressive covert tool for espionage, sabotage and assassinations. He also supported Putin's use of PMCs, further entrenching their role in Russia's strategic operations. These factors make replacing him particularly challenging.

Although the armed forces have historically supported a strong state, they have viewed themselves as shaping Russian society rather than being shaped by civilian control. The Kremlin must then decide whether it is willing to challenge this deeply ingrained institutional military culture, which has long resisted civilian oversight and sought to maintain its autonomy. To reshape military culture, Moscow will have to implement a large-scale recruiting program using its access to a large pool of war veterans who could gradually replace commanders within the MoD and the General Staff.

But this scenario is unlikely. Once the war ends, many veterans will likely choose to demobilize, and the military will selectively filter out those who disagree with the existing, often ineffective rules and practices in the armed forces. Rather than prioritizing combat experience and operational effectiveness, the Kremlin is likely to favor those who demonstrate strict adherence to established rules and loyalty to the president, reinforcing continuity over meaningful institutional change.

Moreover, as Russian history demonstrates, politically adept military leaders have often cultivated parallel relationships with the president and his inner circle, bypassing the formal chain of command. Through these connections, they could challenge or obstruct the MoD's reform agenda, and some officers will not easily be replaced because of their unique knowledge, experience and reputation in the command structure. Hence, these service members can become "first among equals," nominally the same officers as anybody else but informally well-respected and well-connected politico-military leaders. The presidential coalition will have to acknowledge their role in the reform planning.

The MoD's effectiveness in identifying problems, monitoring reform implementation and evaluating outcomes depends on the quality of its monitoring and evaluation systems. While the increasing availability of public information on the Russian military partly mitigates these challenges, the ultimate outcome of the war in Ukraine will shape the narrative—determining whether this body of evidence serves as a record of military success or a chronicle of defeat.

Conclusion

When Russia launched its full-scale invasion of Ukraine in February 2022, I had doubts that Moscow could survive the conflict. Beyond the moral reasons against the war, the invasion is a massive operation requiring vast resources and resilience in the face of potential Ukrainian resistance and Western retaliation. By September 2022, after Russia had lost large portions of occupied territory and reports emerged of severe manpower shortages at the front, it seemed that a full collapse of Russian forces was imminent. But that collapse never came. Russia did not break under the weight of sanctions and Ukrainian strikes; nor did its military disintegrate.

The outcome of the Russo-Ukrainian War remains uncertain, but Russia's experience already provides useful lessons for foreign governments. The interpretation of these lessons will depend on domestic political structures and the beliefs held by the civilian and military leadership.

For democratic states, the war highlights the need to maintain an equilibrium in civil–military relations that supports long-term military preparedness while ensuring strong civilian control. Russia's battlefield failures reflect the dangers of sidelining the civilian coalition and relying on unchecked executive power in military development. A functioning oversight system could have questioned the wisdom of launching a full-scale invasion or have provided a more honest assessment of Russia's military readiness, potentially preventing the war altogether.

In contrast, authoritarian regimes may see Russia's performance differently, unless something happens that causes Russia to lose everything it has gained in Ukraine. Despite heavy sanctions, battlefield setbacks and international isolation, the Kremlin has preserved regime stability, continued military operations and adapted through partial mobilization, repression and economic measures. For these regimes, the lesson may be that tightly controlling civil–military relations and suppressing dissent can ensure survival even in the face of prolonged and costly wars against the West.

CONCLUSION

THE TUG-OF-WAR IN RUSSIA'S CIVIL–MILITARY RELATIONS

Introduction

What drives the development of Russian civil–military relations? Despite appearing to be politically obedient, the Russian military has acted as a veto player in the policy process, obstructing reforms imposed by the civilian leadership—even under Putin's highly centralized rule. Russia's military and civilian leadership have often had divergent expectations of the armed forces' role, the nature of future conflicts and strategic priorities, and followed different decision-making patterns, leading to conflicting visions of national security, defense policies and the optimal structure of the armed forces. The government has had to acknowledge the military's position as no reform could be developed or implemented without military expertise, input from General Staff officers and access to classified defense sector data.

The relationships between the military, civilian and presidential coalitions have often been strained and unproductive within Russia's hierarchical and centralized authoritarian political system. By centralizing authority, the Kremlin has reduced independent oversight while increasing the administrative power of bureaucratic institutions across all ministries, including the MoD. This took shape between 2001 and 2007, as independent politicians advocating for military reform were systematically pushed out of the political arena, and Putin's close ally Sergei Ivanov assumed leadership of the MoD, the first civilian in charge of the Russian military. The Kremlin subordinated the General Staff to the MoD and granted the president substantial authority over military development and command. By 2005, the president had become the sole political and administrative figure capable of supporting or driving changes within the armed forces.

During Putin's first eight years in power, Russia's military and civilian sectors existed in an imperfect equilibrium, where dissatisfaction with the state of the armed forces was widespread, but the Kremlin hesitated to commit the necessary resources and lacked the political will for meaningful reform. Despite a fourfold increase in defense spending during this period, the military lagged far behind key competitors, such as the United States. The turning point came in 2008, when Russia struggled to secure a decisive victory against Georgia's much smaller military. In response, a civilian defense minister launched a series of reforms before being removed in 2012 following a corruption scandal. This led to the return of the imperfect equilibrium that ultimately culminated in the disastrous full-scale invasion of Ukraine.

Civil–military relations and Russian military development

Russian civil–military relations and defense reform outcomes formed a cyclical relationship, wherein each reform initiative was shaped by the prevailing civil–military dynamics of its time. In turn, the reforms introduced new equilibria, redistributing power among the president, the military and civilian actors while also bringing technical and material resources to the armed forces.

However, two features of Russian civil–military relations remained unchanged throughout the 2000–21 period. First, Russia's defense reforms were always initiated by the presidential coalition but implemented by the military. The Russian Constitution and federal laws allow the presidential coalition to formulate defense policy long before any official announcement, giving the president significant control over the reform's direction. But ensuring policy

CONCLUSION

implementation in the defense sector has always been a challenge, requiring the president to build a reliable coalition with a defense minister and a chief of the General Staff who shared his views and were committed to implementing the reforms. While the president set reform goals and the MoD selected policy proposals accordingly, the military could resist critical changes and preserve its autonomy during the implementation stage. Anticipating this, the Kremlin had to work within a limited set of policy choices dictated by existing military structures and ideas. The military coalition benefited from this setup, which reinforced the high level of autonomy of the chief of the General Staff and the personal ties some generals maintained with the president. Avoidable mistakes in policy planning created openings for the military to resist reforms and preserve their institutional interests. Weak monitoring mechanisms further hindered feedback on the policy performance, preventing the presidential coalition from obtaining verifiable evidence on military development. At the same time, a politically controlled legal system undermined accountability, making military oversight dependent on political considerations rather than objective enforcement.

Second, the Russian defense sector's insulation from the civilian coalition meant that defense policy development depended on ideas already circulating within military circles. In 1999, Putin tasked the then Security Council secretary, Sergei Ivanov, with preparing a military reform plan. A similar approach was taken in 2007, when Defense Minister Anatoly Serdyukov was given just over a year to develop his reform program. By the time Sergei Shoigu assumed office in 2012, key policy directions had already been set. Most of these ideas had been discussed within the military long before their adoption, awaiting political endorsement. The minister of defense played a crucial role in translating presidential directives into defense policy, while the chief of the General Staff was responsible for implementing these policies and communicating the military's operational needs. The military coalition protected this arrangement by limiting access to the military and maintaining the monopoly on military expertise.

This turned out badly for the Russian military during the full-scale invasion of Ukraine. Unsatisfied with shallow and demonstrably false official statements about the progress of the war, hundreds of soldiers and affiliated volunteers used blogs and Telegram channels to reveal a more truthful and disturbing picture of Russian military setbacks.

Civilian defeat

The civilian coalition lost its institutional influence in 2003 when the last opposition parties failed to be elected to the Duma. My analysis of parliamentary speeches shows peaks in military-related discussions in 2003, 2007, 2011 and 2015, but the depth and quality of these debates declined over time. In 2003, discussions focused on conscription policies, deferments for various social groups and progress on the 2001–3 military reform. By 2007, after Serdyukov's appointment, parliamentary debates centered on early reform experiments, veteran support and military-industrial exports, though with less substantive engagement than in 2003. In 2011, parliamentary discourse shifted following Serdyukov's dismissal and Shoigu's appointment as defense minister. While parliamentarians criticized Serdyukov for alleged misconduct, they refrained from proposing alternative defense reform strategies—unlike in 2003, when the Duma actively debated military policy. By 2015, during the conflict in Eastern Ukraine—where Russian-backed separatists and covert Russian forces fought the Ukrainian military—and Russia's intervention in Syria, parliamentary debates centered on praising Shoigu's leadership. Speeches often reflected a sense of "victory euphoria" tied to perceived military successes. Simultaneously, the Duma debated more routine matters, such as conscription deferments for rural doctors and amendments to laws on military discharge and defense industry oversight.

The findings suggest that the military reform sparked parliamentary debate before the 2003 Duma election, and subsequent reforms were largely dictated by the executive, with minimal legislative input. The Kremlin's consolidation of control over the Duma after the 2003 elections meant that deputies ceased proposing alternative defense policies, effectively cementing the president's dominance in military affairs. Civilian coalition members could only influence defense policy if they gained direct access to the presidential coalition and aligned with its agenda. That undermined the civilian coalition's unity and incentivized its individual actors to prioritize their relationship with the MoD. In the early 2000s, civilians had some access to the president, but as executive control over policymaking expanded, their role diminished. The alternative strategy was to generate and circulate policy ideas in the hope they would be adopted by a defense minister. But this was a resource-intensive process given civilians' limited military expertise, restricted access to military data and the military coalition's tendency to reject external criticism.

My analysis challenges conventional understandings of civilian supremacy in defense policymaking. The mainstream perspective holds that civilian control benefits the defense sector and democratic development by preventing military interference in domestic political affairs and ensuring the armed forces follow the government's directives.[1] The United States is a clear example of a subordinate military that is allergic to politicization and involvement in domestic affairs.[2] Existing research mostly studies coups as the main outcome of the erosion of civilian control.[3] This study joins a growing stream of research that critically assesses the military's role in public policy, illuminating it as another venue for the military's often discreet influence on the state.[4]

The Russian case demonstrates that civilian supremacy is contingent on the presidential office's openness and accountability. The concentration of power within presidential institutions isolates defense policymaking from broader societal and expert input but still necessitates military involvement in the policy process. Given the Russian military's resistance to power-sharing, this dynamic exacerbates the problem. Thus, while the military remains formally subordinate to civilian leadership, the quality of civil–military relations depends on the extent to which relevant stakeholders are included in decision-making.

Reform enablers

What enabled Moscow to reform its armed forces? The key factors included the strength of the presidential coalition that had the president's strong political will and ensured the administrative access of non-uniformed experts to decision-making. Additionally, an assertive strategic military posture and a militarized foreign policy played a crucial role in driving reform efforts. Each of these elements contributed to the effectiveness of military modernization in Russia.

From 2000 to 2007, the Kremlin deprioritized military effectiveness in favor of consolidating presidential control over the armed forces. Reform efforts remained conservative, and Putin appointed defense ministers who avoided direct conflict with the military. This resulted in an imperfect equilibrium in Russian civil–military relations: both the civilian and military leadership recognized the shortcomings of the armed forces, yet neither side was able or willing to undertake the necessary reforms. The Russian government struggled to push through meaningful military reforms as resistance from the armed forces remained strong. Neither Putin nor Defense Minister Ivanov was willing to challenge military prerogatives or impose significant changes that required the high degree of civil–military consensus needed for policy change. Putin instead leveraged his national security background to bridge this divide by aligning civilian priorities with military ones. His elite recruitment strategy ensured that Russia's civilian leadership became increasingly statist and security-oriented. The Kremlin also centralized control over the military through amendments to federal laws, which the military either ignored or tacitly approved.

The dynamic shifted drastically between Putin's speech in Munich, Germany, in 2007 and his return to the presidency in 2012, as the MoD aggressively imposed reforms, triggering a civil–military crisis in which the armed forces resisted implementation. Eighteen months after Putin's speech in Munich, the war with Georgia exposed critical weaknesses, including logistical failures, outdated equipment and poor coordination, which led to avoidable losses. The MoD responded with sweeping structural reforms that disrupted the previous equilibrium, as the civilian leadership sought to exert greater control over military affairs. The minister imposed his will on the military by greatly reducing its prerogatives via appointing a subordinate chief of the General Staff, civilianizing the MoD and dismissing thousands of officers in exchange for increased financial investment in armaments, infrastructure and personnel benefits. However, the reforms provoked fierce resistance from the military bureaucracy, non-military security agencies and retired officers. In 2012, this opposition culminated in the dismissal of the defense minister and the reestablishment of the imperfect equilibrium, halting further structural changes in the defense sector.

The 2012–21 period marked a shift toward an increasingly assertive use of military power as a central instrument of Russian foreign policy. The MoD began using snap exercises to assess combat readiness, technological tools to oversee finances and infrastructure projects and combat deployments as the ultimate test for military performance. This enabled large-scale rearmament, the introduction of new command-and-control systems and extensive infrastructural investments.

However, the government remained unable to break the imperfect equilibrium. The defense minister relied on the military bureaucracy to implement reforms, leading to the dilution of changes. Over time, the military adjusted to monitoring practices, and, by the time of the full-scale invasion of Ukraine, military development had stagnated once again, with the defense minister struggling to achieve the objectives set by his own office.

These cases of reform demonstrate that the Russian president has to demonstrate strong political will if reform is to be successful. Despite his militaristic image, Putin has rarely displayed the necessary will to push through substantive defense reforms that are unpopular within the military. This requires the alignment of the presidential coalition, including the president and the defense minister, with the military coalition, represented by the chief of the General Staff, all of whom play a central role in shaping defense policy. In Russia's civil–military relations, the president's will must be channeled through a defense minister who is both willing and able to manage the military bureaucracy. The minister has needed be able to lobby for necessary resources and legal changes within Russia's broader government structure. This, in turn, has required a competent and reliable chief of the General Staff, the top military officer responsible for translating the president's strategic objectives into actionable military plans while working constructively with the defense minister. Together, the "troika" of the president, the defense minister and the chief of the General Staff has formed the critical axis for improving military effectiveness.

The president has also needed an assertive, militarized foreign policy orientation that elevates the role of the armed forces as a strategic tool for projecting Russian power abroad. When the state's geopolitical demands for military power were low, the political will to pursue meaningful reform was also limited. The Kremlin remained indifferent to widespread violent crime and systemic dysfunction within the military as long as these issues did not directly interfere with its foreign policy objectives. Incremental changes were often hindered by entrenched interests and bureaucratic inefficiencies. Finally, reformers required direct administrative access to the president to overcome resistance during the implementation phase of reforms and to ensure solid political backing. Without these three factors, military reform was unlikely to succeed in Russia.

The military's deeply embedded institutional culture has further complicated reform efforts. Normative positions have shaped how military actors perceive political–military dynamics and the legitimacy of civilian leadership, influencing their willingness to accept reform. This culture conditioned civil–military relations by defining what service members considered normatively acceptable, reinforcing resistance to civilian-led changes. While the military supports a strong state with a decisive executive capable of enforcing national security policies, it also views itself as a force shaping Russian society, rather than as an institution subject to civilian control. Despite these challenges, reshaping Russian military culture has remained strictly a civilian prerogative. However, the civilian leadership has failed to establish effective mechanisms for monitoring and evaluating military reforms that could enable institutional learning from reform results. Institutionalizing oversight has proved difficult, as the military's resistance prevented its full implementation. Instead, their entrenched normative positions and structural autonomy have continued to obstruct comprehensive reform, leaving the Russian military resistant to external control and slow to adapt to changing strategic realities.

APPENDIX 1

LIST OF INTERVIEWS

No.	Interviewee	Mode	Date and time
1	Major general, ROTC instructor	In person	30/01/20 0:54:10
2	Colonel, ROTC instructor	In person	30/01/20 0:33:19
3	Lieutenant colonel, ROTC instructor	In person	30/01/20 0:33:25
4	Recruitment lawyer, civilian	In person	05/02/20 1:08:07
5	Soldiers' Mothers of Saint Petersburg, human rights lawyer	In person	07/02/20 2:05:50
6	Major, recruitment lawyer	In person	10/01/20 1:46:02
7	Grazhdanin i Armiya (Citizen and Army) movement member	Online	16/01/20 1:45:20
8	Colonel, Military Academy professor	In person	17/02/20 0:50:24
9	Colonel, Military Academy professor	In person	17/02/20 0:43:52

APPENDIX 1

No.	Interviewee	Mode	Date and time
10	Colonel, Military Academy professor	In person	17/02/20 0:20:09
11	Colonel, Military Academy professor	In person	17/02/20 0:29:53
12	Soldiers' Mothers of Saint Petersburg, member	In person	21/02/20 1:20:15
13	Conscientious objectors' movement, member	In person	21/02/20 58:44
14	Colonel, Military Academy professor	In person	02/03/20 1:12:07
15	Lieutenant colonel, Military Academy professor	In person	02/03/20 52:13
16	Military journalist and analyst	Online	12/05/2021 1:01:15
17	Grazhdanin i Armiya (Citizen and Army) movement member	In person	13/05/2021 0:54:05
18	Correspondent of *Komsomolskaya Pravda*	In person	15/05/2021 0:37:21
19	Military journalist	In person	17/05/2021 0:40:18
20	Former high-ranking member of the Russian government, Security Council	In person	18/05/2021 0:33:09
21	Colonel (retired), correspondent	Online	20/05/2021 0:49:24
22	Member of the Social Council of the MoD, journalist	Online	20/05/2021 0:50:24

APPENDIX 1

No.	Interviewee	Mode	Date and time
23	Major general (retired), Council for Foreign and Defense Policy, former member of the Defense Council of the Russian Federation	In person	21/05/2021 0:47:54
24	Member of the Expert Council of the Military-Industrial Commission, journalist	Online	25/05/2021 0:52:29
25	Former member of Yabloko's defense reform group	Online	12/07/2021 0:36:08
26	Research fellow, Center for International and Defense Policy	Email	28/04/18
27	Journalist, MoD press-pool	In person	25/04/18 45:17
28	Professor, Council for Foreign and Defense Policy member	In person	25/04/18 46:58
29	Former State Duma member	In person	23/04/18 30:35
30	Military journalist	In person	20/04/18 20:52
31	Major general, Council for Foreign and Defense Policy member	In person	23/04/18 46:50
32	Political scientist, independent analyst	In person	28/04/18 1:14:36
33	Anti-corruption lawyer	Skype	19/04/18 28:16

APPENDIX 1

No.	Interviewee	Mode	Date and time
34	Associate professor, analyst	Skype	6/04/18 15:21
35	Russian Academy of Science leading research fellow, doctor in political science	In person	23/04/18 45:42
36	Russian Academy of Science leading research fellow	In person	20/04/18 59:07

APPENDIX 2

ADAPTED ADVOCACY COALITION FRAMEWORK

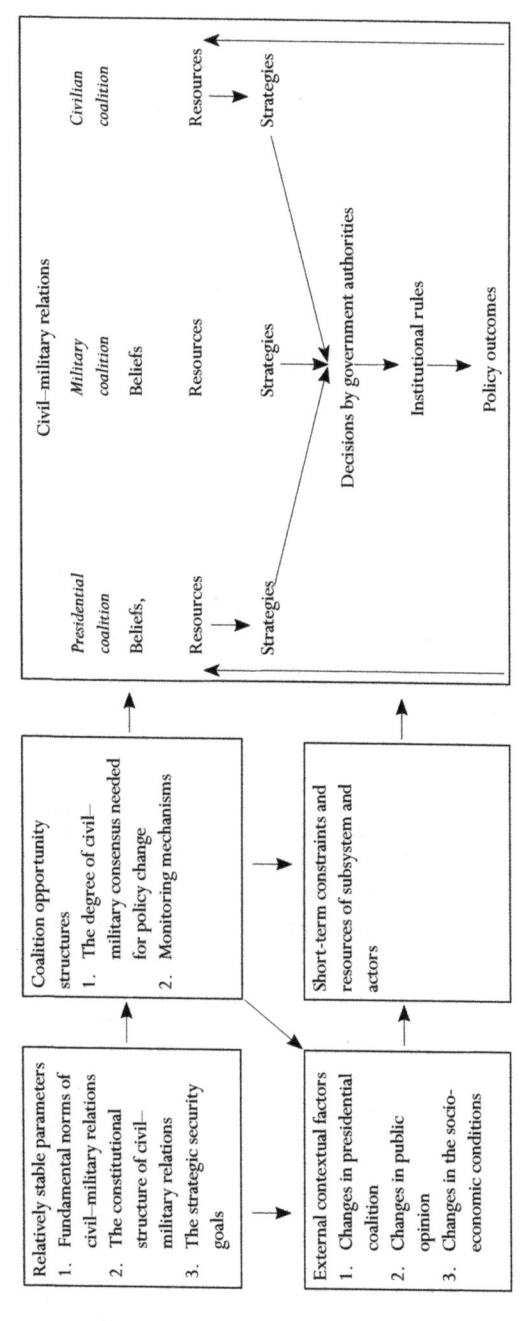

APPENDIX 2.1
OPERATIONALIZATION OF FACTORS USED IN ANALYSIS

Table 1: Relatively stable parameters

Parameter	Operationalization	Measurement
Fundamental norms of civil–military relations	The views of elites on the legitimacy of unquestionable civilian command over the security agencies	Country's history of military *coup d'états* attempts: the number of years without a military coup. Elites' views on military role in civilian politics: opinions on whether the military must always be obedient to civilians.
Constitutional structure	The amount of power key decision-making actors have in the civil–military domain	Provisions in the Constitution on: country's politico-administrative system; number and types of security agencies; role of the president and the parliament.
Strategic military and security goals	Acknowledged national security threats and institutional development plans for the security agencies	Provisions of the military doctrine and national security strategies.

APPENDIX 2

Table 2: Coalition opportunity structures

Structures	Operationalization	Measurement
The degree of civil–military consensus needed for policy change	The level of institutional prerogatives to make a unilateral decision without consulting with other coalitions in national security settings	Institutional prerogatives: analysis of the Constitution, laws and major regulations. Power dynamics: post hoc policy positions.
Monitoring mechanisms	Technological and institutional monitoring mechanisms to assess the conditions in the military	The degree of intrusiveness of the institutional mechanisms of monitoring.

Table 3: External contextual factors

Events	Operationalization	Measurement
Changes in the socio-economic conditions	The number of incentives and resources both coalitions can use in policymaking	Case-specific: available resources for satisfying public and elite demands.
Changes in public opinion	The popularity of political or military leaders among the public. The legitimacy of a selected policy	The popularity of political or military leaders among the public: surveys. Policy legitimacy: rarely surveys, media narratives about a policy change.
Changes in presidential coalition	The level of unequivocal support for security policies	Connections to the security sector in the presidential coalition: biographical research.

APPENDIX 3

DEFENSE POLICY AGENDA

Table 4: Agenda for the 2001–3 reform: Priorities in military development according to the 2000 Military Doctrine

Main priorities	Selected main directions (programming tasks)
The creation of the unified system of command and control	Improving the quality, effectiveness and safety of operation of the technological basis of the military administration.
	Improving the economic support of the military organization based on the concentration and rational use of financial and material resources.
The development of nuclear forces and deterrence	Not mentioned.
The creation and upholding of mobilization resources	Improving the recruitment system (based on the contract-conscription principle, with a gradual increase, as the necessary socio-economic conditions are created, in the proportion of military personnel serving under contract, primarily in the positions of junior commanders and specialists in the leading combat specialties).

APPENDIX 3

Main priorities	Selected main directions (programming tasks)
Manning, equipping, comprehensive support and preparation of formations and military units for permanent combat readiness of general-purpose forces	Bringing the structure, composition and number of components of the state's military organization in line with the tasks of ensuring military security, taking into account the country's economic capabilities.

Source: Voennaya Doktrina Rossiiskoi Federacii [Military doctrine of the Russian Federation] (2000), https://www.ng.ru/politics/2000-04-22/5_doktrina.html

Table 5: Agenda for the 2004–7 period

No.	Main priorities	Selected main directions (programming tasks)
1	Maintaining strategic deterrence	Development of land-based nuclear forces (up to ten divisions by 2008); modernization of Tu-160 strategic bombers; creation of a new sea-based missile complex.
2	Buildup of permanent combat-readiness regiments	No disclosed tasks, general information on the formation of permanently combat-ready units and regiments on the territorial principle.
3	Upgrade of operational preparedness of troops	Exploration of new forms and means of force use under heavy informational and electronic pressure; digitalization of topographic maps; increase of battalion-level exercises and shootings; development of skills of combined arms and joint military actions.
4	Upgrade of manning system	Implementation of the federal program on the transition to all-volunteer forces by 2007; sustaining of mobilization resources.

APPENDIX 3

No.	Main priorities	Selected main directions (programming tasks)
5	Modernization of armaments and equipment	Increase of the share of modern equipment to 35 per cent by 2010 and to 40 to 45 per cent by 2015; full technical modernization by 2020–5; unification of supply systems by 2006; total supply of troops with all logistics support by 2010.
6	Development of military science and education	Implementation of the 2002 federal program "Reforming the Military Education System in the Russian Federation for the Period until 2010"; by 2005, optimization of the network of military academies, installing internet access, establishing a quality monitoring system, piloting military education in civilian institutions with subsequent military service; by 2010, liquidation of unnecessary military education facilities, upgrade of teaching capabilities, expansion of possibilities for military education in civilian institutions, creation of a unified information sharing and management system.
7	Strengthening of social support, upbringing and moral-psychological preparedness	By 2012–15, the reduction of the housing waiting period to one to three months; formation of a funded housing system instead of direct provision of apartments; by 2005, the unification of the upbringing and information systems of the security sector and the re-introduction of military-patriotic education at schools.

Source: MoD, "Aktual'nye zadachi razvitija vooruzhennyh sil Rossijskoj Federacii" [Current development challenges: Armed forces of the Russian Federation], Ministry of Defense of the Russian Federation, 2003, https://web.archive.org/web/20250815002706/http://old.redstar.ru/2003/10/11_10/3_01.html

APPENDIX 3

Table 6: Objectives for military development from 2010

No.	Main priorities	Selected main directions (programming tasks)
1	Developing the command-and-control system and increasing its effectiveness	Increasing the safety and effectiveness of the state and military management; improving military planning; creating the system of integrated material, technical, social, medical and scientific support for the armed forces.
2	Developing the mobilization potential and supporting the mobilization deployment	Adapting the structure and number of personnel to the norms of peaceful and war periods. Allocation of necessary funds for such tasks; improving the system of territorial and civil defense; improving the system of mobilization resources, including armament and vehicle depots.
3	Keeping the necessary level of manning, equipment and logistical support	Improving the air defense system and creating the system of aerospace defense; improving the military-economic support of the military organization; increasing the effectiveness of the system for the operation and maintenance of military vehicles and equipment.
4	Increasing the quality of military higher education and science	Integration of systems of military education, upbringing and research; optimization of the number of military academies and institutions and improving their material and technical equipment.

Source: adapted from "Voennaja doktrina Rossijskoj Federacii" [Military doctrine of the Russian Federation], no. 146 (2010), http://kremlin.ru/supplement/461

APPENDIX 3

Table 7: Defense policy priorities in the 2013–20 period

No.	Main priorities	Operationalized tasks
1	Completing the creation of permanent combat-ready units in all strategic directions	By 31 December 2014: create the National Center for Defense Management. By 31 December 2015: create Centers for Combat Command and Day-to-Day Activities in branch and regional commands. By 31 December 2016: create Centers for Combat Command and Day-to-Day Activities in military districts. By 31 December 2017: create Centers for Combat Command and Day-to-Day Activities in military corps.
2	By the end of 2014, 100 per cent of enlisted personnel must be hired and present	By 31 December 2014: 95–100 per cent of units are fully manned with service members; 240,000 all-volunteer personnel. By 31 December 2015: 350,000 all-volunteer personnel and all service members are equipped with a new uniform. By 31 December 2016–2020: 400–25,000 all-volunteer personnel.
3	Military education	By 31 December 2016: increase the annual hours spend on combat training by 90 per cent. By 31 December 2015: create six new Presidential Cadet Schools in the regions.
4	Increase the quality of combat training and standards for soldiers and officers	Between 2014 and 2020, the Russian military planned gradual increase of time spent on training. For naval crews, the number of days spent at sea had to rise from seventy-five in 2014 to 125 in 2020. Flight hours for various aviation branches: operational-tactical aviation from 100 to 125 hours, military transport aviation from 110 to

APPENDIX 3

No.	Main priorities	Operationalized tasks
		150 hours, army aviation from eighty to 130 hours, and naval aviation from seventy to 120 hours. Practical driving distances for drivers and tank crews increased from 500/350 kilometers to 1,000/500 kilometers per year. The number of parachute jumps per soldier, with reconnaissance units increasing from eleven to twenty-one jumps and paratroopers increasing from seven to twelve jumps.
5	Rearm the military with new weapons and vehicles	By 31 December 2014: 30 per cent of vehicles and weapons must be new. By 31 December 2016–20: 41/48/59/64/70–100 per cent of vehicles and weapons must be new. Increase the quality of repair and upgrade of vehicles by the defense industry.
6	Create the Perspective Research and Development System	By 31 December 2014: create the State Center of Unmanned Aerial Vehicles and the Main Research and Development Center for Robotics Testing.
		By 31 December 2017: create the Main Robotics Research and Development Center. By 31 December 2019: create the Center for Support of Advanced Military Research and Development. Increase the efficacy of research and development spending.
7	Solve the housing problem for active-duty and retired officers	By 1 January 2014: begin the provision of single housing payments based on the average market value per square meter and service experience.

APPENDIX 3

No.	Main priorities	Operationalized tasks
8	Solve the heating problems in garrisons and complete the renovation plan by the end of 2014	By 1 January 2017: reduce the number of garrisons to 495.

Sources: MoD, "Plan deiatel'nosti na 2013–2020 gg." [Activity plan for 2013–20], Ministry of Defense of Russian Federation, 2013, https://mil.ru/mod_activity_plan/constr.htm; "Sozdat' mobil'nye, khorosho osnashchennye vooruzhennye sily" [Create a mobile, well-equipped armed forces], *Rossiiskoye Voennoe Obozrenie* 2, no. 105 (2013): 80.

NOTES

INTRODUCTION

1. Gennady Troshev, *My War: The Chechen Diary of the Trench General* (n.p., 2001), https://www.livelib.ru/book/1000005643-moya-vojna-chechenskij-dnevnik-okopnogo-generala-gennadij-troshev
2. "SIPRI Milex," https://milex.sipri.org/sipri
3. Risa A. Brooks, "The Impact of Culture, Society, Institutions, and International Forces on Military Effectiveness," in *Creating Military Power: The Sources of Military Effectiveness*, ed. Elizabeth A. Stanley and Risa A. Brooks (Stanford University Press, 2007), 9–10, https://stanford.universitypressscholarship.com/view/10.11126/stanford/9780804753999.001.0001/upso-9780804753999
4. Max Weber, *Politics as a Vocation* (Fortress Press, 1965).
5. Alfred C. Stepan, *Rethinking Military Politics: Brazil and the Southern Cone*, 1st edn (Princeton University Press, 1988); Theda Skocpol, *Protecting Soldiers and Mothers: The Political Origins of Social Policy in United States*, reprint edn (Belknap Press of Harvard University Press, 1995); Milan W. Svolik, *The Politics of Authoritarian Rule* (Cambridge University Press, 2012).
6. Brian D. Taylor, *Politics and the Russian Army: Civil–Military Relations, 1689–2000* (Cambridge University Press, 2003); Taylor, "Russia's Passive Army: Rethinking Military Coups," *Comparative Political Studies* 34, no. 8 (2001): 942–52, https://doi.org/10.1177/0010414001034008004
7. Alexander Belkin, "Civil–Military Relations in Russia after 9-11," *European Security* 12, nos. 3–4 (2003): 1–19, https://doi.org/10.1080/09662830390436551; Joss I. Meakins, "Squabbling

Siloviki: Factionalism within Russia's Security Services," *International Journal of Intelligence and CounterIntelligence* 31, no. 2 (2018): 235–70, https://doi.org/10.1080/08850607.2018.1417525

8. Taylor, *Politics and the Russian Army*; Natalia Danilova, "The Development of an Exclusive Veterans' Policy: The Case of Russia," *Armed Forces & Society* 36, no. 5 (2010): 890–916, https://doi.org/10.1177/0095327X09351224; Elizaveta Gaufman, *Security Threats and Public Perception: Digital Russia and the Ukraine Crisis* (Springer, 2016).

9. Olga Kryshtanovskaya and Stephen White, "Putin's Militocracy," *Post-Soviet Affairs* 19, no. 4 (2003): 289–306, https://doi.org/10.2747/1060-586X.19.4.289; Bettina Renz, "Putin's Militocracy? An Alternative Interpretation of Siloviki in Contemporary Russian Politics," *Europe-Asia Studies* 58, no. 6 (2006): 903–24, https://doi.org/10.1080/09668130600831134; David W. Rivera and Sharon Werning Rivera, "Is Russia a Militocracy? Conceptual Issues and Extant Findings Regarding Elite Militarization," *Post-Soviet Affairs* 30, no. 1 (2014): 27–50, https://doi.org/10.1080/1060586X.2013.819681; Rivera and Rivera, "The Militarization of the Russian Elite under Putin," *Problems of Post-Communism* 65, no. 4 (2018): 221–32, https://doi.org/10.1080/10758216.2017.1295812

10. I use the following definition of political will: the ability to collect "committed support among key decision makers for a particular policy solution to a particular problem"; see Lori Ann Post et al., "Defining Political Will," *Politics & Policy* 38, no. 4 (2010): 653–76, at 659, https://doi.org/10.1111/j.1747-1346.2010.00253.x

11. Paul Sabatier, "An Advocacy Coalition Framework of Policy Change and the Role of Policy-Oriented Learning Therein," *Policy Sciences* 21, no. 2/3 (1988): 129–68.

12. Sabatier, "Advocacy Coalition Framework of Policy Change."

13. Gerald B. Thomas, "External Shocks, Conflict and Learning as Interactive Sources of Change in U.S. Security Policy," *Journal of Public Policy* 19, no. 2 (1999): 209–31, https://doi.org/10.1017/S0143814X99000239

14. Hank Jenkins-Smith et al., "Belief System Continuity and Change in Policy Advocacy Coalitions: Using Cultural Theory to Specify Belief Systems, Coalitions, and Sources of Change," *Policy Studies Journal* 42, no. 4 (2014): 484–508, https://doi.org/10.1111/psj.12071

15. Yagil Levy, "Control from Within: How Soldiers Control the Military," *European Journal of International Relations* 23, no. 1 (2017): 192–216, https://doi.org/10.1177/1354066116631807

16. William Zimmerman et al., "Survey of Russian Elites, Moscow, Russia, 1993–2016," Inter-university Consortium for Political and Social Research, 2019, https://doi.org/10.3886/ICPSR03724.v6
17. Federal'nyj zakon "Ob oborone" [Federal law "On defense"], 61, Duma of the Russian Federation, 2021, http://publication.pravo.gov.ru/Document/View/0001202106110007
18. "Russian Losses in the War with Ukraine: Mediazona Count, Updated," Mediazona, July 2025, https://en.zona.media/article/2025/07/18/casualties_eng-trl

1. RUSSIAN CIVIL–MILITARY RELATIONS AFTER THE USSR

1. Francis Fukuyama, *The End of History and the Last Man*, reissue edn (Free Press, 2006), 328.
2. Daniel Nohrstedt, "The Advocacy Coalition Framework: Foundations, Evolution, and Ongoing Research," in *Theories of the Policy Process*, ed. Paul Sabatier and Christopher Weible, 3rd edn (Westview Press, 2014). Wei Li and Christopher M. Weible, "China's Policy Processes and the Advocacy Coalition Framework," *Policy Studies Journal* 49, no. 3 (2021): 703–30, https://doi.org/10.1111/psj.12369
3. Paul Sabatier and Christopher Weible, *The Advocacy Coalition Framework: Innovations and Clarifications* (Westview Press, 2007), https://vtechworks.lib.vt.edu/handle/10919/68212
4. "Gromov, Boris Vsevolodovich," TASS, https://tass.ru/encyclopedia/person/gromov-boris-vsevolodovich
5. RBK, "Sergej Surovikin biografija, foto, kar'era, lichnaja zhizn" [Sergey Surovikin biography, photos, career, and personal life], accessed 13 November 2025, https://www.rbc.ru/; Miodrag Shoric and Vitaly Kropman, "'Sirijskij mjasnik' v Ukraine: zapadnye jeksperty o Surovikine" [The "Syrian Butcher" in Ukraine: Western experts on Surovikin], DW, 16 October 2022, https://www.dw.com/ru/sirijskij-masnik-v-ukraine-zapadnye-eksperty-o-generale-surovikine/a-63441829
6. "V Leningrade Sobchak dogovorilsia s voennymi: V gorode idet zabastovka; V mitinge protiv GKChP uchastvovalo okolo 150 tysiach chelovek" [In Leningrad, Sobchak made a deal with the military; There is a strike in the city; The rally against the GKChP was attended by about 150,000 people], Interfax.ru, 20 August 1991, https://www.interfax.ru/30years/782536; "'Seichas deistvitel'no reshaetsia budushchee': Istoriia putcha v dnevnikovykh zapisiakh avgusta 1991 goda" ["Now the future is really being decided": The history of the

putsch in the diary entries of August 1991], Meduza, 19 August 2016, https://meduza.io/feature/2016/08/19/seychas-deystvitelno-reshaetsya-buduschee

7. Dale R. Herspring, "Samuel Huntington and Communist Civil–Military Relations," *Armed Forces & Society* 25, no. 4 (1999): 557–77, https://doi.org/10.1177/0095327X9902500403; Meakins, "Squabbling Siloviki."
8. Vladimir Gel'man, "Escape from Political Freedom: The Constitutional Crisis of 1993 and Russia's Political Trajectory," *Russian History* 50, nos. 1–2 (2024): 1–20, https://doi.org/10.30965/18763316-12340056
9. Viktor Baranec et al., "Taĭny rasstrela 'Belogo doma'" [Secrets of the "White House" shooting], *Komsomolskaya Pravda* (Moscow), 10 March 2008, https://www.kp.ru/daily/24174/385092/
10. Mark Galeotti, *Putin's Wars: From Chechnya to Ukraine* (Bloomsbury Publishing, 2022).
11. Andrew Cottey et al., "Civil–Military Relations in Postcommunist Europe: Assessing the Transition," *European Security* 14, no. 1 (2005): 1–16, https://doi.org/10.1080/09662830500042452
12. Carolina Vendil, "The Russian Security Council," *European Security* 10, no. 2 (2001): 67–94, https://doi.org/10.1080/09662830108407494
13. OSCE, "Code of Conduct on Politico-Military Aspects of Security," 1994, https://www.osce.org/fsc/41355
14. Igor Dmitrov, "'Seychas tanki voydut, vse razbegutsya': V 1994 godu rossiyskikh soldat poslali v Groznyy i brosili; Komu eto bylo vygodno?" ["Now the tanks will enter, and everyone will scatter": In 1994, Russian soldiers were sent to Grozny and abandoned; Who benefited from this?], Lenta.ru, 31 July 2021, https://lenta.ru/articles/2021/07/31/tankist/
15. "Reforma armii," *Kommersant*, 25 July 1997, https://www.kommersant.ru/doc/181572
16. Federal'nyj zakon "Ob oborone" [Federal law "On defense"].
17. Susan Grant, "5. Stalinist Care: Cadres Decide Everything," in *Soviet Nightingales: Care under Communism* (Cornell University Press, 2022), https://doi.org/10.1515/9781501762604-009
18. Thomas Gomart, *Russian Civil–Military Relations: Putin's Legacy* (Carnegie Endowment for International Peace, 2008).
19. Aaron Belkin and Evan Schofer, "Coup Risk, Counterbalancing, and International Conflict," *Security Studies* 14, no. 1 (2005): 140–77, https://doi.org/10.1080/09636410591002527; Erica De Bruin, "Preventing Coups d'état: How Counterbalancing Works," *Journal of Conflict Resolution* 62, no. 7 (2018): 1433–58, https://

doi.org/10.1177/0022002717692652; Dan Reiter, "Avoiding the Coup-Proofing Dilemma: Consolidating Political Control While Maximizing Military Power," *Foreign Policy Analysis* 16, no. 3 (2020): 312–31, https://doi.org/10.1093/fpa/oraa001

20. Government of Russia, "Federal′nyĭ zakon ot 03.07.2016 N 226-FZ 'O voĭskakh natsional′noĭ gvardii Rossiĭskoĭ Federatsiĭ'" [Federal law of 03.07.2016 N 226-FZ "On the national guard troops of the Russian Federation"], Garant, 3 July 2016, https://base.garant.ru/71433920/

21. Government of Russia, "Federal Constitutional Law No. 4-FKZ 'On the Government of the Russian Federation,'" *Rossiiskaya Gazeta*, 11 June 2020, https://www.consultant.ru/document/cons_doc_LAW_366950/

22. For details on the security agencies and civilians, see: Alexei Makarkin, "The Minister and the Balance," The Daily Journal, 2007, http://ej.ru/?a=note&id=6177; Irina Borogan and Andrei Soldatov, *The New Nobility: The Restoration of Russia's Security State and the Enduring Legacy of the KGB*, 1st edn (PublicAffairs, 2010); Borogan and Soldatov, "Russia's Very Secret Services," *World Policy Journal* 28, no. 1 (2011): 83–91, https://doi.org/10.1177/0740277511402800; "Ex-Minister in Corruption Case Warns Kremlin Elite They Could Be Next," Bloomberg, 7 December 2017, https://www.bloomberg.com/news/articles/2017-12-07/you-may-be-next-ex-minister-in-graft-case-warns-putin-s-elite; Meakins, "Squabbling Siloviki."

23. Peter Feaver, *Armed Servants: Agency, Oversight, and Civil–Military Relations*, revised edn (Harvard University Press, 2005).

24. Feaver, *Armed Servants*, 57.

25. Samuel P. Huntington, *The Soldier and the State: The Theory and Politics of Civil–Military Relations* (Harvard University Press, 1957).

26. Nadine Ansorg and Eleanor Gordon, "Co-operation, Contestation and Complexity in Post-conflict Security Sector Reform," *Journal of Intervention and Statebuilding* 13, no. 1 (2019): 2–24, at 10, https://doi.org/10.1080/17502977.2018.1516392

27. Feaver, *Armed Servants*.

28. Levada Center, "Sbornik obshchestvennoe mnenie 2016" [Public opinion 2016 report], 2017, 272, https://www.levada.ru/sbornik-obshhestvennoe-mnenie/

29. Gel'man, *Authoritarian Russia*, 73.

30. Pekka Sutela, *The Political Economy of Putin's Russia*, 1st edn (Routledge, 2014), 32–45; Vladimir Gel'man, *Authoritarian Modernization in Russia: Ideas, Institutions, and Policies* (Routledge, 2016), 148–200.

31. Joachim Zweynert, *When Ideas Fail: Economic Thought, the Failure of Transition and the Rise of Institutional Instability in Post-Soviet Russia*, 1st edn (Routledge, 2017), 60–70.
32. Program-2010, "Osnovnye napravleniiā sotsīalno-ėkonomicheskoĭ politiki pravitel'stva RF na dolgosrochnuiū perspektivu" [Main directions of the social and economic policy of the government of the Russian Federation for the long-term perspective] (2000), 53–68, https://web.archive.org/web/20100918062948/http://budgetrf.ru/Publications/Programs/Government/Gref2000/Gref2000000.htm
33. Kenneth Wilson, "Modernization or More of the Same in Russia: Was There a 'Thaw' under Medvedev?," *Problems of Post-Communism* 62, no. 3 (2015): 145–58, https://doi.org/10.1080/10758216.2015.1019803
34. Alexey G. Barabashev and Andrey V. Klimenko, "Russian Governance Changes and Performance," *Chinese Political Science Review* 2, no. 1 (2017): 22–39, https://doi.org/10.1007/s41111-017-0057-z
35. Brian D. Taylor, "Police Reform in Russia: The Policy Process in a Hybrid Regime," *Post-Soviet Affairs* 30, nos. 2–3 (2014): 226–55, https://doi.org/10.1080/1060586X.2013.860752
36. Zweynert, *When Ideas Fail*, 92–3.
37. Huntington, *Soldier and the State*; Feaver, *Armed Servants*.
38. Risa Brooks, "Revisiting the Janus-Face: Civil–Military Relations and Strategy-Making," in *Research Handbook on Civil–Military Relations*, ed. Aurel Croissant et al. (Edward Elgar Publishing, 2024), https://www.elgaronline.com/edcollchap/book/9781800889842/book-part-9781800889842-11.xml

2. CIVIL–MILITARY RELATIONS AND RUSSIAN MILITARY CULTURE

1. Mark Moore, "Ex-Russia General Warns Putin against 'Criminal' Ukraine Invasion," *New York Post*, 7 February 2022, https://nypost.com/2022/02/07/ex-russia-general-warns-putin-against-criminal-ukraine-invasion/
2. Parts of this chapters were published in the *Armed Forces and Society* journal in December 2021: Kirill Shamiev, "Civil–Military Relations and Russia's Post-Soviet Military Culture: A Belief System Analysis," *Armed Forces & Society* 49, no. 2 (2021): 252–74, https://doi.org/10.1177/0095327X211062932
3. Joseph Soeters, "Organizational Cultures in the Military," in *Handbook*

of the Sociology of the Military, ed. Giuseppe Caforio and Marina Nuciari, 2nd edn, Handbooks of Sociology and Social Research (Springer International, 2018), 251, https://www.springer.com/gp/book/9783319716008

4. The classic civil–military theorist Morris Janowitz proposed the "civilianization" of the military through mandatory conscription and reservist training programs. These initiatives were designed to promote a convergence of civilian and military values and norms, thereby enhancing mutual understanding and civil–military cohesion; Morris Janowitz, *The Professional Soldier: A Social and Political Portrait* (Free Press, 1960).

5. "Independent International Fact-Finding Mission on the Conflict in Georgia, Report, Volume I–III, 2009," Max Planck Institute for Comparative Public Law and International Law, https://www.mpil.de/en/pub/publications/archive/independent_international_fact.cfm

6. Anatoly Kvashnin, "Perspektivnaiā sistema planirovaniiā stroitel'stva vooruzhennykh sil" [Prospective system of planning for the construction of the armed forces], *Voennaya Mysl* 6, nos. 11–12 (2001), https://militaryarticle.vibrokatok.by/voennaya-mysl/2001-vm/9122-voennoe-stroitelstvo; Yuri Gavrilov and Igor Chernyak, "Īuriĭ Baluevskiĭ: My ne sobiraemsiā voevat' s NATO" [Yury Baluyevsky: We are not going to war with NATO], *Rossiiskaya Gazeta*, 11 January 2005, https://rg.ru/2005/11/01/baluevsky.html

7. These defense policy ideas were proposed by experts such as Alexei Arbatov, Vitaly Shlykov, Makhmut Gareev and Andrei Kokoshin.

8. Vladimir Dvorkin and Alexei Arbatov, "Military Reform in Russia: Current State and Future Prospects," Moscow Carnegie Center, 2013, 79, https://carnegie.ru/2013/07/11/ru-pub-52368; Aleksandr Golts, *Military Reform and Militarism in Russia* (Acta Universitatis Upsaliensis, 2017); Steven Miller and Dmitri Trenin, *Vooryzhennie sily Rossii:Vlast' i politika* [Armed forces of Russia: Power and politics] (Interdialekt+, 2005).

9. Huntington, *Soldier and the State*.

10. John Samuel Fitch, *The Armed Forces and Democracy in Latin America* (Johns Hopkins University Press, 1998).

11. David Pion-Berlin and Danijela Dudley, "Civil–Military Relations: What Is the State of the Field," in *Handbook of Military Sciences*, ed. Anders Sookermany (Springer International, 2020), 10, https://doi.org/10.1007/978-3-030-02866-4_37-1; Sabatier and Weible, *Advocacy Coalition Framework*.

12. Jongseok Woo, "Songun Politics and the Political Weakness of the Military in North Korea: An Institutional Account," *Problems of Post-Communism* 63, no. 4 (2016): 253–62, https://doi.org/10.1080/10758216.2016.1145065
13. Bener Karakartal, "Turkey: The Army as Guardian of the Political Order," in *The Political Dilemmas of Military Regimes*, ed. Christopher Clapham and George Philip (Routledge, 1985); Mark Tessler and Ebru Altinoglu, "Political Culture in Turkey: Connections among Attitudes toward Democracy, the Military and Islam," *Democratization* 11, no. 1 (2004): 21–50, https://doi.org/10.1080/13510340412331294122; "Self-appointed Guardians of Secularism," D+C, Development + Cooperation, 18 September 2008, https://www.dandc.eu/en/article/turkeys-military-self-appointed-guardians-secularism; Yücel Bozdağlioğlu, "The Culture of the Turkish Military: From Intervention to Accommodation," *Journal of South Asian and Middle Eastern Studies* 37, no. 2 (2014): 19–40.
14. Hank Jenkins-Smith et al., "Belief System Continuity and Change in Policy Advocacy Coalitions: Using Cultural Theory to Specify Belief Systems, Coalitions, and Sources of Change; Using Cultural Theory," *Policy Studies Journal* 42, no. 4 (2014): 484–508, https://doi.org/10.1111/psj.12071
15. Soeters, "Organizational Cultures in the Military"; Tamir Libel, *European Military Culture and Security Governance: Soldiers, Scholars and National Defence Universities* (Routledge, 2016), https://doi.org/10.4324/9781315848914; Remi M. Hajjar, "Emergent Postmodern US Military Culture," *Armed Forces & Society* 40, no. 1 (2014): 118–45, https://doi.org/10.1177/0095327X12465261
16. Jenkins-Smith et al., "Belief System Continuity and Change," 493–4.
17. Shushanna Baumann, "A Survey of Military Oaths in Russian History," Special Report, Selection of Papers Presented at the 2019 Fort Leavenworth Ethics Symposium (Lewis and Clark Center, 2019), 204, https://thesimonscenter.org/wp-content/uploads/2019/10/Ethics-Symp-2019-p23-27.pdf
18. In the Soviet Union and Russia, the Great Patriotic War is commemorated as a defining part of the Second World War. In June 1941, Nazi Germany and its allies—Finland, Hungary, Italy and Romania—jointly attacked the Soviet Union, opening the bloodiest and largest theater of the war. The war ended in May 1945, when the Allied Forces (under Soviet, US, UK and French command) captured Berlin and forced Germany to unconditionally surrender. The USSR participated in the war by invading Poland and Finland in 1939,

occupying the Baltic states and taking over Bessarabia and Northern Bukovina from Romania in 1940. The USSR also fought imperial Japan from August to September 1945, effectively defeating Japan's Kwantung Army in China, Korea, Sakhalin and the Kuril Islands.
19. Zimmerman et al., "Survey of Russian Elites, Moscow, Russia, 1993–2016."
20. Interview 6, 10 January 2020.
21. Interview 15, 2 March 2020.
22. Eve Binks and Siobhan Cambridge, "The Transition Experiences of British Military Veterans," *Political Psychology* 39, no. 1 (2018): 125–42, https://doi.org/10.1111/pops.12399
23. John W. R. Lepingwell, "Soviet Civil–Military Relations and the August Coup," *World Politics* 44, no. 4 (1992): 539–72, https://doi.org/10.2307/2010487
24. Zoltan Barany, *Democratic Breakdown and the Decline of the Russian Military* (Princeton University Press, 2009).
25. The elections to the Soviet CPD in March–May 1989 were relatively complex. The CPD comprised 2,250 seats divided equally among three categories: 1,500 direct-elected district deputies and 750 deputies reserved for public organizations such as the Communist Party, trade unions, Komsomol (Communist youth organization), Women's Committee, veterans, scientific bodies, creative unions and cooperatives. Candidates required endorsement from at least 500 voters and over 50 per cent approval at nomination committee meetings.
26. Interview 6, 10 February 2020. Starovoitova was a well-known advocate of democracy, human rights and ethnic minority protections in the Soviet Union.
27. Ivan Dynin, *Posle Afganistana: "Afgantsy" v pis'makh, dokumentakh, svidetel'stvakh ochevidtsev* [After Afghanistan: "Afgantsy" in letters, documents, testimonies] (Profizdat, 1990).
28. Interview 14, 2 March 2020.
29. Interview 14, 2 March 2020.
30. Troshev, *My War*, 24. This view, though less explicitly described, was common among the military respondents and some civilians. The changes happened too rapidly without clearly defined goals.
31. Interview 9, 17 February 2020.
32. Interview 7, 16 February 2020; interview 13, 21 February 2020.
33. Interview 12, 21 February 2020.
34. More details in: "Pavel Grachev," Global Security, n.d., https://www.globalsecurity.org/military/world/russia/grachev.htm

35. Anna Politkovskaya, "Konclager's kommercheskim uklonom" [Concentration camp with a commercial slant], Anna Stepanovna Politkovskaya, 2 June 2001, https://politkovskaya.novayagazeta.ru/pub/2001/2001-14.shtml
36. "Anna Stapnovna Politkovskaya," https://politkovskaya.novayagazeta.ru/bio.shtml
37. Interview 8, 17 February 2020.
38. Interview 8, 17 February 2020; interview 14, 2 March 2020.
39. Interview 14, 2 March 2020.
40. Interview 15, 2 March 2020.
41. Interview 14, 2 March 2020.
42. Interview 14, 2 March 2020; interview 6, 10 February 2020.
43. Lyle J. Goldstein, "Russian Civil–Military Relations in the Chechen War, December 1994–February 1995," *Journal of Slavic Military Studies* 10, no. 1 (1997): 109–27, https://doi.org/10.1080/13518049708430277
44. Goldstein, "Russian Civil–Military Relations," 109–16.
45. Robert Burl Brannon, *Russian Civil–Military Relations* (Ashgate, 2009).
46. Dmitry Okunev, "Na poroge Tret'ej mirovoj: Kak VDV Rossii perehitrili NATO" [On the threshold of World War III: How the Russian Airborne Troops outsmarted NATO], Gazeta.ru, 6 November 2019, https://www.gazeta.ru/science/2019/06/11_a_12407875.shtml
47. Sharon Werning Rivera and James D. Bryan, "Understanding the Sources of Anti-Americanism in the Russian Elite," *Post-Soviet Affairs* 35, nos. 5–6 (2019): 376–92, https://doi.org/10.1080/1060586X.2019.1662194
48. "What Were the Officers Thinking and Talking About, 1992, Moscow," YouTube, 4 September 2011, https://www.youtube.com/watch?v=4KBHP_bLG10&t=1s
49. General Troshev, commander of the joint group of federal forces in the Northern Caucasus in 2000, praised Putin's approach and his energy and decisiveness; see Troshev, *My War*.
50. Vladimir Putin, "V.V. Putin Vstretilsiâ v Kaliningrade s Predstaviteliâmi Organizatsiĭ Veteranov Voĭny, Voennoĭ Sluzhby i Pravookhranitel'nykh Organov" [Vladimir Putin met with representatives of organizations of war veterans, military service and law enforcement agencies in Kaliningrad], 2011, http://archive.government.ru/docs/16950/print/
51. Kryshtanovskaya and White, "Putin's Militocracy."
52. Renz, "Putin's Militocracy?"

53. Neil Robinson, "Russian Neo-patrimonialism and Putin's 'Cultural Turn,'" *Europe-Asia Studies* 69, no. 2 (2017): 348–66, https://doi.org/10.1080/09668136.2016.1265916
54. Interview 6, 10 February 2020.
55. Interview 9, 17 February 2020.
56. Interview 15, 2 March 2020.
57. Interview 12, 21 February 2020.
58. Interview 4, 5 February 2020.
59. Sabatier, "Advocacy Coalition Framework of Policy Change," 145.
60. Jenkins-Smith et al., "Belief System Continuity and Change," 486.
61. Dale R. Herspring, *Civil–Military Relations and Shared Responsibility: A Four-Nation Study* (Johns Hopkins University Press, 2013).
62. Interview 1, 30 January 2020.
63. Interview 13, 21 February 2020.
64. Igor Korotchenko and Viktor Baranec, guests, "Kakova rol' figury Pavla Gracheva v novejshej istorii Rossii?" [What is the role of the figure of Pavel Grachev in modern Russian history?], *GraniVremeni*, dir. Vladimir Kara-Murza, Radio Liberty, 24 September 2012, https://www.svoboda.org/a/24719507.html
65. Troshev, *My War*, 26.
66. Richard Sakwa, "Is Putin an Ism?," *Russian Politics* 5, no. 3 (2020): 255–82, https://doi.org/10.30965/24518921-00503001
67. "Otnoshenie k Vladimiru Putinu" [Attitudes toward Vladimir Putin], Levada Center (blog), 2025, https://www.levada.ru/2025/08/14/otnoshenie-k-vladimiru-putinu-i-massovye-otsenki-ego-deyatelnosti/
68. Interview 7, 16 February 2020.
69. Levada Center, "Sbornik obshchestvennoe mnenie 2016."
70. Interview 3, 30 January 2020.
71. Miller and Trenin, *Vooryzhennie sily Rossii*, 94–6.
72. Interview 5, 7 February 2020.
73. Interview 1, 30 January 2020.
74. Troshev, *My War*, 273–80.
75. Andrew Roth, "Russia Moves to Mask Its Soldiers' Digital Trail with Smartphone Ban," *The Guardian*, 19 February 2019, https://www.theguardian.com/world/2019/feb/19/russia-moves-to-mask-soldiers-digital-trail-with-smartphone-ban
76. "Rossijskim voennym zamenjat smartfony na knopochnye Nokia" [Russian military will replace smartphones with Nokia button phones], Meduza, 15 February 2018, https://meduza.io/news/2018/02/15/rossiyskim-voennym-zamenyat-smartfony-knopochnymi-nokia;

"Matros razgovarival v kazarme po videosvjazi: Kak rossijskih voennyh sazhajut pod arest za smartfony i foto v socsetjah" [A sailor talked in the barracks via video link: How Russian servicemen are put under arrest for smartphones and photos on social networks], Meduza, 8 June 2019, https://meduza.io/feature/2019/08/06/matros-razgovarival-v-kazarme-po-videosvyazi

77. Interview 4, 5 February 2020; interview 5, 7 February 2020; interview 13, 21 February 2020.
78. "Vrachi Tockogo garnizona skryvali sledy dedovshhiny" [Totsk garrison doctors hid traces of hazing], kazan.kp.ru, 18 March 2007, https://www.kazan.kp.ru/daily/23871.5/244115/
79. "Gromko uvolennye voenachal'niki Kamenki tiho vozvrashhajutsja v chast'" [Kamenka's loudly dismissed military leaders quietly return to the unit], Zaks.ru, 15 June 2010, https://www.zaks.ru/new/archive/view/70107
80. Interview 12, 21 February 2020.
81. Vladimir Bondarev, "Vesennij prizyv v Rossijskuju armiju" [Spring call-up to the Russian army], RFI, 9 April 2011, https://www.rfi.fr/ru/obshchii/20110409-vesennii-prizyv-v-rossiiskuyu-armiyu
82. Interview 12, 21 February 2020.
83. Ivan Konovalov, "Kontrol'nyĭ vystrel v generalov" [Check shot at the generals], *Kommersant*, 8 July 2010, https://www.kommersant.ru/doc/1484352
84. Nikolai Makarov, "Put' prob i oshibok vynuzhdennyĭ" [The forced path of trial and error], *Voenno-Promyshlennyi Kurier*, 30 March 2011, https://vpk-news.ru/articles/7369
85. Ivan Safronov, "Sergeĭ Shoĭgu izbavilsia ot lishnikh bumag" [Sergei Shoigu got rid of unnecessary paperwork], *Kommersant*, 22 January 2013, https://www.kommersant.ru/doc/2109874
86. Olesya Ostapchuk, "Tam takoe bratstvo" [There is such brotherhood], 2020, https://holod.media/sparringi-omon
87. "Sentence Upheld of Russian Soldier Who Killed Eight after Brutal Hazing," Radio Free Europe/Radio Liberty, https://www.rferl.org/a/russia-soldier-shooting-spree-hazing-sentence-confirmed/31217223.html
88. "O poriadke raboty Gosudarstvennoĭ Dumy na 22 noiabria 1995 goda" [On the order of work of the State Duma for 22 November 1995], State Duma (1995), http://transcript.duma.gov.ru/
89. For more, see: Dom Russkogo Zarubezhiia imeni Aleksandra Solzhenitsina, "Predmetnye i dokumental'nye Svidetel'stva Pervoj Mirovoj Vojny v Muzee Russkogo Zarubezh'ja" [Object and

documentary evidence of the First World War in the Museum of the Russian Abroad], https://www.domrz.ru/exhibition/56251_predmetnye_i_dokumentalnye_svidetelstva_pervoy_mirovoy_voyny_v_muzee_russkogo_zarubezhya/, and "'My Death for the Motherland is Happiness': Women, Patriotism, and Soldiering in Russia's Great War, 1914–1917," History Cooperative, 29 May 2004, https://historycooperative.org/journal/my-death-for-the-motherland-is-happiness-women-patriotism-and-soldiering-in-russias-great-war-1914-1917/

90. Brannon, *Russian Civil–Military Relations*, 19–23.
91. Clint Reach et al., "Russian Assessments and Applications of the Correlation of Forces and Means," RAND Corporation, 2020, https://www.rand.org/pubs/research_reports/RR4235.html

3. WINDS OF CHANGE?

1. Daria Burlakova, "Khronika gibeli podlodki 'Kursk' i sokhraneniia pamaiti o nei v obshchestve" [Chronicle of the loss of the Kursk submarine and the preservation of its memory in society], *Kommersant*, 12 August 2022, https://www.kommersant.ru/projects/kursk/timeline
2. "'Popytka prezidenta opravdat'sja': Jefir pro 'Kursk' Poslednjaja peredacha Sergeja Dorenko na ORT; Imenno takim on ostanetsja v istorii russkoj zhurnalistiki" ["President's attempt to justify himself": The broadcast about "Kursk" Sergei Dorenko's last program on ORT; This is how he will remain in the history of Russian journalism], Meduza, 5 September 2019, https://meduza.io/feature/2019/05/09/popytka-prezidenta-opravdatsya-efir-pro-kursk
3. Denis Dmitriev, "'We Couldn't Tell the Relatives': Declassified Transcripts Show that Putin as Obsessed with Polling Even as Bill Clinton Consoled Him after the Kursk Submarine Disaster," Meduza, 6 October 2020, https://meduza.io/en/feature/2020/10/06/we-couldn-t-tell-the-relatives
4. Carolina Vendil Pallin, *Russian Military Reform: A Failed Exercise in Defence Decision Making*, 1st edn (Routledge, 2008), 122.
5. Levada Center, "Sbornik obshchestvennoe mnenie 2016."
6. Kimberly Marten, "The 'KGB State' and Russian Political and Foreign Policy Culture," *Journal of Slavic Military Studies* 30, no. 2 (2017): 131–51, https://doi.org/10.1080/13518046.2017.1270053
7. Boris Voicekhovsky, "'Prodali korovu—kupili avtomat': Kak dagestantsy pervymi vstretili boevikov Basaeva i spasli Rossiiu ot

raspada" [Sold a cow and bought a rifle: How Dagestanis were the first to meet Basayev's militants and save Russia from disintegration], Lenta.ru, 8 July 2019, https://lenta.ru/articles/2019/08/07/vtorayachechnya/

8. "Vtorzhenie boevikov v Dagestan (1999)" [Invasion of Dagestan by militants (1999)], Kavkazsky Uzel, 8 July 2024, https://www.kavkaz-uzel.eu/articles/247053
9. Vladimir Putin, "Poslanie Prezidenta Rossii Vladimira Putina Federal'nomu Sobraniju RF" [Russian president Vladimir Putin's address to the Federal Assembly of the Russian Federation], 5 October 2006, http://www.consultant.ru/document/cons_doc_LAW_60109/#dst0
10. Alexei Arbatov, "Yabloko i armiia" [Yabloko and army], Yabloko, 1999, https://www.yabloko.ru/Themes/Defence/yabl-arm.html
11. Sergei Ishenko, "Sluzhit' by rad" [I would love to serve], *Trud*, no. 67, 11 April 2001, http://milprob.narod.ru/11.04.01trud67.htm; Sergei Ishenko, "Armiia ne byvaet besplatnoĭ" [The army doesn't come free], *Trud*, no. 86, 15 May 2001, http://milprob.narod.ru/11.04.01trud67.htm
12. VCIOM, "'Dedovshhina': Glavnaja prichina uklonenija molodyh ljudej ot armii" ["Dedovshchina" is the main reason why young men dodge the draft], VCIOM.ru, 13 February 2006, https://wciom.ru/analytical-reviews/analiticheskii-obzor/dedovshhina-glavnaya-prichina-ukloneniya-molodykh-lyudej-ot-armii
13. Dmitry Litovkin, "Minoborony raskrylo voennuju tajnu" [The Ministry of Defense revealed a military secret], *Izvestiia*, 26 November 2002, https://iz.ru/news/270107
14. Maia Kipp and Aleksandr Golts, *Military Reform and Militarism in Russia* (Lynne Rienner, 2018), 109–10.
15. Vladimir Temnyi, "Grani.Ru: Nepobedimaja i kriminal'naja" [Grani.ru: Invincible and criminal], 25 March 2003, https://graniru.org/War/m.27112.html
16. Nikolai Pankov, "My objazany sberech' oficerskij korpus" [We owe it to ourselves to preserve the officer corps], *Red Star*, 1 September 2003, http://old.redstar.ru/2003/01/09_01/1_01.html
17. Young Russians can receive a deferral from mandatory military service if they are enrolled in full-time education at accredited institutions, such as universities, vocational schools or postgraduate programs. This includes students pursuing bachelor's, specialist, master's or PhD degrees, as well as those in medical residency or scientific training. In some cases, full-time academic staff or researchers at state-approved

institutions may also qualify for deferral based on their professional role. Therefore, some male students pursue academic studies, including at PhD level, solely to avoid the military draft.

18. Vremya Novostei, "S tochnost' do centa Fond INDEM pytaetsja vychislit' masshtaby korrupcii v Rossii" [To the penny, the INDEM Foundation tries to calculate the scale of corruption in Russia], NRU HSE, 21 July 2005, https://www.hse.ru/news/1163615/1122771.html
19. Levada Center, "Rossiĭskaiā armiiā" [Russian army], 2019, https://www.levada.ru/2019/06/18/rossijskaya-armiya-3/
20. Levada Center, "Rol' institutov" [The role of institutions], 3 April 2019, https://www.levada.ru/2019/03/04/rol-institutov-2/
21. Levada Center, "Rossiĭskaiā armiiā."
22. Interview 19, 17 May 2021.
23. "Vstupitel'noe slovo na sovmestnom zasedanii Soveta Bezopasnosti i prezidiuma Gosudarstvennogo soveta 'Ob osnovah politiki v oblasti razvitija oboronno-promyshlennogo kompleksa na period do 2010 goda i dal'nejshuju perspektivu'" [Opening remarks at the joint meeting of the Security Council and the Presidium of the State Council on "The fundamentals of policy in the field of defense industry development for the period up to 2010 and beyond"], President of Russia, 16 November 2001, http://kremlin.ru/events/president/transcripts/21383
24. Ilja Bulavinov, "Voenno-promyshlennyj kompleks" [Military-industrial complex], *Kommersant*, 4 December 2001, https://www.kommersant.ru/doc/300259
25. Vladimir Mukhin, "Gosudarstvennaja ideja nedovooruzhenija" [The state idea of disarmament], 19 January 2009, http://nvo.ng.ru/wars/2009-01-19/1_idea.html
26. Parts of this section were included in a report published by the Center for Strategic and International Studies (CSIS): Kirill Shamiev, "Understanding Senior Leadership Dynamics within the Russian Military," Understanding the Russian Military Today, CSIS, 2021, https://www.csis.org/analysis/understanding-senior-leadership-dynamics-within-russian-military
27. Interview 19, 17 May 2021.
28. "Sergei Ivanov: Ot KGB do prirodoohrannoj dejatel'nosti" [Sergei Ivanov: From the KGB to environmental activities], diletant.media, 8 December 2016, https://diletant.media/articles/30369167/
29. Sergei Ivanov, "Sergej Ivanov: 'Velika Rossija, veliki i ee problemy'"

[Sergei Ivanov: "As big as Russia is, so big are its problems"], 26 April 2000, https://aif.ru/archive/1638930
30. Interview 16, 12 May 2021.
31. Katia Arenina, "Unnatural Numbers: Part Two," Proekt, 7 July 2022, https://www.proekt.media/en/narrative-en/putin-ratings/
32. Roman Shleinov, "Put' Sergeja Ivanova ot razvedchika do administratora" [Sergei Ivanov's journey from intelligence officer to administrator], Vedomosti, 18 March 2013, https://www.vedomosti.ru/library/articles/2013/03/18/nu_kakoj_ya_ministr_oborony
33. Ivanov, "Sergei Ivanov."
34. Miller and Trenin, Vooryzhennie sily Rossii.
35. Interview 24, 25 May 2021.
36. Aleksandr Golts, "Mal'chik zamechatel'no igral Olivera Tvista" [The boy played Oliver Twist wonderfully], New Times, 26 February 2007, https://newtimes.ru/articles/detail/10119
37. Interview 22, 20 May 2021.
38. Interview 17, 13 May 2021.
39. Sergei Krivenko, "Alternativnaya grazhdanskaya zluzhba v Rossiiskoy Federacii," in Al'ternativnaja grazhdanskaja sluzhba: Standarty i podhody k reformirovaniju; Sbornik statej i dokumentov [Alternative civil service: Standards and approaches to reform; A collection of articles and documents], ed. Mikhail Pashkevich et al. (Lawtrend, 2010), https://www.lawtrend.org/social-actions/alternativnaya-grazhdanskaya-sluzhba-standarty-i-podhody-k-reformirovaniyu-sbornik-statej-i-dokumentov-tsentr-pravovoj-transformatsii-sost-m-pashkevich-e-tonkacheva-o-domorad-e-kovaleva-minsk-monli
40. Interview 17, 13 May 2021.
41. Pavel Gazukin, "Russian Armed Forces in the Post-Soviet Period: Problems of Reforming and Military Building; 1992–2001," Politeia: Journal of Political Theory, Political Philosophy and Sociology of Politics 20, no. 2 (2001): 66–7, https://doi.org/10.30570/2078-5089-2001-20-2-44-71
42. Interview 20, 18 May 2021.
43. Interview 20, 18 May 2021.
44. Interview 20, 18 May 2021.
45. Artem Krechetnikov, "Geroi i antigeroi Kavkaza: Anatolii Kvashnin" [Heroes and anti-heroes of the Caucasus: Anatoly Kvashnin], BBC Russian Service, 3 December 2004, http://news.bbc.co.uk/hi/russian/russia/newsid_4067000/4067153.stm
46. Aleksandr Tolmachev, "Glava Genshtaba Kvashnin dovel podchinennogo do infarkta so smertel'nym ishodom" [Chief of

General Staff Kvashnin drove a subordinate to a fatal heart attack], Compromat.ru, 20 February 2002, http://www.compromat.ru/page_11552.htm
47. Aleksandr Golts, "Mertvyj mozg Genshtaba" [Dead brain of the General Staff], Compromat.ru, 7 May 2004, http://www.compromat.ru/page_15171.htm
48. Konstantin Lantratov, "Armija budet napolovinu kontraktnoj" [The army will be half contract], 11 July 2003, https://www.kommersant.ru/doc/395115
49. Alexander Babakin, "Sekretnoe zaveshchanie generala Kvashnina" [General Kvashnin's secret will], *Nezavisimaya Gazeta*, 23 July 2004, https://www.ng.ru/politics/2004-07-23/1_kvashnin.html
50. Prominent Russian politicians, reformers and public figures who played important roles in shaping Russia's post-Soviet transition during the 1990s and early 2000s. Most were associated with liberal economic reforms and democratic politics. Nemtsov served as deputy prime minister under Boris Yeltsin and was once seen as a possible presidential successor. Gaidar was the architect of Russia's early 1990s "shock therapy" economic reforms as acting prime minister and minister of economy under Yeltsin. Kirienko briefly served as prime minister of Russia in 1998 during a major financial crisis and later led Rosatom (the state nuclear energy corporation). Khakamada is an economist, public intellectual and one of the few prominent female politicians in post-Soviet Russia; she has been a consistent advocate of liberal democracy, women's rights and small business development. Chubais was the key architect of privatization in the 1990s and a top economic official under Yeltsin. He served as head of the State Property Committee, first deputy prime minister and later as head of the national energy monopoly RAO UES.
51. Kipp and Golts, *Military Reform and Militarism in Russia*, 87–90.
52. The Council of Ministers under Kasyanov refers to the Russian federal government. Kasyanov, a former finance official and debt negotiator, was appointed prime minister in May 2000, succeeding Putin as acting prime minister. The Council of Ministers was responsible for implementing federal policy in areas such as the economy, social development, defense and law enforcement. It was composed of the prime minister, deputy prime ministers, federal ministers and heads of major federal agencies.
53. The pension reform under Mikhail Kasyanov's government was a complex restructuring of Russia's pension system aimed at addressing long-term financial sustainability and demographic pressures. It

introduced a three-pillar pension structure in 2002. The reform faced limited public awareness, low trust in private asset managers and poor financial literacy, reducing its effectiveness. See Ivan Grigoriev and Anna Dekalchuk, "School of Autocracy: Pensions and Labour Reforms of the First Putin Administration," SSRN Scholarly Paper no. 2572992 (Social Science Research Network, 3 March 2015), https://doi.org/10.2139/ssrn.2572992; Sarah Wilson Sokhey, "Market-Oriented Reforms as a Tool of State-Building: Russian Pension Reform in 2001," *Europe-Asia Studies* 67, no. 5 (2015): 695–717, https://doi.org/10.1080/09668136.2015.1045453

54. Interview 20, 18 May 2021.
55. Arbatov, "Yabloko i armiia."
56. Pavel Nastin, "General Armii Andreĭ Nikolaev otmetil 70-letniĭ iubileĭ" [Army general Andrey Nikolaev celebrates seventieth anniversary], TV Zvezda, 21 April 2019, https://tvzvezda.ru/news/20194221236-NvoJc.html
57. Interview 17, 13 May 2021.
58. Celestine Bohlen, "Putin's Team Hammers Out a Plan to Untwist, Level and Streamline Russia's Economy," *New York Times*, 2 April 2000, https://www.nytimes.com/2000/04/02/world/putin-s-team-hammers-out-a-plan-to-untwist-level-and-streamline-russia-s-economy.html
59. Putin's reform of the federal districts in May 2000 was one of his earliest attempts to centralize political authority. The reform created seven federal districts, each headed by a presidential envoy appointed directly by the president. The envoys were empowered to monitor regional governors, oversee local courts and coordinate federal agencies within the district.
60. Sutela, *Political Economy of Putin's Russia*, 32–45; Gel'man, *Authoritarian Modernization in Russia*, 148–200.
61. Vladimir Putin, "Annual Address to the Federal Assembly of the Russian Federation, 2001," President of Russia, 2001, http://en.kremlin.ru/events/president/transcripts/21216; Vladimir Putin, "Annual Address to the Federal Assembly of the Russian Federation, 2002," President of Russia, 2002, http://en.kremlin.ru/events/president/transcripts/21567
62. Dmitry Krylov, "Programma-2000: Chto sdelano" [Program-2000: What is done], Nauchno-obrazovatel'nyĭ portal IQ, 25 January 2010, https://iq.hse.ru/news/177674728.html
63. Interview 20, 18 May 2021.
64. Vitaly Tsymbal and Vasilii Zacepin, "Reforma armii" [Army reform],

Kommersant, 29 October 2007, https://www.kommersant.ru/doc/819269

65. "Voennaya Doktrina Rossiiskoi Federacii" [Military Doctrine of the Russian Federation], 2000, https://www.ng.ru/politics/2000-04-22/5_doktrina.html
66. Interview 23, 21 May 2021.
67. Federal'nyj zakon "Ob oborone."
68. Interview 23, 21 May 2021.
69. Gazukin, "Russian Armed Forces in the Post-Soviet Period."
70. Yabloko, "Povyshenie boesposobnosti vooruzhennyh sil RF, ih strukturnaja perestrojka, napravlennaja na sohranenie strategicheskoj stabil'nosti v mire" [Improving the combat effectiveness of the armed forces of the Russian Federation and restructuring them to maintain strategic stability in the world], Epicenter, 2003, https://www.yabloko.ru/Publ/Army/yabloko_ar0002.html
71. Interview 20, 18 May 2021.
72. Interview 24, 25 May 2021.
73. Interview 21, 20 May 2021; interview 24, 25 May 2021.
74. Interview 21, 20 May 2021.
75. MoD, "Zadachi vooruzhennyh sil Rossijskoj Federacii" [Tasks of the armed forces of the Russian Federation], 2021, https://structure.mil.ru/mission/tasks.htm
76. Interview 23, 21 May 2021.
77. Sergei Minaev, "Egor Gaĭdar: Prizyv v armiĭu; Éto nalog, kotoryĭ nado snizhat'" [Yegor Gaidar: Conscription is a tax that must be reduced], *Vechernyaya Moskva*, 19 December 2001.
78. Early military training in Russian schools involves preparing youth for future military service, patriotic education and basic defense readiness. Most Russian secondary schools include elements of "initial military training," often integrated into the "Basics of Life Safety" course.
79. Mikhail Demidenko, "'Jabloko' nachalo vojnu s SPS" ["Yabloko" started a war with the SPS], *Kommersant*, 21 June 2003, https://www.kommersant.ru/doc/390524
80. Interview 25, 12 July 2021.
81. Interview 21, 20 May 2021.
82. Interview 17, 13 May 2021.
83. Interview 19, 17 May 2021.
84. Kvashnin, "Perspektivnaia sistema planirovaniia stroitel'stva vooruzhennykh sil."

85. Kvashnin, "Perspektivnaia sistema planirovaniia stroitel'stva vooruzhennykh sil."
86. Egor Gaidar, "Gaidar's Letter to Putin," personal communication, 14 May 2003.
87. Gazukin, "Russian Armed Forces in the Post-Soviet Period," 67.
88. Interview 21, 20 May 2021.
89. Vladimir Putin, "Ob obespechenii stroitel'stva i razvitiia vooruzhennykh sil Rossiĭskoĭ Federatsii, sovershenstvovanii ikh struktury" [On ensuring the construction and development of the armed forces of the Russian Federation and improving their structure], President of Russia, 24 March 2001, http://kremlin.ru/acts/bank/14927
90. Putin, "Annual Address to the Federal Assembly of the Russian Federation, 2002."
91. Golts, *Military Reform and Militarism in Russia*, 88–9.
92. Interview 19, 2021.
93. Yabloko, "Povyshenie boesposobnosti vooruzhennyh sil RF."
94. Government of Russia, "O federal'noj celevoj programme 'Perehod k komplektovaniju voennosluzhashhimi, prohodjashhimi voennuju sluzhbu po kontraktu, rjada soedinenij i voinskih chastej' na 2004–2007 gody" [About the federal targeted program "Transition to manning a number of formations and military units with servicemen serving under a contract" for 2004–7], 25 August 2003, http://pravo.gov.ru/proxy/ips/?doc_itself=&backlink=1&nd=102083123&page=1&rdk=5#I0
95. Golts, *Military Reform and Militarism in Russia*, 95–101; "Kak menjalas' shtatnaja chislennost' vooruzhennyh sil RF: Dos'e" [How the staff strength of the armed forces of the Russian Federation changed: Dossier], TASS (Moscow), 17 November 2017, https://tass.ru/info/4135532
96. Interview 5, 2021.
97. Interview 17, 13 May 2021.
98. Francesca Mereu, "Russia: Duma Backs Government-Sponsored Alternative to Army," Archive, Radio Free Europe/Radio Liberty, https://www.rferl.org/a/1099447.html; Mikhail Zherebyatev, "Alternative Community Service in Russia: The Results of Ten Years of Debate," Jamestown Foundation, 28 February 2002, https://jamestown.org/program/alternative-community-service-in-russia-the-results-of-ten-years-of-debate/
99. Interview 17, 13 May 2021.
100. Interview 20, 18 May 2021.

101. Interview 23, 21 May 2021.
102. Interview 16, 12 May 2021.
103. Bulavinov, "Voenno-promyshlennyj kompleks."
104. Irina Granik, "'Budem delat' stavku ne na chiny, a na menedzhment'" ["We will focus on management rather than rank"], *Kommersant*, 30 October 2001, https://www.kommersant.ru/doc/289371
105. Vladimir Putin, "Osnovy gosudarstevennoĭ politiki RF po voennomu stroitelstvu na period do 2010 g." [Basics of state policy on military buildup for the period to 2010], 2002, http://old.nasledie.ru/vlact/5_3/article.php?art=7
106. Vladimir Putin, "Ukaz prezidenta Rossijskoj Federacii 'Voprosy Ministerstva oborony Rossijskoj Federacii i General'nogo shtaba vooruzhennyh sil Rossijskoj Federacii'" [Decree of the president of the Russian Federation "Issues of the Ministry of Defense of the Russian Federation and the General Staff of the armed forces of the Russian Federation"], President of Russia, 9 October 2003, https://www.consultant.ru/document/cons_doc_LAW_44269/
107. Pallin, *Russian Military Reform*, 132.
108. Svetlana Babaeva, "Liubov' Kudelina: 'Ia ne stroiu generalov; Ia prosto s nikh strogo sprashivaiu'" [Lubov Kudelina: "I don't parade generals; I just ask them strictly"], *Izvestiia*, 3 May 2004, https://iz.ru/news/287691
109. Golts, *Military Reform and Militarism in Russia*, 95.
110. Krasnaya Zvezda, "Aktual'nye zadachi razvitija vooruzhennyh sil Rossijskoj Federacii" [Current tasks for development of the armed forces of the Russian Federation], *Krasnaya Zvezda*, 11 October 2003, https://web.archive.org/web/20250715084742/http://old.redstar.ru/2003/10/11_10/3_01.html
111. Vitaly Shlykov, "Voennaja reforma v plany ili blagie namerenija?" [Military reform: Plans or good intentions?], *Otechestvennye zapiski* 8, no. 9 (2002), https://strana-oz.ru/2002/8/voennaya-reforma-v-plany-ili-blagie-namereniya
112. Pallin, *Russian Military Reform*, 128–34.
113. Bulavinov, "Voenno-promyshlennyj kompleks."
114. Granik, "'Budem delat' stavku ne na chiny, a na menedzhment.'"
115. Granik, "'Budem delat' stavku ne na chiny, a na menedzhment.'"
116. Bulavinov, "Voenno-promyshlennyj kompleks."
117. Zweynert, *When Ideas Fail*.
118. MoD, "Aktual'nye zadachi razvitija vooruzhennyh sil Rossijskoj Federacii" [Current development challenges armed forces of the Russian Federation], 2003, https://web.archive.org/

web/20250815002706/http://old.redstar.ru/2003/10/11_10/3_01.html
119. "Mikhail Fradkov: Neodnoznachnye ėpizody biografii" [Mikhail Fradkov: Ambiguous episodes of his biography], Kompromat.ru, 3 February 2004, http://www.compromat.ru/page_10665.htm; Komitet Narodnogo Kontrolya, "Fradkov Mihail Efimovich," 2016, http://comnarcon.com/index.php?id=481
120. Mikhail Glikin, "Sil'nyĭ administrator" [Strong administrator], *Nezavisimaya Gazeta*, 3 February 2004, http://www.ng.ru/politics/2004-03-02/1_fradkov.html
121. "M.Fradkov rasskazal o prioritetakh novogo pravitel'stva" [Mikhail Fradkov spoke about the priorities of the new government], RBC, 3 May 2004, https://www.rbc.ru/politics/05/03/2004/5703b5ef9a7947783a5a52a5
122. Ekaterina Adamova et al., "Vse pravitel'stvo" [All of the government], *Kommersant*, 28 June 2004, https://www.kommersant.ru/doc/485775
123. Adamova et al., "Vse pravitel'stvo."
124. "Biografija Aleksej Kudrin" [Biography of Alexei Kudrin], Peoples.ru, Luydi: Biographii, istoriim facty, fotograpfii, 19 March 2004, https://www.peoples.ru/state/minister/russia/kudrin/index.html
125. Rinat Tairov, "Kudrin rasskazal o spasshem ėkonomiku Rossii reshenii Putina" [Kudrin told about Putin's decision that saved Russia's economy], Forbes.ru, 25 December 2019, https://www.forbes.ru/newsroom/obshchestvo/390145-kudrin-rasskazal-o-spasshem-ekonomiku-rossii-reshenii-putina
126. Yuri Baluyevsky, "Strategicheskaĭa stabil'nost' v ėpokhu globalizat͡sii: Obshchaĭa povestka dnĭa dlĭa Rossii i SShA" [Strategic stability in an era of globalization: A common agenda for Russia and the United States], in *Voennaja bezopasnost' Rossijskoj Federacii v 21 Veke* [Military security of the Russian Federation in the twenty-first century] (Flot, 2004), https://flot.com/publications/books/shelf/safety/4.htm; Baluyevsky, "Teoreticheskie i metodologicheskie osnovy formirovanija voennoj doktriny Rossijskoj Federacii" [Theoretical and methodological foundations of the military doctrine of the Russian Federation], *Voennaya Mysl* [Military thought], March 2007, 14–21; Sergei Migulin, "I͡uriĭ Nikolaevich Baluevskiĭ: Nachal'nik General'nogo Shtaba VS RF" [Yury Baluyevsky: Chief of the General Staff of the Russian armed forces], Encyclopedia of the Ministry of Defense, 2017, https://topwar.ru/115035-yuriy-nikolaevich-baluevskiy-nachalnik-generalnogo-shtaba-armii.html

127. Alexei Kozlov, "Baluevskiĭ 'zaigralsi͡a'" [Baluyevsky is "overdoing it"], The Moscow Post, 21 March 2008, http://www.moscow-post.su/politics/baluevskij_zaigralsja/
128. "After the INF Treaty: An Objective Look at US and Russian Compliance, plus a New Arms Control Regime," Russia Matters, 7 December 2017, https://www.russiamatters.org/analysis/after-inf-treaty-objective-look-us-and-russian-compliance-plus-new-arms-control-regime; Greg Thielmann, "Moving beyond INF Treaty Compliance Issues," Arms Control Association, https://www.armscontrol.org/blog/2014-09-05/moving-beyond-inf-treaty-compliance-issues
129. In the Russian military, brigades and divisions are both large military formations, but they differ in size, structure, command role and operational purpose. A division usually has 10,000–15,000 personnel on paper, while an average brigade houses around 3,000–5,000 service members.
130. Gavrilov and Chernyak, "I͡uriĭ Baluevskiĭ: My ne sobiraemsi͡a voevat' s NATO."
131. Roman Streshnev and Yuriya Shapilova, "Most k dialogu" [Bridge to dialogue], Krasnaya Zvezda, 4 April 2006, https://web.archive.org/web/20240728175800/http://old.redstar.ru/2006/04/04_04/1_02.html
132. Yuri Baluevsky, "Global Peace Security Index: The Russian Dimension," Index Bezopasnosti 81, no. 1 (2007), https://web.archive.org/web/20240901211217/https://pircenter.org/wp-content/uploads/2023/12/2007-SI-INT-%E2%84%961-81.pdf
133. Miriam Elder, "Vladimir Putin Expected to Face Questions over Protests on Live TV Show," The Guardian, 14 December 2011, https://www.theguardian.com/world/2011/dec/14/vladimir-putin-question-protests-live-tv
134. Boris Nemtsov was a former physicist turned reformist politician who became one of the most prominent liberal voices in post-Soviet Russia. Rising to national prominence as the governor of Nizhny Novgorod oblast (1991–7), he later served as deputy prime minister and minister of fuel and energy under President Yeltsin. In 1999, he co-founded the SPS and became a leading critic of Putin, denouncing government corruption, democratic backsliding and Russia's interventions abroad. Nemtsov continued to champion democracy, transparency and human rights through mass protests and

investigative reports—remaining in active opposition until he was assassinated near the Kremlin in 2015.
135. Alexander Piskunov is a Russian statesman and retired major general who served in the Strategic Missile Forces. He was a People's Deputy of the RSFSR Supreme Soviet (1990–3), deputy chairman of its Defense Committee and later served in the State Duma, where he chaired or held senior positions in the defense and budget committees. In 2001, Piskunov was appointed auditor of the Accounts Chamber of the Russian Federation, overseeing federal budget expenditures until 2013.
136. Interview 23, 21 May 2021.
137. United Russia initially won 222 seats out of 450, which is short of the 300 needed for a constitutional majority (two-thirds of the Duma). However, it formed a pro-Kremlin supermajority by allying with other smaller pro-government factions and deputies from single-mandate districts. United Russia consolidated control over more than 300 seats, giving it the power to amend the Constitution, including changes like abolishing direct gubernatorial elections (2004), dominate committee appointments and legislative procedures and limit the influence of independent deputies and opposition parties.
138. Mikhail Lukin, "'Vlast'" predstavlíaet spravochnik'" ["The Vlast" presents the guidebook], *Kommersant*, 19 January 2004, https://www.kommersant.ru/doc/441446
139. Federal'nyj zakon "O vnesenii izmenenij v nekotorye zakonodatel'nye akty Rossijskoj Federacii i priznanii utrativshimi silu nekotoryh zakonodatel'nyh aktov Rossijskoj Federacii v svjazi s osushhestvleniem mer po sovershenstvovaniju gosudarstvennogo upravlenija" [Federal law "On introducing amendments to certain legislative acts of the Russian Federation and the repeal of certain legislative acts of the Russian Federation in connection with the implementation of measures to improve public administration], 58, the State Duma 4, FZ (2004), http://www.consultant.ru/document/cons_doc_LAW_48233/
140. Three major Russian state-owned corporations central to the country's industrial and technological policy. Rusnano was tasked with developing Russia's nanotechnology and innovation sectors, aiming to modernize the economy beyond raw materials, though it struggled with profitability and governance issues. Rosatom, the state nuclear energy corporation, plays a dual role as a domestic energy provider and a key actor in global nuclear exports, managing both civilian and military nuclear infrastructure. Rostec integrates hundreds of firms in

aerospace, electronics and arms production, serving as a cornerstone of Russia's military-industrial complex and a strategic tool for import substitution and defense modernization.

141. Yakov Pappe and Ekaterina Drankina, "Kak razvivaiut Rossiiu: Gosudarstvo i ko" [How Russia is developed: State and corp], *Kommersant*, 29 September 2008, https://www.kommersant.ru/doc/1031363
142. Sutela, *Political Economy of Putin's Russia*, 66–70.
143. Karen Agamirov, "Tragediia riadovogo Andreia Sycheva: Ocherednoe ChP v rossiiskoi armii ili ee sistema" [The tragedy of Private Andrey Sychev: Another emergency in the Russian army or its system], Radio Liberty, 31 January 2006, https://www.svoboda.org/a/130299.html
144. "'Delo Sycheva' zavershilos': Glavnogo obviniaemogo posadili na 4 goda" ["Sychev's case" is over: The main defendant was jailed for four years], NEWSru.com, 26 September 2006, https://palm.newsru.com/russia/26sep2006/verdict.html
145. Yelena Pankratieva, "'London' Andreia Sycheva: Kak zhivet soldat, stavshii tiazhelym invalidom posle izdevatel'stv v Cheliabinskom tankovom uchilishche" [Andrei Sychev's "London": How a soldier who became severely disabled after abuse at the Chelyabinsk Tank School lives], 74.ru, 9 January 2024, https://74.ru/text/health/2024/01/09/73099079/
146. "Voennyi prokuror RF: 'Nekachestvennye' prizyvniki oslabili VS Rossii" [Military prosecutor of the Russian Federation: "Substandard" conscripts have weakened the Russian armed forces], RBC, 3 June 2003, https://www.rbc.ru/society/03/06/2003/5703bb449a7947afa08c8a43
147. Interview 22, 20 May 2021.
148. Interview 20, 18 May 2021.
149. Igor Plugatarev, "Minoborony: Vekhi i veshki 2006 goda" [Ministry of Defense: Milestones and landmarks of 2006], *Nezavisimoye Voennoe Obozrenie*, 29 December 2006, http://nvo.ng.ru/forces/2006-12-29/1_minoborony.html
150. Andrei Garavsky, "OPK: Starye problemy i novye zadachi" [Defense industry: Old problems and new challenges], *Krasnaya Zvezda*, 2 November 2006, http://old.redstar.ru/2006/02/11_02/4_01.html
151. Alexandra Gritskova et al., "Sergeĭ Chemezov sygral v monopoliiu" [Sergei Chemezov played Monopoly], *Kommersant*, no. 235, 15 December 2006.

152. Rosoboronzakaz, "Federalnaya sluzhba po oboronnomy zakazu (Rosoboronzakaz)" [Federal service on defense order (Rosoboronzakaz)], Rosoboronzakaz, 17 February 2012, https://web.archive.org/web/20120217190506/http://www.fsoz.gov.ru/about/head/index.html
153. Garavsky, "OPK: Starye problemy i novye zadachi."
154. Ilja Bulavinov, "Prezident rasporjadilsja integrirovat' oboronku" [The president ordered the integration of the defense industry], *Kommersant*, 31 October 2001, https://www.kommersant.ru/doc/289595
155. "Thesis," Klub Voenachalnikov Rossiiskoi Federacii, 20 May 2009, 19, https://web.archive.org/web/20250428124404/https://kvrf.org/wp-content/uploads/2015/11/sovremennyj-etap-voennogo-stroitelstva-v-rossijskoj-federatsii-soderzhanie-sroki-metody.pdf
156. Interview 24, 25 May 2021.
157. Kulikov, "Thesis," 7–8.
158. Golts, *Military Reform and Militarism in Russia*, 97–101.
159. Kira Vasilieva, "Dedovshhina po kontraktu" [Contract hazing], Newizv.ru, 2 December 2009, https://web.archive.org/web/20231204233937/https://newizv.ru/news/2009-02-12/dedovschina-po-kontraktu-100865
160. Alexei Maslov, "Armii nuzhny professionaly" [The army needs professionals], *Armeisky Sbornik*, no. 1 (January 2008): 70.
161. World Bank, "Military Expenditure (Current USD): Russian Federation Data,"World Development Indicators, World Bank Group, 2008, https://data.worldbank.org/indicator/MS.MIL.XPND.CD?end=2008&locations=RU&start=2000
162. Mukhin, "Gosudarstvennaja ideja nedovooruzhenija"; "Gosudarstvennye programmy vooruzhenija Rossijskoj Federacii: Problemy ispolnenija i potencial optimizacii" [State armament programs of the Russian Federation: Implementation issues and potential for optimization], CAST, 21 April 2015, http://cast.ru/news/opublikovan-analiticheskiy-doklad-gosudarstvennye-programmy-vooruzheniya-rossiyskoy-federatsii-probl.html; "Gosudarstvennye programmy vooruzhenija Rossii: Dos'e" [Russian state armament programs: Dossier], TASS, 26 February 2018, https://tass.ru/info/4987920
163. Garavsky, "OPK: Starye problemy i novye zadachi."
164. Igor Plugatarev, "'Innovacionnaja armija': Chto jeto?" ["Innovative army": What is that?], *NezavisimoyeVoennoe Obozrenie*, 15 February 2008, http://nvo.ng.ru/forces/2008-02-15/1_innovations.html?print=Y
165. Interview 17, 13 May 2021.

166. Tsymbal and Zacepin, "Reforma armii."
167. Pallin, *Russian Military Reform*, 135.
168. Pallin, *Russian Military Reform*, 136–7.
169. Vladimir Putin, "Opublikovano interv'ju Vladimira Putina glavnym redaktoram gazet 'Izvestija,' 'Komsomol'skaja pravda,' 'Moskovskij komsomolec' i 'Trud'" [Published an interview with Vladimir Putin to the chief editors of Izvestia, Komsomolskaya Pravda, Moskovsky Komsomolets and Trud], President of Russia, 21 March 2001, http://kremlin.ru/events/president/news/40661
170. Mark Episkopos, "Conspiracy Theories about the Sunken Kursk Submarine Resurface in Russia," *The National Interest*, 23 November 2021, https://nationalinterest.org/blog/buzz/conspiracy-theories-about-sunken-kursk-submarine-resurface-russia-196991/

4. FROM COMBAT EFFECTIVENESS TO OVERSIGHT OVERLOAD

1. "Voina Rossii s Gruziei: Khronologiia 2008 goda" [Russia's war with Georgia: Chronology of 2008], Refworld, 8 April 2014, https://www.refworld.org/ru/coi/countrynews/iwpr/2014/ru/136499
2. Olga Allenova, "Pervaia mirotvorcheskaia voina" [The first peacekeeping war], *Kommersant*, 9 August 2008, https://www.kommersant.ru/doc/1009540
3. Mikhail Kirillov, "Osetino–gruzinskii konflikt: Piatidnevnaia voina; Prichiny, khod boev, posledstviia [Ossetian–Georgian conflict: Five-day war; Causes, course of fighting, consequences], Lenta.ru, 8 August 2023, https://lenta.ru/articles/2023/08/08/08_08_08/
4. "Tsentr Analiza Strategii i Tekhnologii provel nezavisimyi podschet poter' Rossiiskoi tekhniki v voine s Gruziei" [The Center for Analysis of Strategies and Technologies conducted an independent calculation of Russian equipment losses in the war with Georgia], Kavkazsky Uzel, 8 April 2010, https://www.kavkaz-uzel.eu/articles/172524
5. Michael Kofman, "Russian Performance in the Russo-Georgian War Revisited," War on the Rocks, 4 September 2018, https://warontherocks.com/2018/09/russian-performance-in-the-russo-georgian-war-revisited/
6. Viktor Litovkin, "Genshtab informiruet zagranitsu" [The General Staff informs abroad], *Nezavisimaya Gazeta*, 26 December 2008, https://nvo.ng.ru/forces/2008-12-26/1_genshtab.html
7. Wilson, "Modernization or More of the Same in Russia."
8. Dvorkin and Arbatov, *Military Reform in Russia*; Bettina Renz, *Russia's Military Revival* (Polity, 2018).

9. Vladimir Putin, "Speech and the Following Discussion at the Munich Conference on Security Policy," 10 February 2007, http://en.kremlin.ru/events/president/transcripts/24034
10. Julie Newton and William Tompson, *Institutions, Ideas and Leadership in Russian Politics* (Springer, 2010).
11. Interview 19, 17 May 2021.
12. Several citizens of the UAE, Saudi Arabia and Qatar participated in or funded the Chechen separatist movement. One of the most famous was Ibn al-Khattab (Saudi Jihadist, killed by a poisoned letter in 2002). Ayman al-Zawahiri, Bin Laden's deputy, reportedly stated: "[I]f the Chechens and other Caucasus mujahideen reach the shores of the oil-rich Caspian, the only thing that will separate them from Afghanistan will be the neutral state of Turkmenistan. This will form a mujahid Islamic belt to the south of Russia." See "The Rise and Fall of Foreign Fighters in Chechnya," Jamestown Foundation, 31 January 2006, https://jamestown.org/program/the-rise-and-fall-of-foreign-fighters-in-chechnya/
13. Interview 20, 18 May 2021.
14. Allen C. Lynch, *How Russia Is Not Ruled: Reflections on Russian Political Development* (Cambridge University Press, 2005).
15. Vladimir Putin, "Obrashchenie prezidenta Rossii Vladimira Putina" [Address by Russian president Vladimir Putin], President of Russia, 9 April 2004, http://kremlin.ru/events/president/transcripts/22589
16. Interview 29, 23 April 2018.
17. Andrew E. Kramer and Thom Shanker, "Russia Steps Back from Key Arms Treaty," *New York Times*, 14 July 2007, https://www.nytimes.com/2007/07/14/world/europe/14cnd-russia.html
18. Interview 30, 20 April 2018.
19. Parts of this section were included in a report published by CSIS: Shamiev, "Understanding Senior Leadership Dynamics within the Russian Military."
20. Henry E. Hale and Timothy J. Colton, "Russians and the Putin–Medvedev 'Tandemocracy': A Survey-Based Portrait of the 2007–2008 Election Season," *Problems of Post-Communism* 57, no. 2 (2010): 3–20, https://doi.org/10.2753/PPC1075-8216570201
21. Irina Vyunova, "Kremlevskiĭ vizir'" [The Kremlin vizier], *Profil*, 17 November 2003, http://www.compromat.ru/page_26199.htm
22. Ilya Zhegulev, "Druz'ja i poputchiki Medvedeva" [Medvedev's friends and companions], SmartMoney, 17 September 2007, http://www.compromat.ru/page_21421.htm
23. Zweynert, *When Ideas Fail*, 92–3.

24. Zweynert, *When Ideas Fail*, 86–90.
25. Interview 32, 28 April 2018.
26. Alexei Nikolsky et al., "Anatoly Serdyukov: 'Not a Person, a Function,'" *Vedomosti*, 23 April 2012, https://www.vedomosti.ru/library/articles/2012/04/23/eto_ne_chelovek_eto_funkciya
27. Nikolsky et al., "Anatoly Serdyukov: 'Not a Person, a Function.'"
28. Steven Lee Myers and Andrew E. Kramer, "From Ashes of Yukos, New Russian Oil Giant Emerges," *New York Times*, 27 March 2007, https://www.nytimes.com/2007/03/27/world/europe/27russia.html
29. Associated Press, "Russia Violated Rights of Yukos Oil Company, Rules European Court," *The Guardian*, 20 September 2011, https://www.theguardian.com/world/2011/sep/20/russia-violated-yukos-rights-court
30. Charles K. Bartles, "Defense Reforms of Russian Defense Minister Anatolii Serdyukov," *Journal of Slavic Military Studies* 24, no. 1 (2011): 55–80, https://doi.org/10.1080/13518046.2011.549038
31. Nikolsky et al., "Anatoly Serdyukov: 'Not a Person, a Function.'"
32. Interview 29, 23 April 2018.
33. Aleksandra Zaitseva, "Est' u oficera test,'" Gazeta.ru, 19 September 2007, https://www.gazeta.ru/politics/2007/09/19_a_2172876.shtml
34. A high-level advisory and coordination body that discusses and approves major decisions related to defense planning, military development, procurement and organizational reforms. It is chaired by the minister of defense and includes senior military officials, such as the chief of the General Staff, service branch commanders and heads of military districts. It also includes civilian officials from the ministry and occasionally external participants like representatives of other ministries or the Presidential Administration.
35. Aleksandr Yakovenko, dir., "Sergeĭ Ivanov bol'she ne ministr oborony" [Sergei Ivanov is no longer defense minister], *Segodnia*, NTV, 15 February 2007, 20:00, https://www.ntv.ru/video/103656/
36. Interview 21, 20 May 2021.
37. Interview 21, 20 May 2021.
38. Alyona Pavlova, "Zhenskaia Dolia Ministra Serdyukova," 12 February 2012, http://www.mk.ru/politics/2012/12/02/781903-zhenskaya-dolya-ministra-serdyukova.html
39. Interview 23, 21 May 2021.
40. "Kurirovat' VPK Rossii naznachen Dmitrij Rogozin" [Dmitry Rogozin was appointed to supervise the Russian military-industrial complex], BBC News Russian Service, 23 December 2011, https://www.bbc.

com/russian/russia/2011/12/111223_rogozin_appointment_defence
41. "Biografija Dmitrija Rogozina" [Biography of Dmitry Rogozin], TASS, 24 May 2018, https://tass.ru/info/5230231
42. Kirill Shishov, "Modernizatsiia VPK: Den'gi na veter ili ryvok vpered" [Modernization of the military-industrial complex: Money for the wind or a breakthrough], RBC, 29 February 2012, https://www.rbc.ru/economics/29/02/2012/5703f3f19a7947ac81a65570
43. Redakcija Forbes, "Kudrin protiv Medvedeva: Kak sostojalas' otstavka ministra finansov" [Kudrin vs. Medvedev: How the resignation of the minister of finance took place], Forbes.ru, 19 June 2013, https://www.forbes.ru/sobytiya/vlast/240906-kudrin-protiv-medvedeva-kak-sostoyalas-otstavka-ministra-finansov
44. "Biografija Antona Siluanova" [Biography of Anton Siluanov], TASS, 18 May 2018, https://tass.ru/info/5213072
45. Interview 16, 12 May 2021.
46. "Genshtab menjaet furazhku, a Baluevskogo na Makarova," Radio Svoboda, 6 March 2008, https://www.svoboda.org/a/450478.html
47. Interviews 17, 30, 36, April 2018; Alexei Kozlov, "Baluevskij 'zaigralsja,'" Moscow Post, 25 March 2008, http://www.moscow-post.com/politics/baluevskij_zaigralsja/
48. Interviews 28, 16, April 2018.
49. "Nikolaĭ Makarov, èks-nachal'nik Genshtaba: Biografiia" [Nikolai Makarov, ex-chief of the General Staff: Biography], Echo Moskvy, 11 February 2012, https://echo.msk.ru/blog/echomsk/949501-echo/
50. Aleksandr Tikhonov, "Armiia Rossii: Novyĭ oblik" [The Russian army: A new look], *Krasnaya Zvezda*, 15 February 2012, http://archive.redstar.ru/index.php/mohov/item/645-armiya-rossii-novyiy-oblik
51. Elizaveta Orlova, "Na konferentsiiu v Moskvu" [To a conference in Moscow], *Krasnaya Zvezda*, 4 June 2012, http://archive.redstar.ru/index.php/newspaper/item/1637-na-konferentsiyu-v-moskvu
52. Sergei Konovalov, "General'skiĭ demarsh" [General's demarche], *Nezavisimoye Voennoe Obozrenie* (Moscow), 7 May 2011, http://nvo.ng.ru/nvo/2011-07-05/1_demarsh.html
53. Interview 22, 20 May 2021.
54. Dmitry Kartsev, "Nepotopliaemyi" [Unsinkable], *Profil*, 10 December 2009, https://profile.ru/archive/nepotoplyaemyy-121428/
55. Ruslan Pukhov, "Serdyukov Cleans Up the Arbat," Moscow Defense Brief 1/2008, 6–9.
56. Tikhonov, "Army of Russia."

57. Interview 21, 20 May 2021.
58. Yuri Timofeev and Mumin Shakirov, "Armiīa na mitinge" [Army at the rally], Glavnye Razdely, Radio Liberty, 17 November 2010, https://www.svoboda.org/a/2213147.html
59. Egor Mostovshhikov et al., "Sshibka," *New Times*, no. 35 (October 2010), https://newtimes.ru/articles/detail/29355
60. Pavel Vasiliev, "V Cheliābinske proshel miting protiv zakrytiīa avtomobil′nogo instituta" [A rally was held in Chelyabinsk against the closure of the Automobile Institute Army], 74.ru, 20 September 2010, https://web.archive.org/web/20220603124500/https://74.ru/text/gorod/2010/09/20/58840291/
61. Pavel Aksenov, "Konstruktor 'Topolej': Gosoboronzakaz-2011 sorvan" ["Topol" constructor: State defense order-2011 failed], BBC News Russian Service, 6 July 2011, https://www.bbc.com/russian/russia/2011/07/110706_russia_missiles_building
62. Ivan Safronov, "Minoborony pereshlo ot slov k 19 trillionam" [Ministry of Defense went from words to 19 trillion], *Kommersant* (Moscow), 25 February 2011, https://www.kommersant.ru/doc/1591146
63. Vadim Soloviev, "Voennaja reforma 2009–2012 godov" [Military reform 2009–12], *Nezavisimoe Voennoe Obozrenie*, 12 December 2008, http://nvo.ng.ru/forces/2008-12-12/1_reform.html
64. Viktor Litovkin, "Nachal'nik Genshtaba postavil diagnoz" [The chief of the General Staff diagnosed], *Nezavisimoe Voennoe Obozrenie*, 30 March 2011, http://nvo.ng.ru/nvo/2011-03-30/10_genshtab.html
65. Interview 23, 21 May 2021.
66. "Vitaliy Vasilievich Shlykov: Biographicheskaia spravka," RIA Novosti, 30 November 2011, https://web.archive.org/web/20240302075406/https://ria.ru/20111120/493601651.html
67. Interviews 28, 16 April 2018.
68. Gavrilov and Chernyak, "Iuriĭ Baluevskiĭ: My ne sobiraemsiā voevat′ s NATO."
69. Interview 27, 25 April 2018.
70. Mikhail Barabanov, *Russia's New Army*, ed. Mikhail Barabanov, 1st edn (Center for Analysis of Strategies and Technology, 2011).
71. Interview 31, 23 April 2018.
72. Viktor Baranec, "Armiīa shla na voĭnu v starykh latakh" [The army went to war in old amor], *Komsomolskaya Pravda*, 26 August 2008, https://www.kp.ru/daily/24152/368191/
73. Interview 18, 15 May 2021.
74. Interview 35, 23 April 2018.

75. Interview 37, 25 April 2018.
76. "Chto kroetsja za otstavkoj Serdjukova?" [What lies behind Serdyukov's resignation?], BBC News Russian Service, 6 November 2012, https://www.bbc.com/russian/russia/2012/11/121106_serdyukov_dismissal
77. Interview 31, 23 April 2018.
78. Aleksandr Golts, *Voennaja reforma i rossijskij militarizm* (Acta Universitatis Upsaliensis, 2017), http://urn.kb.se/resolve?urn=urn:nbn:se:uu:diva-328939
79. Keir Giles, "Who Gives the Orders in the New Russian Military?," NATO Defense College, 2012, http://www.jstor.org/stable/resrep10414. Rosstat, "Spravka o chislennosti i oplate truda grazhdanskih sluzhashhih federal'nyh gosudarstvennyh organov" (2012), 5, https://web.archive.org/web/20230802162812/https://mgoprofgos.ru/files/30082012-12_45_59.pdf
80. Anatoliy Ermolin, "Razrushiteli Otechestva," *New Times*, 21 February 2011, https://newtimes.ru/articles/detail/34773
81. Dvorkin and Arbatov, *Military Reform in Russia*.
82. Lyudmila Vakhnina, "Tragedija beglecov" [The tragedy of the fugitives], Media, Rosbalt, 5 April 2010, https://polit.ru/article/2010/05/04/vahnina/
83. Interview 17, 13 May 2021.
84. Dada Lindell and Margarita Alekhina, "Dedovshhina vyhodit iz stroja" [Hazing is going out of business], RBC, 29 November 2019, https://www.rbc.ru/newspaper/2019/11/29/5dd6b5749a79479efffb5771
85. Interview 29, 23 April 2018.
86. In a military, service commands (or service branches) refer to the main parts of the armed forces, such as the army, navy and air force. Each of these branches has its own leadership and command structure. At the top of each branch is a service chief.
87. Interview 24, 25 May 2021.
88. Golts, *Voennaja reforma i rossijskij militarizm*.
89. Vadim Soloviev, "Generaly pereshli v kontrataku" [The generals counterattacked], *Nezavisimaia Gazeta*, 28 May 2009, http://www.ng.ru/politics/2009-05-28/1_generals.html
90. Viktora Litovkin, "Brigady pod 'zontikom' desantnykh divizii" [Brigades under "umbrella" of airborne divisions], *Nezavisimoe Voennoe Obozrenie*, 3 February 2012, http://nvo.ng.ru/forces/2012-03-02/1_desant.html
91. The Federal Prosecutor's Office, the SKR and the FSB are three state institutions responsible for overseeing legal compliance, investigating

crimes and maintaining internal security. The Prosecutor's Office ensures that commanders and military officials follow legal procedures and do not violate the rights of service members. Military prosecutors, a branch of this office, conduct oversight within military units and can intervene in cases of abuse or misconduct. The SKR is Russia's main criminal investigation body. It handles serious crimes, including those committed by or against military personnel: hazing, corruption, abuse of power or deaths in service. The committee has specialized military investigative departments to handle cases within the armed forces. The FSB is Russia's primary internal security and counterintelligence agency. Within the military, the FSB monitors discipline, loyalty, subversion, espionage and ideological threats. It operates military counterintelligence units embedded in formations and sometimes investigates criminal cases involving state secrets or extremism.

92. Dale R. Herspring and Roger N. McDermott, "Serdyukov Promotes Systemic Russian Military Reform," *Orbis* 54, no. 2 (2010): 284–301, https://doi.org/10.1016/j.orbis.2010.01.004
93. Vladimir Vashenko, "Ne ponimau, chem zanimaetsya voennaya poliziia," Gazeta.ru, 11 January 2016, https://www.gazeta.ru/social/2016/11/01/10297829.shtml
94. Interview 27, 25 April 2018.
95. Interview 17, 13 May 2021.
96. Colonel Kvachkov is a former spetsnaz colonel who was convicted and sentenced for plotting an "armed mutiny" in 2010–13. He is known for far-right views and for founding the "People's Militia Named after Minin and Pozharsky," which was banned in 2015 as a terrorist organization. "Jailed Former Russian Intelligence Officer Kvachkov to Be Released," Radio Free Europe/Radio Liberty, https://www.rferl.org/a/jailed-former-russian-intelligence-officer-kvachkov-to-be-released/29756715.html
97. Ilya Polonsky, "Vezhlivye liudi: Den' sil spetsial'nykh operatsii Rossii" [Polite people: Day of the Russian special operations forces], *Voennoe Obozrenie*, 26 February 2018, https://topwar.ru/136719-vezhlivye-lyudi-den-sil-specialnyh-operaciy-rossii.html
98. Christopher Marsh, *Developments in Russian Special Operations: Spetsnaz, SOF, and Russian Special Operations Forces Command* (Canadian Forces Special Operations Forces Education and Research Centre, 2017), https://www.academia.edu/29576160/Developments_in_Russian_Special_Operations_Spetsnaz_SOF_and_Russian_Special_Operations_Forces_Command

99. Alexei Mikhailov, "Boĭtsy chetvertogo izmereniia" [Fighters of the fourth dimension], VPK.name, 20 April 2016, https://vpk.name/news/153815_boicy_chetvertogo_izmereniya.html
100. Dmitrii Bykov, "Voennye normativy" [Military standards], *Kommersant*, 29 June 2015, https://www.kommersant.ru/doc/2757166
101. Interview 32, 28 April 2018.
102. Interviews 27, 34 and 35, April 2018.
103. Interview 32, 28 April 2018.
104. A major Russian oil company, formed as a joint venture between British Petroleum and the Russian AAR Consortium (Alfa-Access-Renova).
105. Sergei Mashkin, "General pokonchil s kvartirnym voprosom" [The general is done with the apartment issue], *Kommersant*, 22 May 2024, https://www.kommersant.ru/doc/855771
106. Pukhov, "Serdyukov Cleans Up the Arbat."
107. Golts, *Voennaja reforma i rossijskij militarizm*.
108. Interviews 27 and 32, April 2018.
109. Interview 27, 25 April 2018.
110. Interview 27, 25 April 2018
111. Irina Granik et al., "Aleksej Kudrin poluchil dvojnuju otstavku" [Alexei Kudrin received a double resignation], *Kommersant* (Moscow), 27 September 2011, https://www.kommersant.ru/doc/1781828
112. Redakcija Forbes, "Kudrin protiv Medvedeva: Kak sostojalas' otstavka ministra finansov" [Kudrin vs. Medvedev: How the resignation of the minister of finance took place], recollection of Evgeniya Pismennaya, *Sistema Kudrina: Istoriya klyuchevogo ekonomista putinskoy Rossii* (Mann, Ivanov i Ferber, 2013).
113. "Interview/Voennoe Obrazovanie/Viktor Goremykin," *Voenyi Sovet*, dir. Viktor Goremykin, Echo-Moskvy, 14 March 2009, https://echo.msk.ru/programs/voensovet/577758-echo/
114. Ministerstvo oborony Rossijskoj Federacii, "Ministr Oborony General Armii Sergej Shojguvystupil na prieme v chest' luchshih vypusknikov voennyh vuzov [Minister of Defense General of the Army Sergei Shoigu spoke at a reception in honor of the best graduates of military universities], 28 June 2016, https://function.mil.ru/news_page/country/more.htm?id=12088746@egNews
115. Herspring and McDermott, "Serdyukov Promotes Systemic Russian Military Reform."
116. Multiple interviews in April 2018.
117. Interview 29, 23 April 2018.
118. Interviews 26, 35, 36, April 2018.

119. Interviews 36, 20 April 2018.
120. Interview 27, 25 April 2018.
121. Interview 29, 23 April 2018.
122. Interviews 30, 36, April 2018.
123. Soloviev, "Generaly pereshli v kontrataku."
124. Valery Shiryaev, "'Vezhlivye liudi' v Krymu: Kak ėto bylo; 'I togda priniali reshenie: otlozhit' oruzhie i idti vrukopashnuiu'" ["Polite people" in Crimea: How it was; "And then they made a decision: To put aside weapons and go hand to hand"], *Novaya Gazeta*, 17 April 2014, https://novayagazeta.ru/articles/2014/04/17/59255-171-vezhlivye-lyudi-187-v-krymu-kak-eto-bylo
125. Sergei Goryashko and Ivan Safronov, "Oni vtorgalis' na rodinu" [They were invading the homeland], *Kommersant*, 18 March 2015, https://www.kommersant.ru/doc/2688725
126. Charles K. Bartles and Roger N. McDermott, "Russia's Military Operation in Crimea," *Problems of Post-Communism* 61 (2014): 46–63, https://www.tandfonline.com/doi/abs/10.2753/PPC1075-8216610604.2014.11083050
127. "Voennaja doktrina Rossijskoj Federacii" [Military doctrine of the Russian Federation], no. 146 (2010), http://kremlin.ru/supplement/461
128. "Delo Obornservisa" [The case of Oboronservis], *Kommersant*, 11 June 2017, https://www.kommersant.ru/doc/2347295
129. Kira Latukhina, "Sergeĭ Shoĭgu rasskazal o prioritetakh na postu ministra oborony" [Sergei Shoigu spoke about his priorities as defense minister], *Rossiiskaya Gazeta* (Moscow), no. 256, 11 July 2012, https://rg.ru/2012/11/06/ministr-site.html
130. Elena Rykovceva, "Putin i Shoĭgu: Istoriia liubvi" [Putin and Shoigu: A love story], Licom k Sobytiu, Radio Liberty, 22 March 2021, https://www.svoboda.org/a/31163798.html
131. "Prezident naznachil Sergeia Shoĭgu ministrom oborony" [President appoints Sergei Shoigu as minister of defense], *Rossiiskaya Gazeta* (Moscow), 11 June 2012, https://rg.ru/2012/11/06/ministr-anons.html
132. Interview 23, 21 May 2021.
133. Roman Feygin, "Vozglavivshaia federatsiiu triatlona doch' Shoĭgu poobeshchala stroit' bazy" [Shoigu's daughter, who headed the triathlon federation, promised to build bases], RBC Sport (Moscow), 12 May 2020, https://sportrbc.ru/news/5fcb58399a7947407c2d312a
134. Sergei Chapnin, "Khorosho li molilis' generaly" [Did the generals pray

well], *Vedomosti* (Moscow), 15 June 2020, https://www.vedomosti.ru/opinion/articles/2020/06/14/832551-horosho-molilis
135. Ilja Kramnik, "Armiia" [army], Facebook, 24 September 2019, https://meduza.io/news/2019/09/26/izvestiya-uvolili-voennogo-obozrevatelya-ilyu-kramnika-za-narushenie-standartov-posle-kolonki-s-kritikoy-shoygu
136. Alexei Nikolsky, "Sergeĭ Shoĭgu provel pervye kadrovye perestanovki v Minoborony" [Sergei Shoigu held the first personnel reshuffle in the Defense Ministry], *Vedomosti* (Moscow), 11 December 2012, https://www.vedomosti.ru/politics/articles/2012/11/12/shtatskie_uhodyat
137. Interview 24, 25 May 2021.
138. Alexei Nikolsky, "Putin naznachil zamestiteleĭ Shoĭgu" [Putin appointed Shoigu's deputies], *Vedomosti* (Moscow), 11 September 2012, https://www.vedomosti.ru/management/articles/2012/11/09/putin_odobril_kandidaturu_valeriya_gerasimova_na_post
139. Valery Gerasimov, "Doklad NGSh VS RF na ezhegodnom sobranii Akademii voennyh nauk" [Report of the RF armed forces national General Staff at the annual meeting of the Academy of Military Sciences], Akademiia Voennyh Nauk, 2 March 2014, http://www.avnrf.ru/index.php/component/content/article/72-novosti-sajta/607-generalnyj-shtab-i-oborona-strany
140. Valery Gerasimov, "Cennost' nauki v predvidenii" [The value of science in foresight], *Voenno-Promyshlennyi Kurier* (Moscow), 26 February 2013, https://vpk-news.ru/articles/14632
141. Nabi Nabiev, "Goriachie budni Generala Gerasimova" [Hot routine of General Gerasimov], *Krasnaya Zvezda* (Moscow), 3 December 2001, https://web.archive.org/web/20250913043717/http://old.redstar.ru/2001/03/12_03/a_t21.html
142. Roman Biryulin, "Iz suvorovcev—v strategi" [From Suvorov to strategists], *Krasnaya Zvezda* (Moscow), 9 September 2020, https://web.archive.org/web/20210414075405/http://redstar.ru/iz-suvorovtsev-v-strategi/
143. "Vektory razvitiia voennoĭ strategii" [Vectors of military strategy development], *Krasnaya Zvezda* (Moscow), 3 April 2019, http://redstar.ru/vektory-razvitiya-voennoj-strategii/
144. "Otnoshenie k Vladimiru Putinu."
145. "Russia Bans Smartphones for Soldiers over Social Media Fears," BBC, 20 February 2019, https://www.bbc.com/news/world-europe-47302938
146. Svetlana Prokopieva, "'Pisat' nel'zia voobshche ni o chëm': Chto FSB

skryvaet ot inostrantsev" ["You can't write about anything at all": What the FSB hides from foreigners], Sever.Reallii, 22 July 2021, https://www.severreal.org/a/perechen-svedenij-fsb-inoagent/31369983.html

147. "Russia: New 'Foreign Agents' Bill Further Erodes Freedom of Expression and Association," Amnesty International, 19 November 2020, https://www.amnesty.org/en/latest/press-release/2020/11/russia-new-foreign-agents-bill-further-erodes-freedom-of-expression-and-association/

148. Almaz-Antey is Russia's producer of air and missile defense systems. The United Aircraft Corporation unites Russia's major aircraft manufacturers and is responsible for both civilian and military aviation projects. The United Shipbuilding Corporation manages Russia's naval shipyards and builds submarines, surface vessels and icebreakers for military and civilian use. The Tactical Missiles Corporation specializes in guided missile systems and supplies the Russian armed forces with air-to-air, air-to-surface and naval strike weapons.

149. Pavel Luzin, "Russia's GPV-2027 State Arms Programme," Riddle Russia, 18 April 2018, https://ridl.io/russias-gpv-2027-state-arms-programme/

150. Pavel Luzin, "Russia's Arms Manufacturers Are a Financial Black Hole," Riddle Russia, 30 January 2020, https://ridl.io/russia-s-arms-manufacturers-are-a-financial-black-hole/; Luzin, "Sanctions and the Russian Defence Industry," Riddle Russia, 30 October 2020, https://ridl.io/sanctions-and-the-russian-defence-industry/

151. Lev Gudkov, "Doverie institutam" [Trust in institutions], Levada Center, 21 September 2020, https://www.levada.ru/2020/09/21/doverie-institutam/

152. Sergei Smirnov, "Tonkaia shlifovka armii" [Army fine grinding], Gazeta.ru (Moscow), 27 February 2013, https://www.gazeta.ru/politics/2013/02/27_a_4990925.shtml; "Putin i voennaia reforma" [Putin and military reform], Interfax (Moscow), 27 February 2013, https://www.interfax.ru/russia/292810

153. "Shoigu zachistil voennoe obrazovanie" [Shoigu has cleaned up military education], Interfax, 12 July 2012, https://www.interfax.ru/russia/279810

154. For example, the police do not have the right to conduct independent operational and investigative activities.

155. Smirnov, "Tonkaia shlifovka armii."

156. Kira Latukhina, "Oborona na perspektivu" [Defense for the future],

Rossiiskaya Gazeta (Sochi), no. 271, 12 February 2013, https://rg.ru/2013/02/27/armiya-site.html

157. "Shoĭgu nazval t͡selʹ reform VS Rossii" [Shoigu named the goal of reforms of the Russian armed forces], Interfax, 11 September 2013, https://www.interfax.ru/russia/339760
158. Roger Mcdermott and Charles Bartles, "The Russian Military Decision-Making Process & Automated Command and Control," GIDSresearch no. 02/2020, German Institute for Defence and Strategic Studies, 2020, 71, https://gids-hamburg.de/the-russian-military-decision-making-process-automated-command-and-control/
159. Mcdermott and Bartles, "Russian Military Decision-Making Process," 55–62.
160. "Zasedanie kollegii Ministerstva oborony" [Meeting of the Collegiate Board of the Ministry of Defense], President of Russia, 25 December 2019, http://kremlin.ru/events/president/news/62401
161. Dmitriĭ Bykov, "Voennye normativy" [Military standards], *Kommersant*, 29 June 2015, https://www.kommersant.ru/doc/2757166
162. Alexander Trushin, "'Voennai͡a nagruzka stala tormozom'" ["The military workload has become a brake], *Kommersant*, 17 October 2016, https://www.kommersant.ru/doc/3114479
163. Trushin, "'Voennai͡a nagruzka stala tormozom.'"
164. Ivan Safronov and Dmitry Butrin, "Vooruzhenii͡a vstupili v boĭ s vozrazhenii͡ami" [The armaments have entered the fray with objections], *Kommersant*, 19 February 2015, https://www.kommersant.ru/doc/2670562
165. Richard Connolly and Mathieu Boulègue, "Russia's New State Armament Programme: Implications for the Russian Armed Forces and Military Capabilities to 2027," Chatham House Research Paper, Royal Institute for International Affairs, 2018, 298–300, https://www.degruyter.com/document/doi/10.1515/sirius-2018-3017/html
166. Pavel Luzin, "Russia's GPV-2027 State Arms Programme," Riddle Russia, 18 April 2018, https://ridl.io/russias-gpv-2027-state-arms-programme/
167. Aleksandr Mikhailovsky and Kharis Sayfetdinov, "Kompʹi͡uternye formy obuchenii͡a dolzhnostnykh lit͡s Nat͡sionalʹnogo t͡sentra upravlenii͡a oboronoĭ Rossiĭskoĭ Federat͡sii" [Computer-based forms of training for officials of the National Defense Management Center of the Russian Federation], *Voennaya Mysl*, no. 5 (2016): 57–8, https://elibrary.ru/item.asp?id=25934000
168. Mcdermott and Bartles, "Russian Military Decision-Making Process."

169. Viktor Khudoleev, "Operativnost′ priniatiia reshenii povyshena v razy" [The speed of decision-making is increased many times over], *Krasnaya Zvezda*, 9 September 2019, http://redstar.ru/operativnost-prinyatiya-reshenij-povyshena-v-razy/

170. Konstantin Legkov and Vadim Orkin, "Osnovnye napravlenija razvitija edinogo informacionnogo Prostranstva Vozdushno-Kosmicheskih Sil v Sovremennyh Uslovijah" [Main areas of development of the unified information space of the Air and Space Forces in modern conditions], *Voennaya Mysl*, 13 August 2020, https://vm.ric.mil.ru/Stati/item/260339/

171. Mikhail Osipenkov and Ilmir Uzyakaev. "Osnovnye problemy dostizheniia interoperabel′nosti informatsionnykh sistem organov gosudarstvennogo i voennogo upravleniia pri reshenii zadach oborony" [Main problems in achieving interoperability of information systems of state and military administration bodies when solving defense tasks], *Voennaya Mysl* (Moscow), no. 5 (2020).

172. "V Rossii pojavjatsja chastnye armii" [Private armies will appear in Russia], BFM.ru, business portal, 19 September 2012, https://www.bfm.ru/news/194024

173. At the time of writing, Russia had not legalized PMCs. However, initially, the Kremlin even refused to acknowledge that such organizations existed.

174. Irina Malkova and Anton Baev, "Chastnaja armija dlja prezidenta: Istorija samogo delikatnogo poruchenija Evgenija Prigozhina" [A private army for the president: The story of Yevgeny Prigozhin's most delicate assignment], The Bell, 29 January 2019, https://thebell.io/41889-2

175. Malkova and Baev, "Chastnaja armija dlja prezidenta."

176. Malkova and Baev, "Chastnaja armija dlja prezidenta."

177. Anna Borshchevskaya, "Russian Private Military Companies: Continuity and Evolution of the Model," Foreign Policy Research Institute, 18 December 2019, https://www.fpri.org/article/2019/12/russian-private-military-companies-continuity-and-evolution-of-the-model/

178. Tor Bukkvoll and Åse G. Østensen, "The Emergence of Russian Private Military Companies: A New Tool of Clandestine Warfare," *Special Operations Journal* 6, no. 1 (2020): 1–17, https://doi.org/10.1080/23296151.2020.1740528

179. Herman Petelin and Elizaveta Maetnaya, "Kto i kak kormit Rossijskuju armiju: Rassledovanie 'Gazety.Ru'" [Who and how to feed the Russian army: Rassledovanie 'Gazety.ru'], Gazeta.ru, 24 December 2015,

https://www.gazeta.ru/social/2015/12/03/7933403.shtml; "Prigozhin vstretilsja s roditeljami posle zhalob na edu v shkolah i detsadah" [Prigozhin meets with parents after complaints about food in schools and kindergartens], RBC, 2 December 2019, https://www.rbc.ru/society/12/02/2019/5c62c3579a7947eaaca0577b

180. Lilia Yapparova et al., "Grubo govorja, my nachali vojnu Kak otpravka ChVK Vagnera na front pomogla Prigozhinu naladit' otnoshenija s Putinym—i chto takoe 'sobjaninskij polk'" [Roughly speaking, we started the war: How sending PMC Wagner to the front helped Prigozhin to establish relations with Putin—and what is "Sobyanin's regiment"], Meduza, 13 July 2022, https://meduza.io/feature/2022/07/13/grubo-govorya-my-nachali-voynu

181. Il'ja Barabanov and Denis Korotkov, *"Naš biznes—smert'": Polnaja istorija ČVK "Vagner" i ee osnovatelja Evgenija Prigožina* (Meduza, 2024).

182. "Russian MP Demands Government Regulate Private Military Companies," TASS, 14 February 2018, https://tass.com/politics/989972

183. Vitaly Tsymbal and Vasilii Zacepin, "Novaia sistema upravleniia oboronoĭ Rossii: Reforma ili imitatsiia?" [Russia's new defense management system: Reform or imitation?], *Jekonomicheskoe Razvitie Rossii* (Moscow) 22, no. 5 (2015): 5; Philippe Lagassé and Stephen M. Saideman, "When Civilian Control Is Civil: Parliamentary Oversight of the Military in Belgium and New Zealand," *European Journal of International Security* 4, no. 1 (2019): 20–40, https://doi.org/10.1017/eis.2018.17

184. Interviews 17, 18, 13 and 15, May 2021.

185. Interview 22, 20 May 2021.

186. Aleksandra Dzordzhevich and Ivan Safronov, "FAS beret na pritsel vooruzheniia" [The chief of the General Staff diagnosed], *Kommersant*, 3 April 2019, https://www.kommersant.ru/doc/3931759

187. Anna Trunina, "FAS nachala massovye proverki oboronnyh predprijatij" [FAS launches mass inspections of defense companies], RBC, 2 April 2019, https://www.rbc.ru/society/02/04/2019/5ca3178f9a7947db48fafa44

188. "Plan deiatel'nosti na 2013–2020 gg." [Activity plan for 2013–20], MoD, 2013, https://mil.ru/mod_activity_plan/constr.htm

189. "Defense Chief Praises Russian Military's Success in Syria," TASS, 22 February 2017, https://tass.com/defense/932437

190. Interview 22, 20 May 2021.

191. MoD, "Plan deiatel'nosti na 2013–2020 gg."

192. Konstantin Bogdanov, "Poslednii otschet: Do starta novoi

gosprogrammy vooruzhenii ostaiutsia mesiatsy" [The final countdown: Months to go before the start of the new state arms program], Lenta. ru, 25 May 2017, https://lenta.ru/articles/2017/05/25/gpv/

193. "Vystuplenie Nachal'nika General'nogo Shtaba Vooruzhennykh Sil Rossiiskoi Federatsii: Pervogo Zamestitelia Ministra Oborony Rossiiskoi Federatsii Generala Armii Valeriia Gerasimova na Otkrytom Zasedanii Kollegii Minoborony Rossii 7 Noiabria 2017 g.; Ministerstvo Oborony Rossiiskoi Federatsii" [Speech by Valery Gerasimov, chief of the General Staff of the armed forces of the Russian Federation: First deputy minister of defense of the Russian Federation, Army General Valery Gerasimov, at the open session of the Collegium of the Russian Ministry of Defense on 7 November 2017; Ministry of Defense of the Russian Federation], 11 July 2017, https://function.mil.ru/news_page/intrel/more.htm?id=12149743@egNews [no longer active].

194. "OPK pomog Vooruzhjonnym silam RF v 2021 godu vyjti po novomu vooruzheniju bolee chem na 71%—Shojgu" [The defense industry has helped the Russian armed forces reach more than 71 per cent in 2021 in terms of new weapon—Shoigu], VPK.name, 29 December 2021, https://vpk.name/news/568707_opk_pomog_vooruzhennym_silam_rf_v_2021_godu_vyiti_po_novomu_vooruzheniyu_bolee_chem_na_71-shoigu.html

195. Kirill Shamiev, "Brass Tacks: Why Russia's Military Fails to Reform," European Council on Foreign Relations, 15 May 2024, https://ecfr.eu/publication/brass-tacks-why-russias-military-fails-to-reform/

196. Sarah A. Topol et al., "The Deserter: An Epic Story of Love and War," podcasts, *New York Times*, 21 September 2024, https://www.nytimes.com/2024/09/21/podcasts/russia-ukraine-deserter-audio.html

5. RUSSIAN CIVIL–MILITARY RELATIONS AND THE FULL-SCALE INVASION OF UKRAINE

1. Jonas J. Driedger and Mikhail Polianskii, "Utility-Based Predictions of Military Escalation: Why Experts Forecasted Russia Would Not Invade Ukraine," *Contemporary Security Policy* 44, no. 4 (2023): 544–60, https://doi.org/10.1080/13523260.2023.2259153
2. Julian Borger, "All Options Fraught with Risk as Biden Confronts Putin over Ukraine," *The Guardian*, 25 November 2021, https://www.theguardian.com/us-news/2021/nov/25/all-options-fraught-with-risk-as-biden-confronts-putin-over-ukraine; Ivan Timofeev, "War between Russia and Ukraine: A Basic Scenario?," Russian Council, 25 November 2021, https://russiancouncil.ru/en/analytics-and-

comments/analytics/war-between-russia-and-ukraine-a-basic-scenario/; Dmitri Trenin, "Russia's National Security Strategy: A Manifesto for a New Era," Russian Council, 9 July 2021, https://russiancouncil.ru/en/analytics-and-comments/comments/russias-national-security-strategy-a-manifesto-for-a-new-era/; Harun Yilmaz, "No, Russia Will Not Invade Ukraine," Al Jazeera, 2 September 2022, https://www.aljazeera.com/opinions/2022/2/9/no-russia-will-not-invade-ukraine; Harlan Ullman, "Why Putin Won't Invade Ukraine," Atlantic Council, 16 February 2022, https://www.atlanticcouncil.org/blogs/new-atlanticist/why-putin-wont-invade-ukraine/; Frank Gardner, "Ukraine Crisis: Five Reasons Why Putin Might Not Invade," BBC, 21 February 2022, https://www.bbc.com/news/world-europe-60468264

3. Mike Eckel, "How Did Everybody Get the Ukraine Invasion Predictions So Wrong?," Radio Free Europe/Radio Liberty, 17 February 2023, https://www.rferl.org/a/russia-ukraine-invasion-predictions-wrong-intelligence/32275740.html

4. Rowena Mason, "UK Must Be Ready for War with Russia, Says Armed Forces Chief," *The Guardian*, 14 November 2021, https://www.theguardian.com/uk-news/2021/nov/14/uk-must-be-ready-for-war-with-russia-says-armed-forces-chief

5. Natasha Bertrand, "Biden Keeping Ukraine at Arm's-Length," Politico, 13 March 2021, https://www.politico.com/news/2021/03/13/biden-ukraine-kyiv-putin-475546; Borger, "All Options Fraught with Risk"; Michael Crowley and Julian E. Barnes, "How Far Would Biden Go to Defend Ukraine against Russia?," *New York Times*, 25 November 2021, https://www.nytimes.com/2021/11/25/us/politics/biden-putin-russia-ukraine.html; Ken Dilanian et al., "Biden Admin Carefully Examining Legal Issues around Providing Arms to Ukraine," NBC News, 25 February 2022, https://www.nbcnews.com/politics/national-security/biden-admin-carefully-examining-legal-issues-providing-arms-ukraine-rcna17758

6. For a detailed discussion of the analytical challenges with predicting the invasion, see Kirill Shamiev, "Chekhov's Gun: Security Services and Blind Spot of Russia Studies," in *Studying Russia Anew: An Academic Audit in Times of Insecurity*, ed. Yulia Kurnyshova and Andrey Makarychev (Brill, forthcoming).

7. Scott Neuman, "Referendum in Russia Passes, Allowing Putin to Remain President until 2036," NPR, 1 July 2020, https://www.npr.org/2020/07/01/886440694/referendum-in-russia-passes-allowing-putin-to-remain-president-until-2036

8. "Putin Targets U.S. Social Media, Secret Agent Leaks and Protests with New Laws," Reuters, 30 December 2020, https://www.reuters.com/business/finance/putin-targets-us-social-media-secret-agent-leaks-protests-with-new-laws-2020-12-30/
9. Pjotr Sauer, "Chemical Burns, Poisoning and Prison: The Persecution of Alexei Navalny," *The Guardian*, 16 February 2024, https://www.theguardian.com/world/2024/feb/16/chemical-burns-poisoning-prison-alexei-navalny-persecution
10. Sabine Fischer, "Repression and Autocracy as Russia Heads into State Duma Elections," Stiftung Wissenschaft und Politik (SWP), 30 June 2021, https://www.swp-berlin.org/publikation/repression-and-autocracy-as-russia-heads-into-state-duma-elections
11. Andrew Roth, "Russian Court Outlaws Alexei Navalny's Organisation," *The Guardian*, 9 June 2021, https://www.theguardian.com/world/2021/jun/09/russian-court-expected-to-outlaw-alexei-navalnys-organisation
12. "Obostrenie v Donbasse" [Aggravation in Donbass], Levada Center, 14 December 2021, https://www.levada.ru/2021/12/14/obostrenie-v-donbasse/
13. William Zimmerman et al., "Survey of Russian Elites, Moscow, Russia, 1993–2020," Inter-university Consortium for Political and Social Research, 1 June 2023, https://doi.org/10.3886/ICPSR03724.v8
14. "Official: Russian Military Build-Up near Ukraine Numbers More than 100,000 Troops, EU Says," Reuters, 19 April 2021, https://www.reuters.com/world/europe/russian-military-build-up-near-ukraine-numbers-more-than-150000-troops-eus-2021-04-19/
15. Vladimir Putin, "Article by Vladimir Putin 'On the Historical Unity of Russians and Ukrainians,'" President of Russia, 14 July 2021, http://en.kremlin.ru/events/president/news/66181
16. "Contextualizing Putin's 'On the Historical Unity of Russians and Ukrainians,'" Ukrainian Research Institute, 2 August 2021, https://www.huri.harvard.edu/news/putin-historical-unity
17. Alberto Nardelli and Jennifer Jacobs, "U.S. Intel Shows Russia Plans for Potential Ukraine Invasion," Bloomberg, 21 November 2021, https://www.bloomberg.com/news/articles/2021-11-21/u-s-intel-shows-russian-plans-for-potential-ukraine-invasion
18. "Russia Says Ukraine Has Deployed Half Its Army to Donbass Conflict Zone," Reuters, 1 December 2021, https://www.reuters.com/world/europe/russia-says-ukraine-has-deployed-half-its-army-donbass-conflict-zone-2021-12-01/
19. "Soglashenie o Merah Obespechenija Bezopasnosti Rossijskoj Federacii

i Gosudarstv-Chlenov Organizacii Severoatlanticheskogo Dogovora" [Agreement on security measures between the Russian Federation and the member states of the North Atlantic Treaty Organization], Ministry of Foreign Affairs of Russian Federation, 17 December 2021, https://mid.ru/ru/foreign_policy/rso/nato/1790803/; "Dogovor Mezhdu Rossijskoj Federaciej i Soedinennymi Shtatami Ameriki o Garantijah Bezopasnosti" [Agreement between the Russian Federation and the United States of America on security assurances], Ministry of Foreign Affairs of Russian Federation, 17 December 2021, https://mid.ru/ru/foreign_policy/rso/nato/1790818/

20. Pjotr Sauer, "'You Shake at the Smallest of Noises': Russian Soldier Tells of Life as a PoW," *The Guardian*, 26 May 2022, https://www.theguardian.com/world/2022/may/26/russian-soldier-pow-ukraine; Andrew Roth and Pjotr Sauer, "'I Don't See Justice in this War': Russian Soldier Exposes Rot at Core of Ukraine Invasion," *The Guardian*, 17 August 2022, https://www.theguardian.com/world/2022/aug/17/i-dont-see-justice-in-this-war-russian-soldier-exposes-rot-at-core-of-ukraine-invasion

21. Tony Selhorst MMAS, "Limits of Russian Operational Art," Militaire Spectator, 15 May 2023, https://militairespectator.nl/artikelen/limits-russian-operational-art

22. "The Gulf War II Air Campaign, by the Numbers," *Air & Space Forces Magazine*, July 2023, https://www.airandspaceforces.com/PDF/MagazineArchive/Magazine%20Documents/2003/July%202003/0703Numbers.pdf

23. Greg Miller and Catherine Belton, "Russia's Spies Misread Ukraine and Misled Kremlin as War Loomed," *Washington Post*, 19 August 2022, https://www.washingtonpost.com/world/interactive/2022/russia-fsb-intelligence-ukraine-war/

24. "The Battle of Hostomel Airport: A Key Moment in Russia's Defeat in Kyiv," War on the Rocks, 10 August 2023, https://warontherocks.com/2023/08/the-battle-of-hostomel-airport-a-key-moment-in-russias-defeat-in-kyiv/

25. Mikhail Tukmakov, "Osnovnye napravleniia sovershenstvovaniia voenno-politicheskoĭ raboty pri podgotovke operatsiĭ" [Main directions for improving military-political work in preparation for operations], *Voennaya Mysl* (Moscow), no. 2 (2023): 5, https://vm.ric.mil.ru/upload/site178/KTKcn4mdSu.pdf

26. Peter Feaver and Richard H. Kohn, "Civil–Military Relations in the United States," *Strategic Studies Quarterly* 15, no. 2 (2021): 12–37.

27. For a more detailed and technical discussion about Russian wartime

civil–military relations, please see my policy report for Center for Naval Analysis (CNA): Kirill Shamiev, "Dynamics of Russian Civil–Military Relations during the War with Ukraine: Legal Reforms, Elite Dynamics, and Societal Perceptions," CNA, August 2025, https://www.cna.org/analyses/2025/08/dynamics-of-russia-civil-military-relations

28. "Poslanie prezidenta Federal′nomu Sobraniiu" [Presidential address to the Federal Assembly], Kremlin.ru, 29 February 2024, https://web.archive.org/web/20241223202038/http://www.kremlin.ru/events/president/news/73585

29. "'Novaia élita' ne vydvigaetsia" [The "new elite" is not being nominated], Vazhnye Istorii, 24 December 2024, https://web.archive.org/web/20241224034829/https://istories.media/stories/2024/09/06/novaya-elita-ne-vidvigaetsya/

30. "Regional′nye vlasti nachali sozdavat′ desiatki dolzhnostei pod 'novuiu élitu' Putina" [Regional authorities have begun creating dozens of positions for Putin's "new elite"], Agentstvo, 14 February 2025, https://web.archive.org/web/20250217011418/https://www.agents.media/regionalnye-vlasti-nachali-sozdavat-desyatki-dolzhnostej-pod-novuyu-elitu-putina/

31. "Veterany 'SVO' poiaviatsia v rukovodstve krupnykh goskompanii" [SVO veterans will appear in the management of large state-owned companies], Verstka, 28 February 2025, https://web.archive.org/web/20250228034843/https://verstka.media/fetish-nachalstva-uchastnikov-vojny-v-ukraine-naznachat-v-rukovodstvo-krupnejshih-goskompanij-rossii

32. "Putin sozdal vidimost′ kar′ernogo lifta dlia uchastnikov voiny" [Putin has created the appearance of a career elevator for war veterans], Agentstvo, 11 May 2024, https://t.me/agentstvonews/7960

33. "Naemniki ChVK Vagnera ob″iavili, chto zakryvaiut svoiu glavnuiu bazu v krasnodarskom Mol′kino" [The mercenaries of the PMC Wagner announced that they were closing their main base in Krasnodar's Molkino], Meduza, 17 July 2023, https://meduza.io/news/2023/07/17/naemniki-chvk-vagnera-ob-yavili-chto-zakryvayut-svoyu-glavnuyu-bazu-v-krasnodarskom-molkino

34. "Prigozhin ob″iasnil vysshim chinam rossiiskoi armii, chto s nim nado govorit′ na vy Prezritel′nye peregovory osnovatelia ChVK s zamministra oborony Evkurovym i zamnachal′nika Genshtaba Alekseevym. Rasshifrovka besedy" [Prigozhin explained to the highest ranks of the Russian army that it is necessary to speak with him on you: Contemptuous talks of the PMC founder with Deputy Defense

Minister Yevkurov and Deputy Chief of the General Staff Alekseev: Transcript of the conversation], Meduza, 24 June 2023, https://meduza.io/feature/2023/06/24/prigozhin-ob-yasnil-vysshim-chinam-rossiyskoy-armii-chto-s-nim-nado-govorit-na-vy

35. "TSentr 'Dos'e' poluchil dostup k pochte Ministra Oborony Belousova i uznal, chto tot kuriroval rabotu Evgeniia Prigozhina" [The Dossier Center accessed the mail of Defense Minister Belousov and learned that he supervised the work of Yevgeny Prigozhin], The Insider, 21 May 2024, https://theins.ru/news/271757

36. "Ugolovnye dela protiv generalov i chinovnikov Minoborony: Infografika" [Criminal cases against generals and officials of the Ministry of Defense: Infographics], RBC, 18 September 2024, https://www.rbc.ru/politics/30/08/2024/66d0b0689a7947d54fce35a3

37. "Nikolaĭ Pankov naznachen stats-sekretarem Minoborony" [Nikolai Pankov appointed state secretary of the Ministry of Defense], Kommersant, 19 September 2005, https://www.kommersant.ru/doc/986388; "Siloviki" [Security forces], Kommersant, 4 June 2002, https://www.kommersant.ru/doc/325689

38. "Minoborony: Kto takie Leonid Gornin, Anna TSivilëva i Pavel Fradkov" [Ministry of Defense: Who are Leonid Gornin, Anna Tsivilyova and Pavel Fradkov?], Vyorstka, 24 March 2025, https://web.archive.org/web/20250324025359/https://verstka.media/anna-tsivileva-zamministra-oborony

39. "Minfin Ob"iasnil Poiavlenie Eshche Odnogo Pervogo Zamestiteliā u Siluanova" [The Ministry of Finance explained the appearance of another first deputy to Siluanov], Vedomosti, 28 May 2018, https://web.archive.org/web/20180528182925/https://www.vedomosti.ru/economics/news/2018/05/28/770933-minfin-obyasnil-poyavlenie-esche-odnogo-pervogo-zamestitelya-u-siluanova

40. "Pavel Fradkov stal blizhe k Staroĭ ploshchadi" [Pavel Fradkov became closer to the Old Square], Kommersant, 21 May 2015, https://www.kommersant.ru/doc/2731094

41. "Proekt o lishenii svobody na srok do 5 let za prizyvy k sanktsiiam protiv RF odobren dliā I chteniiā" [The bill on imprisonment for up to five years for calls for sanctions against Russia has been approved for the first reading], Interfax.ru, 28 March 2025, https://www.interfax.ru/russia/1017104

42. "V Gosdume reshili popolnit' Ugolovnyĭ kodeks stat'iami na sluchaĭ voennykh deĭstvii" [The State Duma decided to add articles to the Criminal Code in case of military operations], BBC News Russian Service, 25 May 2022, https://www.bbc.com/russian/news-61584618

43. "After Weeks of Chaos, Russia Says Partial Mobilisation Is Complete," Reuters, 31 October 2022, https://www.reuters.com/world/europe/russia-completes-partial-mobilisation-defence-ministry-2022-10-31/
44. Josh Pennington and Jessie Yeung, "Protests Erupt in Russia's Dagestan Region over Putin's Mobilization Orders," CNN, 26 September 2022, https://www.cnn.com/2022/09/26/europe/russia-dagestan-protests-mobilization-intl-hnk
45. "Russian Universities Admit Twice as Many Ukraine War Veterans for 2024–25 Academic Year," Moscow Times, 22 August 2024, https://www.themoscowtimes.com/2024/08/22/russian-universities-admit-twice-as-many-ukraine-war-veterans-for-2024-25-academic-year-a86114
46. Thibault Spirlet, "A New Way for Russia to Cement Its Hold on Ukraine: Dirt-Cheap Mortgages," Business Insider, 1 November 2024, https://www.businessinsider.com/russia-way-to-cement-hold-on-ukraine-dirt-cheap-mortgages-2024-11; "After Waiting Years for Social Housing, Russians Are Losing Their Place in Line to Veterans of the Kremlin's War against Ukraine," Meduza, 20 September 2024, https://meduza.io/en/feature/2024/09/20/after-waiting-years-for-social-housing-russians-are-losing-their-place-in-line-to-veterans-of-the-kremlin-s-war-against-ukraine
47. The links to the rejected bills are at the bottom of this summary: "Spetsial′naia Voennaia Operatsiia, mobilizatsiia 2022–2025" [Special Military Operation, mobilization 2022–5], Garant, https://base.garant.ru/77188369/
48. "Spetsial′naia Voennaia Operatsiia, mobilizatsiia 2022–2025."
49. "Rasporiazhenie Pravitel′stva RF Ot 6 Maia 2023 g. № 1168-r Ob Utverzhdenii Ustava Gosudarstvennogo Fonda Podderzhki Uchastnikov Spetsial′noi Voennoi Operatsii Zashchitniki Otechestva" [Order of the government of the Russian Federation of 6 May 2023, no. 1168-r: On approval of the charter of the state fund for support of participants of the Special Military Operation defenders of the fatherland], 15 May 2023, Garant, https://www.garant.ru/products/ipo/prime/doc/406762562/
50. "Pekhota pushche nevoli: Desiatki vooruzhennykh grupp—ChVK 'Vagnera,' Kadyrovtsy, Neonatsisty—Prinimaiut v riady 'pushechnogo miasa' na voinu v Ukraine vsekh, vkliuchaia zekov i bol′nykh; my popytalis′ stat′ dobrovol′tsami" [More infantry than captivity: Dozens of armed groups—the Wagner PMC, the Kadyrovtsy, the Neo-Nazis—are accepting everyone, including convicts and the sick, as "cannon fodder" for the war in Ukraine; We tried to become volunteers],

253

Novaya Gazeta Evropa, 8 October 2022, https://novayagazeta.eu/articles/2022/08/10/pekhota-pushche-nevoli

51. Josh Pennington, "Wagner Boss Threatens Bakhmut Withdrawal Unless His Forces Get More Munitions," CNN, 30 April 2023, https://www.cnn.com/2023/04/30/world/wagner-head-threatens-withdrawal-bakhmut-intl

52. "Ukraine War: Russia Moves to Take Direct Control of Wagner Group," BBC, 11 June 2023, https://www.bbc.com/news/world-europe-65871232

53. "Kontrakt s Minoborony podpisali bolee 20 dobrovol'cheskih formirovanij" [More than twenty volunteer units signed a contract with the Ministry of Defense], RBC, 22 June 2023, https://www.rbc.ru/rbcfreenews/6493ac0a9a794710648f4177

54. "Chto izvestno ob 'Afrikanskom korpuse' Rossii" [What is known about Russia's "African Corps"?], *Vedomosti*, 22 December 2023, https://www.vedomosti.ru/politics/articles/2023/12/22/1012398-chto-izvestno-ob-afrikanskom-korpuse-rossii; "Afrikanskiĭ korpus MO: platiat $5 tys, no ne otpravliaiut domoĭ" [African Defense Corps: Paid $5k but not sent home], Vyorstka, 8 November 2024, https://verstka.media/iz-vagnera-v-minoborony-kto-verbuet-rossiyan-v-afrikanskij-korpus

55. Ilya Barabanov and Anastasia Lotareva, "Chto proiskhodit s voennym naslediem Evgeniia Prigozhina i ChVK 'Vagner' cherez god posle miatezha" [What happens to the military legacy of Yevgeny Prigozhin and PMC "Wagner" a year after the insurgency?], BBC News Russian Service, 21 June 2024, https://www.bbc.com/russian/articles/c0dd3rp0344o

56. "Spetsial'naia Voennaia Operatsiia, mobilizatsiia 2022–2025."

57. "Proekt Federal'nogo Zakona N 848123-8 'O Vnesenii Izmeneniĭ v Stat'i 2 i 4 Federal'nogo Zakona "Ob Al'ternativnoĭ Grazhdanskoĭ Sluzhbe"'" [Draft Federal Law no. 848123-8 "On amending Articles 2 and 4 of the federal law 'On alternative civilian service'"], Garant, 24 February 2025, https://base.garant.ru/76868930/

58. "Federal'nyĭ Zakon Ot 08.08.2024 N 300-FZ 'O Vnesenii Izmeneniĭ v Federal'nyĭ Zakon "Ob Osobennostiakh Regulirovaniia Korporativnykh Otnosheniĭ v Khoziaĭstvennykh Obshchestvakh, Iavliaiushchikhsia Ėkonomicheski Znachimymi Organizatsiiami"'" [Federal law of 08.08.2024 no. 300-FZ "On amendments to the federal law 'On peculiarities of regulation of corporate relations in business companies that are economically significant organizations'"], Garant, 8 August 2024, https://base.garant.ru/409494263/

CONCLUSION

1. Huntington, *Soldier and the State*; Herspring, "Samuel Huntington and Communist Civil–Military Relations"; Aurel Croissant and David Kuehn, *Reforming Civil–Military Relations in New Democracies: Democratic Control and Military Effectiveness in Comparative Perspectives* (Springer International, 2017).
2. "The Precarious State of Civil–Military Relations in the Age of Trump," War on the Rocks, 28 March 2018, https://warontherocks.com/2018/03/the-precarious-state-of-civil-military-relations-in-the-age-of-trump/; Andrew Radin and Thomas Szayana, "Another 'Crisis' in Civil–Military Relations?," War on the Rocks, 8 July 2021, https://warontherocks.com/2021/07/another-crisis-in-civil-military-relations/; "To Support and Defend: Principles of Civilian Control and Best Practices of Civil–Military Relations," War on the Rocks, 6 September 2022, https://warontherocks.com/2022/09/to-support-and-defend-principles-of-civilian-control-and-best-practices-of-civil-military-relations/
3. Risa A. Brooks, "Integrating the Civil–Military Relations Subfield," *Annual Review of Political Science* 22 (2019): 379–98, https://doi.org/10.1146/annurev-polisci-060518-025407
4. Polina Beliakova, "Erosion of Civilian Control in Democracies: A Comprehensive Framework for Comparative Analysis," *Comparative Political Studies* 54, no. 8 (2021): 1393–423, https://doi.org/10.1177/0010414021989757; Karabekir Akkoyunlu and José Antonio Lima, "Brazil's Stealth Military Intervention," *Journal of Politics in Latin America* 14, no. 1 (2022): 31–54, https://doi.org/10.1177/1866802X211039860; Anit Mukherjee and David Pion-Berlin, "The Fulcrum of Democratic Civilian Control: Reimagining the Role of Defence Ministries," *Journal of Strategic Studies* 45, nos. 6–7 (2022): 783–97, https://doi.org/10.1080/01402390.2022.2127094

SELECTED BIBLIOGRAPHY

Barabanov, Mikhail. *Russia's New Army*. Edited by Mikhail Barabanov. 1st edition. Center for Analysis of Strategies and Technology, 2011.

Barany, Zoltan. *Democratic Breakdown and the Decline of the Russian Military*. Princeton University Press, 2009.

——— *The Soldier and the Changing State: Building Democratic Armies in Africa, Asia, Europe, and the Americas*. Princeton University Press, 2012. https://www.jstor.org/stable/j.ctt7rgt7

Brannon, Robert Burl. *Russian Civil–Military Relations*. Ashgate, 2009.

Brooks, Risa. *Creating Military Power: The Sources of Military Effectiveness*. Stanford University Press, 2007.

Colton, Timothy J., and Thane Gustafson, eds. *Soldiers and the Soviet State: Civil–Military Relations from Brezhnev to Gorbachev*. Princeton University Press, 2014.

Croissant, Aurel, and David Kuehn, eds. *Reforming Civil–Military Relations in New Democracies: Democratic Control and Military Effectiveness in Comparative Perspectives*. Springer International, 2017. https://www.springer.com/gp/book/9783319531885

Feaver, Peter. *Armed Servants: Agency, Oversight, and Civil–Military Relations*. Revised edition. Harvard University Press, 2005.

Finer, Samuel Edward. *The Man on Horseback: The Role of the Military in Politics*. Transaction Publishers, 2002.

Gel'man, Vladimir. *Authoritarian Russia: Analyzing Post-Soviet Regime Changes*. 1st edition. University of Pittsburgh Press, 2015.

Golts, Aleksandr. *Military Reform and Militarism in Russia*. Acta Universitatis Upsaliensis, 2017.

Gomart, Thomas. *Russian Civil–Military Relations: Putin's Legacy*. Carnegie Endowment for International Peace, 2008.

SELECTED BIBLIOGRAPHY

Huntington, Samuel P. *The Soldier and the State: The Theory and Politics of Civil–Military Relations*. Harvard University Press, 1957.

Janowitz, Morris. *The Professional Soldier: A Social and Political Portrait*. Free Press, 1960.

Lynch, Allen C. *How Russia Is Not Ruled: Reflections on Russian Political Development*. Cambridge University Press, 2005.

Newton, Julie, and William Tompson. *Institutions, Ideas and Leadership in Russian Politics*. Springer, 2010.

Renz, Bettina. *Russia's Military Revival*. Polity, 2018.

Sabatier, Paul, and Christopher Weible. *The Advocacy Coalition Framework: Innovations and Clarifications*. Westview Press, 2007. https://vtechworks.lib.vt.edu/handle/10919/68212

Sakwa, Richard. *The Crisis of Russian Democracy: The Dual State, Factionalism and the Medvedev Succession*. Cambridge University Press, 2010.

Taylor, Brian D. *Politics and the Russian Army: Civil–Military Relations, 1689–2000*. Cambridge University Press, 2003.

——— *State Building in Putin's Russia: Policing and Coercion after Communism*. 1st edition. Cambridge University Press, 2011.

INDEX

Note: Page numbers followed by "*f*" refer to figures, "*n*" refer to notes.

Abkhazia, 35
Academy of the General Staff, 74
Accounts Chamber, 110
advocacy coalition framework (ACF), 8–9
Afghan War, 20, 40, 42–3
Afghanistan, 18, 20, 87
Africa, 156
Airborne Forces (VDV) Institute, 86–7, 135
Alekseev, Vladimir, 173
Allende, Salvador, 4
Almaz-Antey, 101, 149, 243n148
Arbatov, Alexei, 77, 83
Arctic, 180
Argentina, 4
Armata armored platform (for tanks and IFVs), 153
Armenia, 3, 96
Armored Forces Academy, 74
al-Assad, Bashar, 3
Aushev, Ruslan, 40
Azerbaijan, 3
Azov-Black Sea Regional Administration, 142

Baku, 40–1
Balaklava, 142
Baltic states, 214–15n18
Baluyevsky, Yuri, 30, 84, 97, 122, 125, 130–1
Basayev, Shamil, 65
Baturin, Yurii, 23
Belarus, 169
Belbek military airfield, 142
Belgrade, 88
Belyaninov, Andrei, 72, 104
Berlusconi, Silvio, 137
Beslan school hostage crisis (2004), 118
Biden, Joe, 166
Black Book, The, 55
Black Sea, 168
Blinken, Antony, 166
Borrell, Josep, 166
Botlikh, 65
British Special Air Service, 136

"cadres decide everything" principle, 24
Central African Republic, 156

INDEX

Central Asia region, 86
Chechen War I, 1, 2, 22, 43, 46, 68, 75
Chechen War II, 2, 23, 43, 65, 74, 110–11
Chechnya, 1–2, 20, 22, 30, 40, 43, 47, 51, 54, 64–7, 74, 75, 89, 136
   campaign in, 48
Chelstov, Boris, 126
Chelyabinsk Armor Institute, 101
Chelyabinsk, 128, 138
Chemezov, Sergei, 138
Chile, 4
China, 118, 166, 214–15n18
Chubais, Anatoly, 76
"Civic Forum", 71
Committee for External Economic Relations, 124
Committee for Military-Technical Cooperation, 72
Communism, 17
Communist Party of Russia, 77
Communist Party of Ukraine, 18
Communist Party, 17, 21, 40, 79
Congress of People's Deputies (CPD), 18
Conventional Armed Forces, Treaty on, 117
Council of Europe, 89
Council on Foreign and Defense Policy (SVOP), 130
COVID-19 pandemic, 165
Crimea, 3, 23, 50, 142–3, 168, 169
Crimea, annexation of, 31, 50, 117, 137, 148, 152, 153, 181
Criminal Code, 133, 176, 177

Dagestan, 64, 65, 69
Defense Committee of the Duma, 109

Deir ez-Zor, Battle of, 156
Directorate of Special Operations, 136–7
Dmitriev, Mikhail, 72
Donetsk region, 3
Dorenko, Sergei, 62
Dudayev, Dzhokhar, 20, 22
Duma, 75–6, 77, 83, 89, 99, 124, 162, 176–7, 188
Duma's Defense Committee, 76

East Germany (Dresden), 69
East Germany, 96
Eastern Regional Command, 131
Eastern Ukraine, 3, 23, 117, 143, 148, 168, 169, 181, 188
economically significant organizations (EZOs), 180
"the end of history", 17
English Channel, 20
EU (European Union), 96, 125, 166
Europe, 97, 117–18, 170, 176
European Court of Human Rights, 122
Expert Council of the Military-Industrial Commission, 146
Export Control, 91

Fatherland Foundation, 178
Federal Agency for Special Construction, 91, 109
Federal Counterintelligence Service (Federal Security Service) (FSB), 22, 24, 25, 43, 65, 69, 73, 100, 135–6, 162
Federal Guards Service (FSO), 24, 25
Federal Prosecutor's Office, 135
Federal Service for Military-

INDEX

Technological Cooperation, 91, 109
Federal Service for Technological, 91, 109
Federal Service for the Defense Order, 91
Federal Service of Labor and Employment (Rostrud), 108
Federal Service on Defense Order, 108, 109
Federal Target Program, 104
Federal Tax Policy Service, 95
Federal Tax Service, 30, 55, 122, 137, 174
Federal Treasury, 179
Feodosia, 142
financial crisis (1998), 107
financial crisis (2008), 96
Finland, 69, 214–15n18
Foreign Intelligence Service (SVR), 24, 25, 72, 73
45th Separate Airborne Regiment, 142
45th Special Purpose Airborne Regiment, 43
Fradkov, Mikhail, 95, 135
Fradkov, Pavel, 175
France, 137
FSB Alpha, 136
Fukuyama, Francis, 17

Gaidar, Yegor, 76, 81, 83, 85
Gareev, Makhmut, 76
Gazprom, 79, 120
Gel'man, Vladimir, 29
"General Armageddon", 18
General Staff, 5, 9, 15–16, 21–3, 29, 30, 38, 69, 71, 75, 81–2, 87, 94, 97, 116, 125–7, 130–1, 146, 163, 181, 185, 187, 190–2
radical reform package, 132–41

Russia, policy changes in, 99–105
Shoigu, military development under, 149–51, 150f
Georgia, 35, 55, 77, 94, 96, 107, 117, 131, 186
Georgian forces, 115–16
Gerasimov, Valery, 127, 146–7, 155, 161, 181
Germany, 43, 167, 190
GLONASS navigation system, 149
Gorbachev, Mikhail, 18, 40
Gori, 116
Gornin, Leonid, 175
GPV. *See* State Armament Program (GPV), 68
GPV-2020 program. *See* State Rearmament Program 2020 (GPV-2020)
GPV-2027 program, 153
Grachev, Pavel, 22, 42–3, 47, 51
Great Patriotic War (the June 1941–May 1945 part of the Second World War), 38, 39, 214n18
See also World War I; World War II
Gromov, Boris, 18, 46
Grozny, 2, 75
Gryzlov, Boris, 99
Gulf War (1991), 128

Hamilton College, 38–9
"Hero of the Soviet Union", 18
Hungary, 214n18
Huntington, Samuel, 26

infantry fighting vehicle (IFV), 18
Infantry Headquarters, 75
Ingushetia, 40

INDEX

Institute of Economics of the Soviet Academy of Sciences, 96
Intermediate-Range Nuclear Forces (INF) Treaty, 96–7, 125
Investigative Committee (SKR), 135–6, 143–4
Iraq War (2003), 128
Iraq, 170
Islamist ideology, 65
Italy, 137, 214n18
Ivanov, Sergei, 5, 28, 30, 63, 66, 69–73, 81, 92, 95, 101–2, 105–6, 123, 131, 144, 186, 188
Ivashov, Leonid, 33

Japan, 214–15n18
Joint Group of Forces, 2

Kadetsky, 145
Kantemirovskaya, 141
Kasyanov, Mikhail, 72, 91–2, 95, 96, 110, 223n52, 223–4n53
Kazakhstan, 3, 143, 181
Kazan, 146
Kenya, 69
Kerch Strait, 168
KGB (Komitet Gosudarstvennoi Bezopasnosti, or Committee for State Security), 10, 18, 69, 73, 104, 108
Khabarovsk, 93
Khakamada, Irina, 76
Khasavyurt Accords, 46, 75
al-Khattab, Ibn, 65
Khodorkovsky, Mikhail, 122
Khrulyov, Anatoly, 115
Khursevich, Sergei, 137
Kiev Military District, 18
Kirienko, Sergei, 76
Kislitsyn, Mikhail, 65–6
Kolesnikov, Dmitry, 61–2

Kolomensky High Artillery Command School, 140
Komsomolsk-on-Amur aviation plant (KnAAPO), 93
Korea, 214–15n18
Kosovo, 75
Krai, Krasnoyarsk, 47
Kubinka-2, 136
Kudelina, Lyubov, 72–3, 91–2
Kudrin, Alexei, 95–6, 124, 138–40
Kulikov, Anatoly, 105
Kurgan Machine-Building Institute, 74
Kuril Islands, 214–15n18
Kursk nuclear submarine, 28, 61, 62–3, 65, 109, 112
Kvashnin, Anatoly, 23, 30, 74–5, 84–5, 96, 130
Kwantung Army, 214–15n18
Kyiv, 142, 166, 170

Lebed, Alexander, 23, 46–7
Leningrad, 19
Libya, 156
"Little Green Men", 142
Luhansk region, 3
Lukin, Vladimir, 77

Maev, Sergei, 104
Main Cathedral of the Armed Forces, 145
Main Directorate of Combat Training and Service, 135
Main Financial and Economic Department, 91–2
Main Intelligence Directorate (GRU) officer, 130, 132, 136
Main Operations Directorate, 96
Main Organizational and Mobilization Directorate, 81
Main Personnel Directorate, 132

INDEX

Makarov, Nikolai, 55, 116, 125–8, 132, 138, 146, 155
Mali, 156
Martyanov, Oleg, 136
Maskhadov, Aslan, 46
Maslov, Alexei, 107
Masorin, Vladimir, 126
Mazurkevich, Anatoly, 126
Medvedev, Dmitry, 2, 6, 30–1, 116, 119–21, 123–4, 125–7, 131, 139, 143, 147, 149
Mikhailov, Vladimir, 126
military culture, 33–6
  Russian deep core beliefs, 37–51, 44*f*
  Russian policy core beliefs, 51–8
Military-Industrial Commission, 134
Ministry of Defense (MoD), 9, 21–2, 26, 28, 31, 38, 55, 68, 71–3, 75, 81, 82, 87–8, 92, 94, 108–9
  media, 145
  policy changes (2004–7), 99–105
  radical reform package, 132–41
  reform results, 141–2
  Shoigu, military development under, 149–51, 150*f*
  Shoigu's plan, 151–60
Miroshnichenko, Alexander, 136
Mishustin, Mikhail, 149
Mk 41 Vertical Launching System, 97
Moscow. *See* Russia
Moskovsky, Alexei, 126
Moskva River, 20
Motorin, Mikhail, 137
Motsak, Mikhail, 28
Mulino, 137

Munich Security Conference, 117, 143
Munich, 190
Murmansk region, 28

Nagorno-Karabakh, 3, 143, 181
National Defense Management Center (NDMC), 152, 154, 160
National Guard, 24, 25, 170, 178–9
National Security Advisor, 47
NATO (North Atlantic Treaty Organization), 20, 33, 58, 70, 88–90, 94, 109, 123–4, 125, 143, 166–7, 169
  Russia's military needs, 117–19
Navalny, Alexei, 167–8
Nazi Germany, 214n18
Nemtsov, Boris, 76–7, 81, 85, 229–30n134
"The New Look", 128
Nikolaev, Andrei, 77
Nizhny Novgorod region, 137, 229n134
Nizhny Tagil, 138
North Caucasus, 22, 65, 96
North Korea, 36, 37
North Ossetia, 118
North Ossetian republic, 115
Northern Fleet, 62
Novichok, 167
Novolaksky district, 65

Oboronservis company, 143–4
October 1917 Revolution, 40
Officers (Soviet film), 38
"On the Election of People's Deputies", 40
Organization for Security and Co-

263

INDEX

operation in Europe (OSCE), 22

Pankov, Nikolai, 103, 174
"Pasha Mercedes", 43
Perestroika, 17–18
Perón, Juan, 4
Pinochet, Augusto, 4
Piskunov, Alexander, 230n135
Pochinok, Alexander, 72
Pohlebenina, Yulia, 121
Poland, 214–15n18
"Polite People", 142
Politkovskaya, Anna, 42, 43
Popov, Vyacheslav, 28, 112
Popovkin, 138–9
Presidential Administration, 82, 120, 136, 174
Presidential Council for Civil Society and Human Rights, 12
Prigozhin, Yevgeny, 156, 173–4, 179
Pristina airport dash (1999), 75, 96
private military companies (PMCs), 155
Private Ramil Shamsutdinov, 57
Privolzhsky Military District, 86
Putin, Vladimir, 2, 5, 14, 19, 33, 43, 61–4, 131, 152, 155–6, 186, 188, 223n52, 224n59
   bombings, 64–6
   civil–military disaster, 169–72
   civil–military relations and defense reform, 110–13
   civil–military relations and reform, 7–11, 8f
   defense policy, 105–10
   initial reform plan, 79–85
   invasion, preparing for, 166–9
   military coalition, 92–3
   military culture, 33–6
   military violence and corruption, 66–7, 67f
   Putin's first civil–military coalitions, 68–79, 78f
   reform results, 141–2
   reforms, substance of, 86–92
   Russia's military needs, 117–19
   Russian MoD, civilian, 121–8
   Russian policy core beliefs, 51–8
   security services, controlling of, 24–9
   strong government, 48–51
   struggling defense industry, 67–8
   See also Ivanov, Sergei
Pyotr Velikiy (battle cruiser), 62

Regional Defense Management Centers, 154
Republic of Chechnya, 1, 20, 30
Reserve Officers' Training Corps (ROTC), 123
Rheinmetall, 137
"Right Cause" party, 128
Rodionov, Igor, 22–3
Rogozin, Dmitry, 123–4
Roki Tunnel, 115
Romania, 214n18
Rosatom, 101, 173, 230–1n140
Roskomnadzor, 175–6
Rosoboronexport, 72, 104, 109
Rostec, 149
Rostec140, 101
RSFSR Supreme Soviet, 230n135
Rusnano, 100–1
Russia
   bombings, 64–6
   civil–military disaster, 169–72
   civil–military relations and

INDEX

defense reform, 110–13
civil–military relations and reform, 7–11, 8*f*
Civil–military relations and Russian military development, 186–8
defense policy, 105–10
initial reform plan, 79–85
invasion, preparing for, 166–9
policy changes in, 99–105
Putin's first civil–military coalitions, 68–79, 78*f*
reform results, 141–2
reforms, substance of, 86–92
research, 11–15
Russia's military needs, 117–19
Russian civil–military instability, 17–24
Russian MoD, civilian, 121–8
Russian policy core beliefs, 51–8
security services, controlling of, 24–9
struggling defense industry, 67–8
violence and corruption, 66–7, 67*f*
Russian 4th Air Army, 115–16
Russian 58th Army, 115, 146–7
Russian Civil War, 38
Russian Constitution, 110, 186
Russian deep core beliefs, 37–51, 44*f*
  deep core belief convergence, 48–51
  military and militarism, 38–9
  military marginalization, 42–5, 44*f*
  military, politicization of, 39–42
  strong leadership, 46–8
Russian defense policy, 4, 26, 68–9

Russian military intelligence, 3, 173
Russian military, 1
  bombings, 64–6
  civil–military disaster, 169–72
  civil–military relations and defense reform, 110–13
  deep core belief convergence, 48–51
  defense policy, 105–10
  initial reform plan, 79–85
  military and militarism, 38–9
  military marginalization, 42–5, 44*f*
  military, politicization of, 39–42
  needs, 117–19
  new-look Russian military, 128–30, 129*f*
  Putin's first civil–military coalitions, 68–79, 78*f*
  radical reform package, 132–41
  reform ideas, 130–2
  reform results, 141–2
  Russian deep core beliefs, 37–51, 44*f*
  Russian MoD, civilian, 121–8
  Shoigu, military development under, 149–51, 150*f*
  Shoigu's plan, 151–60
  strong leadership, 46–8
  struggling defense industry, 67–8
  violence and corruption, 66–7, 67*f*
Russian parliament, 20, 22, 57, 99
Russian PMCs, 156
Russian Railways, 79
Russian Stabilization Fund, 30, 96
Russian White House, 43
Russo-Georgian War, 130

265

INDEX

Russo-Ukrainian War, 183
Rutskoy, Alexander, 20
Ryazan, 86–7

Saint Petersburg International Economic Forum, 155
Saint Petersburg Mayor, 124
Saint Petersburg State University, 120
Saint Petersburg, 93, 96, 119–20, 122, 125, 140
Sakhalin, 214–15n18
Samsonov, Viktor, 19
Saratov, 173
Sarkozy, Nicolas, 137
Serdyukov, Anatoly, 118, 119, 121–4, 125–8, 131–4, 135, 137–8, 141, 143–6, 162–3, 174, 188
   reform results, 141–2
   Shoigu, military development under, 149–51, 150f
Serdyukov, Anatoly, 6, 54–6, 187
Sergeyev, Igor, 23, 52, 69, 112
76th Airborne Division, 87, 142
Shamanov, Vladimir, 54, 135, 146–7
Shamsutdinov, Ramil, 57
Shevtsov, Leontiy, 90
Shevtsova, Tatiana, 175
Shlykov, 130
Shoigu, Ksenia, 145
Shoigu, Sergei, 6, 56, 119, 144–9, 167, 174, 187, 188
   military development under, 149–51, 150f
   plan, 151–60
   reform results, 160–2
Siberian Military District, 125
Siluanov, Anton, 124, 140, 175
Simferopol Airport, 142

Simferopol Border Guard Detachment, 142
Sivyakov, Alexander, 101
16th Special Purpose Brigade, 142
Sobchak, Anatoly, 19
Sochi, 61
South Ossetia, 35, 115
Souz Pravykh Sil (Union of Right Forces, SPS) party (1999–2003), 47, 72, 76, 77, 79, 81, 83, 85, 99, 110, 229n23
Soviet Armed Forces, 18
Soviet coup attempt (1991), 171
Soviet CPD, 40
Soviet Union, 17, 61, 74, 96, 143, 214n18
   defense policy, 105–10
   Russian civil–military instability, 17–24
   Russian deep core beliefs, 37–51, 44f
Space Forces, 75, 81
Special Operations Center (Kubinka), 136
Special Operations Forces Command (KSSO), 136, 137
Spetsstroy, 91
Stalin, Joseph, 126
Stanford University, 38–9
Starovoitova, Galina, 40
State Armament Program (GPV), 68
State Duma's Defense Committee, 77
State Rearmament Program 2020 (GPV-2020), 137, 152–3, 160–1
Strategic Missile Forces, 75, 81, 135
Sukhoi, 93
Surovikin, Sergei, 18, 171

INDEX

Suvorov, Alexander, 145, 147
SVR. *See* Foreign Intelligence Service (SVR)
Switzerland, 130
Sychev, 109
Sychyov, Andrey, 101–3
Syria, 3, 23, 50, 117, 143, 148, 149, 156, 159–60, 167, 171, 181, 188

Tactical Missiles Corporation, 101, 149, 243n148
Tajikistan, 87
"tandemocracy", 121
Tbilisi, 40–1
13th Guards Tank Regiment, 22
TNK-BP, 137
Tokayev, Kassym-Jomart, 3
Tomahawk cruise missiles, 97
Tomsk, 138
Transmash plant, 68
Troshev, Gennady, 1–2, 42, 52, 54
Tsivilev, Sergei, 174
Tsivileva, Anna, 174, 178
Tskhinvali, 35, 115–16
Tsumadin, 65
Turkestan Military District, 74
Türkiye, 36–7

Ukraine, 33, 94, 142, 156, 160, 162, 165–6, 176
 Russia's preparation, 166–9
 Russian soldiers, 1
 See also NATO (North Atlantic Treaty Organization); Russia
Ukraine, invasion of, 13–14, 18, 152, 157, 191
Ukrainian military installations, 142
Ukrainian troops, 142
Ulyanovsk region, 135

Unified Energy System of Russia (RAO UES), 79
Union of Airborne Veterans, 127–8
United Aircraft Corporation, 149
United Engine, 101
United Group of Forces, 22
United Kingdom (UK), 166
United Russia party, 127, 144, 176, 177, 230n137
United Shipbuilding Corporation, 149
United States (U.S.), 31–2, 58, 65, 96, 97, 109, 117, 169, 186, 189
University of Michigan, 38–9
unmanned aerial vehicles (UAVs), 157, 161
Ural Military District, 86
Uralvagonzavod, 68, 138
US Joint Special Operations Command, 136
USSR (Union of Soviet Socialist Republics), 15, 40, 41–3, 95, 214–15n18

VDV. *See* Airborne Forces (VDV) Institute
Vidyaevo naval base, 62
Viktor Ishaev of Khabarovsk, 104
Vladivostok, 140
Vorobyev, Eduard, 47
Vysotsky, Vladimir, 126

Wagner Group, 155–7, 173–4, 179
Warsaw Pact countries, 117
World War I, 57
World War II, 76, 141, 214n18

Yabloko, 76–7, 81, 83, 99, 110

Yakutia, 173
Yavlinsky, Grigory, 77
Yeltsin, Boris, 19–20, 43, 47,
    76–7, 82, 90–1, 141
    defense reform, 21–4
Yevkurov, Yunus-bek, 173
Yugoslavia, 88

Yukos, 122
"YunArmiya" (Young Army), 145

Zavarzin, Viktor, 99, 121, 122, 127
"Zvezda" military television channel, 145